Kotaro Isaka

THREE
ASSASSINS

Translated from the Japanese
by Sam Malissa

VINTAGE

3 5 7 9 10 8 6 4 2

Vintage is part of the Penguin Random House group of companies whose
addresses can be found at global.penguinrandomhouse.com

Penguin
Random House
UK

First published in Vintage in 2023
First published in hardback by Harvill Secker in 2022

penguin.co.uk/vintage

A CIP catalogue record for this book is available from the British Library

ISBN 9781529115512

Typeset in 10.14/14.85pt Scala by Jouve (UK), Milton Keynes
Printed and bound in Great Britain by Clays Ltd, Elcograf S.p.A.

The authorised representative in the EEA is Penguin Random House Ireland,
Morrison Chambers, 32 Nassau Street, Dublin D02 YH68

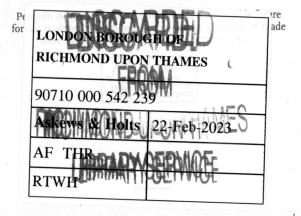

THREE
ASSASSINS

SUZUKI

LOOKING OUT AT THE CITY, Suzuki thinks about insects. It's night but the scene is ablaze with gaudy neon and streetlamps. People everywhere. Like a writhing mass of luridly colored insects. It unsettles him, and he thinks back to what his college professor once said: 'Most animals don't live on top of each other in such great numbers. In some ways, humans are less like mammals and closer to insects.' His professor had seemed pleased with the conclusion. 'Like ants, or locusts.'

'I've seen photos of penguins living in groups all bunched together,' Suzuki had responded, gently needling. 'Are penguins like insects too?'

His professor flushed. 'Penguins have nothing to do with it.' He sounded endearingly childlike, and Suzuki had felt that he wanted to be the same way as he got older. He still remembers it.

Then a memory of his wife flashes through his mind. His wife died two years ago. She used to laugh at the story about his professor. 'You're supposed to just answer, "You're absolutely right, professor," and then everything works out,' she used to say.

It was certainly true that she loved it anytime he had agreed with her and said, 'You're absolutely right, honey.'

'What are you waiting for? Get him in the car.'

Hiyoko's urging startles him. Suzuki shakes his head to ward off the memories, then pushes the young guy in front of him. The guy tumbles into the back seat of the sedan. He's tall, blond hair. Unconscious. He has a black leather jacket on over a black shirt, with a pattern of little insects. The unsavory pattern matches the guy's general unsavory vibe. Also in the back seat, on the other side, is a girl. Suzuki had forced her into the car as well. Long black hair, yellow coat, in her early twenties. Her eyes are closed and her mouth slightly open as she sleeps sprawled on the seat.

Suzuki tucks the guy's legs into the car and closes the door.

'Get in,' says Hiyoko. Suzuki gets in on the passenger side.

The car is parked just outside the northernmost entrance to the Fujisawa Kongocho subway station. In front of them is a big intersection with a busy pedestrian crossing.

It's ten thirty at night in the middle of the week, but this close to Shinjuku things are busier after dark than they are in the daytime, and the area is thronged with people. Half of them are drunk.

'Wasn't that easy?' Hiyoko sounds totally relaxed. Her white skin has a luster like porcelain, seeming to float in the dark car interior. Her chestnut hair is cut short, coming just to the top of her ears. Something about her expression is cold, maybe because of her single eyelids. The red of her lipstick shines brightly. Her white shirt is open down to the middle of her chest and her skirt doesn't quite reach her knees. She's apparently in her late twenties, same as Suzuki, but she often shows the craftiness of someone far older. She looks like a party girl, but he can tell she's sharp, with the benefit of a proper education. She's wearing black high heels, and has one foot on the brake. *It's amazing she can drive in those*, he thinks.

'It wasn't easy or hard, I mean, all I did was get them in the car.' Suzuki frowns. 'I just carried these two unconscious people and put them in the back seat.' *I take no further responsibility*, he wanted to say.

'If this sort of thing rattles you, you won't get very far. Your trial period is almost over, so you better get used to jobs like this. Although I bet you never imagined you'd be kidnapping people, huh?'

'Of course not.' Though the truth is that Suzuki isn't all that surprised. He never thought his employer was a legitimate company. 'Fräulein means "maiden" in German, doesn't it?'

'Very good. Apparently, Terahara named the company himself.'

When she says that name his body tenses. 'The father?' That is, the CEO.

'Obviously. His idiot son could never come up with a company name.'

Suzuki has a momentary vision of his dead wife and his emotions boil. He clenches his stomach and feigns calm. The idiot son, Terahara's son – anytime Suzuki thinks of him he can barely contain himself. 'I just never thought that a company with a name that means "maiden" would actually prey on young women,' he somehow manages to say.

'It does seem strange.'

Hiyoko may be the same age as Suzuki but she's been with the company for a long time, and has the according rank. In the month since Suzuki joined as a contractor, he's been reporting to her.

As for what he's been doing in that month, it was all standing in shopping arcades, hailing passing women.

He stood in the busy spots, calling out to women walking by. They would say no, they would ignore him, they would swear at

3

him, but he still kept trying. Almost all of the women just walked away, regardless of his delivery, effort, technique or skill. They scowled at him, they looked at him warily, they avoided him, but still he kept calling out to every woman who walked by.

But there was usually one woman each day, maybe one in a thousand, who showed interest. He would take her to a cafe and give her a pitch for makeup products and diet drinks. He had a basic script: 'You won't see the effects right away, but after about a month you'll see dramatic changes.' He would improvise, saying whatever felt most appropriate, then show her the pamphlets. They were printed in color, full of graphs and figures, but not a single thing written in them was true.

The gullible girls would sign an agreement right then and there. The more suspicious ones would leave saying they'd think about it. If he could sense that there was still a chance, he would follow them. After that, another group would take over, far more persistent, starting their illegal solicitation. They would force their way into the woman's home and refuse to leave, keep constant surveillance on her, until she finally gave in and signed the agreement. Or so Suzuki understood. But that part of the arrangement was still all hearsay to him.

'Well, you've been with us for a month. Shall we take you to the next level?' Hiyoko had said this to him an hour earlier.

'The next level?'

'I can't imagine you planned to spend the rest of your life soliciting women on the street.'

'Well, I mean,' he answered vaguely, 'the rest of my life is a long time.'

'Today's job is different. When you get someone into a cafe, I'll be coming with you.'

'It's not that easy to get someone to listen,' he said with a pained smile, thinking of the last month.

But for better or for worse, inside of thirty minutes Suzuki had found two people willing to hear him out. The guy and girl who are currently passed out in the back of the car.

First the girl showed interest. 'Hey, don't you think if I lost a little weight I could do modeling?' she asked the guy casually. He answered encouragingly, 'Sure, babe, you could definitely be a model, for sure. You could be, like, a supermodel.'

Suzuki called Hiyoko, took the couple to a cafe, and started introducing products as he normally would. Whether it was because they were young and stupid or just gullible, the young man and woman seemed almost comically willing to go along with what Suzuki and Hiyoko were pitching. Their eyes lit up at the barest of compliments, and they nodded enthusiastically at all the bogus data from the pamphlets.

Their complete lack of skepticism was enough to make Suzuki feel concerned for their futures. He had a surge of memories of his students from when he was still a teacher. The first place his mind went, for some reason, was to one poorly behaved kid. He remembered the boy saying, 'See, Mr Suzuki, I can do good too.' He was always acting out, and the other students didn't like him much, but one time he surprised everybody by catching a purse-snatcher in a shopping district. 'I can do good too,' he had said to Suzuki, smiling with both pride and embarrassment. Then he said, 'Don't give up on me, teach,' looking like a much younger boy.

Come to think of it . . . The guy in front of him flipping through the pamphlet, face pockmarked from acne scars, somehow reminded him of that student. He knew he had never met this person before, but the resemblance was striking.

Then he noticed that Hiyoko had gone to the counter to order refills of coffee. He took another look and saw that she was doing something with her hands over the cups, then realized: she was drugging the coffee.

5

Before long the guy's and girl's eyes glazed over and their heads started sagging. The girl said, 'They call me Yellow, and he's Black. Just nicknames, you know? That's why I'm wearing a yellow coat, and he's dressed in black.' Then she mumbled, 'Hey, I'm like, sleepy.' And she nodded off. Next to her, the guy said, 'Yeah, but my hair's blond, and yours is black,' slurring nonsensically. 'Why is that . . .' Then he passed out too.

'Well then,' said Hiyoko. 'Let's get them to the car.'

'Depending on how we use them, these two dummies could make us some decent money,' she says, sounding bored.

Would you do this to my students? Suzuki has to tell himself not to ask it out loud. 'Are we . . . just staying here?'

'Normally we'd be leaving now.' Her voice sharpens. 'But tonight's different.'

A sense of foreboding runs up his spine. 'Different, how?'

'I need to test you.'

'What are you testing?' Suzuki's voice quavers a bit.

'We don't trust you.'

'You don't trust me?' He swallows. 'Why not?'

'If you're asking what's fishy about you, well, there's plenty. You were really determined to join our company. And you seem like a pretty strait-laced guy. What was it you did before?'

'Teacher,' Suzuki answers. He doesn't see any reason to hide it. 'I worked at a middle school. I taught math.'

'Yeah. You *seem* like you taught math. That's why we didn't trust you from the get-go. You're clearly wrong for this. A middle-school math teacher going out of their way to get involved with a company like ours. I mean, we scam young people – does that seem like work a teacher would ever do?'

'It doesn't matter what most teachers would do, here I am doing it.'

'I'm telling you it would never happen.'

She's right. Of course it would never happen. 'You may not be affected, but there's a recession on, and it's tough trying to find work. So when I heard about this company called Fräulein that was looking for contract workers, I applied.'

'Bullshit.'

'It's true.' It was bullshit. Suzuki hadn't found out about Fräulein randomly. He had been searching for them. He realizes that his breathing is becoming rough, and his chest is starting to rise and fall. *This isn't casual conversation. It's an interrogation.*

He looks out the window. Young people are gathered in front of a fountain outside a hotel. It's only the beginning of November but there are already Christmas decorations on the trees lining the sidewalks and the signs hanging from the buildings. The clamor of car horns and young voices laughing seems to fill the air, mixing with the curtain of cigarette smoke.

'I'm sure you knew we weren't a strictly above-board company, but do you know exactly how dirty we are?'

'I don't quite know how to answer that,' he says with a forced grin, shaking his head. 'Now, this is just what I imagine . . .'

'Your imagination is fine. Go ahead.'

'Well, I've thought that maybe the things I'm selling aren't health products, but something else. Something habit forming, something that's, uh, how might you put it . . . ?'

'Illegal?'

'Right. That.'

Over the past month, he had met several of the women using the Fräulein brand products. All of them were jittery, with bloodshot eyes. Most of them had begged him with unsettling urgency to send more. Their skin was chapped and their throats painfully dry. It would be far easier to believe that they were on drugs than on a health regimen.

'Correct.' Hiyoko's color doesn't change even a shade.

Like she's testing me. Suzuki grimaces. 'But is it actually

7

effective to solicit people on the street like we do? It's fishing with a rod instead of a net, I mean, it feels like the ratio of effort to profit is all off.'

'Don't you worry. We have much more ambitious scams too.'

'Ambitious, how?'

'Like sometimes we'll hold a beauty seminar at a venue and invite lots of girls. Like a big sales event, and we sell plenty of products.'

'People fall for that?'

'The majority of the women are plants. If fifty come, forty of them are with us, and they get the buying rush started.'

'So then others join in?' He had heard about schemes like that targeting seniors.

'Do you know about the Performers?'

'Performers? Like a theater troupe?'

'Not quite. The Performers work in our industry.'

He's starting to get a sense of what she means by 'our industry': people in the business of illegal, illicit activities. The more that's revealed to him the more improbable it all seems. Apparently in the world of professional criminals everyone has eccentric aliases.

'There's a group called the Performers – I don't know how many of them there actually are, but they have all kinds of actors. You can hire them to play basically any part. Do you remember a while back when a Foreign Ministry official was killed in a bowling alley in Yokohama?'

'Um, I missed that story.'

'All the people at the bowling alley were members of the Performers. They were all in on it. But nobody ever found out.'

'And so?'

'We hire them too, to come to our sales events. That's how we get our plants.'

'So people in our industry help each other out.'

'Well, now there's some friction.'

'Friction?'

'What got paid, what didn't get paid, it turns into trouble.'

'I see.' Suzuki isn't all that interested.

'Then there's the organ business.'

'Sorry, what?'

'Hearts,' Hiyoko says like she's listing off products, 'kidneys.' She pushes the climate control button and cranks the temperature dial.

'Ah. That kind of organ.' Suzuki does his best to look calm. *Yes, internal organs, of course I knew that, naturally.*

'Do you know how many people in Japan are waiting for organ transplants? Plenty. Which means there's plenty of business. We really rake it in with that.'

'I could be mistaken about this, but I'm pretty sure it's not legal in Japan to buy and sell internal organs.'

'That's my understanding as well.'

'Which means you can't have a company that operates that way.'

'That isn't a problem.'

'Why not?'

Hiyoko shifts to an indulgent tone, as if she's explaining the way the world works to a naive student. 'Say, for example, a little while ago, a certain bank went out of business.'

'A certain bank.'

'But it ended up getting rescued by an infusion of trillions of yen.'

'And?'

'Or take another example – an employment insurance scheme, which all company employees paid into. Did you know that several hundred billion yen of that was used for unnecessary building projects?'

'I might have heard about that on the news.'

'Buildings no one needed that cost hundreds of billions and never recouped the expenditure. Sounds strange, right? And then they say that the employment insurance fund doesn't have enough to cover what's needed. Doesn't that make you angry?'

'Yes it does.'

'But the person responsible for that needless spending goes unpunished. They could throw away hundreds of billions of yen, trillions in taxes, and not get in any trouble. Not only that, they still get a nice fat bonus when they retire. Footloose and fancy-free. It's crazy. And you know why it happens that way?'

'Because the Japanese citizenry is so kind and forgiving?'

'Because the people at the top have a shared understanding.' Hiyoko raises her index finger. 'Life has nothing to do with right and wrong. The people with the power make the rules. So if they're on your side, you have nothing to worry about. That's how it is with Terahara. He and the politicians have a give-and-take. They work together like they're in a three-legged race, basically inseparable. If a politician says that someone is in the way, Terahara takes care of it. In exchange, the politicians never go after Terahara.'

'I've never met Mr Terahara.'

Hiyoko adjusts the angle of the rearview mirror and touches her eyelashes. Then fixes Suzuki with a sidelong gaze. 'But your business is with his idiot son.'

Suzuki shudders, as if an arrow has been shot straight into his core. 'I have business with Mr Terahara's son?' His voice is flat, and he's barely able to get the words out.

'And this takes us back to the beginning of our conversation.' She makes a little circle with her finger. 'We don't trust you.' She sounds like she's enjoying herself. 'I meant to ask, but forgot – are you married?'

He clearly has a ring on his left ring-finger. 'No,' he answers. 'I'm not. I was.'

'But you still wear a ring?'

'I gained weight and I can't get it off.'

Another lie. If anything, his ring is loose. He's lost weight since he was married. It always feels like his ring might slip off just from walking around.

Don't lose your ring, his wife would say with great gravity, when she was still alive. *It's the symbol of our connection. Whenever you look at it, I want you to think of me.* If he lost it, she'd be furious, even now that she's dead.

'Shall I guess?' Hiyoko's eyes glitter.

'This isn't a quiz.'

'I'm guessing that your wife died because of Terahara's idiot son.'

How does she – He struggles to keep himself still. His eyes want to dart around. His throat wants to swallow hard. His brow wants to tremble. His ears want to turn bright red. His panic wants to burst out of every pore. At the same time, he pictures his wife, crushed between the SUV and the telephone pole. He clenches his stomach, tries to block the memory out.

'Why would Mr Terahara's son kill my wife?'

'Killing for no good reason is just part of the idiot son doing his idiot thing.' Hiyoko's face says that she expects Suzuki to know this. 'That moron causes all kinds of trouble. He's always stealing cars in the middle of the night and going on joyrides. Getting drunk, running people down. He does it all the time.'

'That's terrible.' Suzuki tries to keep any emotion out of his voice. 'It's just terrible.'

'Isn't it though? Hard to forgive and forget. So, how did your wife die?'

'Why would you assume that she's dead?'

He's picturing his wife's mangled body again. He thought the memory had faded away, but now it roars back, all too vivid. He sees her: soaked in blood, face crushed in, shoulders shattered and askew. Suzuki had stood there, rooted to the spot, while next to him the middle-aged forensics cop got up from examining the ground and muttered, *They didn't even try to brake – looks like they actually sped up.*

'Wasn't she hit by a car?' Bullseye. That's exactly what happened.

'Don't make assumptions.'

'As far as I recall, two years ago the idiot son ran over a woman whose family name was Suzuki.'

That was also right on the nail. 'That can't be true.'

'Oh, it's true all right. The idiot son is always bragging about his adventures. No matter what he does, he never faces any consequences. And do you know why?'

'No idea.'

'Because everyone loves him so much.' Hiyoko raises her eyebrows. 'His father, the politicians.'

'Like with what you were saying about taxes and employment insurance.'

'Exactly. And I'm sure you're aware that he never got into any trouble after killing your wife. Because you looked into it. And you found out that he works for his father's company. You found out about Fräulein. So you joined us as a contract worker.' Hiyoko reels off the facts, like she's reciting a report from memory. 'Isn't that right?'

'Why would I do all of that?'

'Because you want revenge.' She says it like it's obvious. 'You're waiting for a chance to get back at the idiot son. So you've stuck it out for a month. Am I wrong?'

She was not wrong. 'These are baseless accusations.'

'And that,' she continues, raising the corners of her red lips, 'is why you are currently under suspicion.' Over her shoulder, the garish lights from signs blink off and on.

Suzuki swallows hard.

'Which is why yesterday I got special orders.'

'Orders?'

'I'm supposed to find out if you're just working for us or if you're out for vengeance. We have plenty of use for dumb employees, not so much smart guys with vendettas.'

Suzuki says nothing, only smiles vaguely.

'Oh, and by the way, you're not the first one.'

'Sorry?'

'There have been others like you who have a bone to pick with Terahara and his idiot son and joined the company looking for revenge. We're used to dealing with this sort of thing. So we let them work for a month and keep an eye on them. And if something still feels off, then we test them.' Hiyoko shrugs. 'Like we're doing with you today.'

'You're wrong about me.' As he says this Suzuki feels a deep hopelessness wash over him.

The fact that others have tried this before makes his vision go dark. Working for a shady company like Fräulein, spending a month selling young women what he was sure were drugs, it was all so he could avenge his wife. He told himself that the women he was scamming should have known better, trying to smother his guilt, to push aside his fear and sense of decency, to focus only on his plan.

But now he's finding out that his mission is a rerun, a rerun of a rerun, and it's like the bottom drops out from under him. He feels scattered, powerless, lost in darkness.

'So now it's time to test you. To find out whether you're actually interested in working for us.'

'I'm sure I can live up to your expectations.' But as he says it Suzuki is aware that his voice sounds tiny.

'In that case,' Hiyoko says, jabbing her thumb at the back seat, 'why don't you kill those two back there? Just some guy, some girl, nothing to do with you.'

*

Nervously Suzuki turns his head to look between the front seats at the back. 'Why me?'

'To clear up any suspicions, obviously.'

'Doing this won't prove anything.'

'What does proof matter? The way we operate is very straight-forward. Potentialities, evidence – we don't care about any of that. We just have some simple rules and rituals. So it's like this: if you kill the two of them, right here, right now, you'll be a full member of the team.'

'A full member?'

'We'll get rid of the contract part of your contract employee title.'

'But why do I have to do *this*?'

The car is off, and it's quiet. Suzuki can feel vibrations, but he realizes that it's the thrumming of his own heart. With each breath his whole body seems to rise and fall, and the expansion and contraction transmits through the seat and shakes the whole car. He exhales, then inhales, the smell of the leather seats filling his nose.

In a daze, he turns back to the front and looks out the wind-shield. The green of the pedestrian signal at the intersection starts to blink. It looks like it's in slow motion. It feels like it might never turn red.

How long is it going to keep flashing?

'All you have to do is shoot those two back there and we'll be good. Shoot them and kill them. That's your only option.' Her voice brings him back to reality.

'But what's killing them going to achieve?'

'Who knows. If they've got good organs we might cut those out and sell them. The girl might end up as a decoration.'

'A . . . decoration?'

14

'Sure, if we cut off her arms and legs.'

He can't tell if she's joking.

'Well? Are you going to do it? The gun is right here, sir, at your disposal.' Hiyoko's overly polite word choice is mocking, as she produces the dull-colored instrument from under her seat. Then she aims it at Suzuki's chest. 'And if you try to run away, I'll shoot you.'

Suzuki freezes. The blunt reality of a gun pointed at him takes away his ability to move. It's like someone is staring at him from deep within the black hole of the barrel, fixing him in place. Hiyoko's finger is on the trigger. *All she has to do is bend her finger, apply just the barest pressure, and a bullet will rip into my chest.* The realization of just how easy it would be drains his blood.

'You're going to use this gun to shoot our friends in the back seat.'

'What if,' he begins, afraid to even move his lips, 'you give me the gun and I aim it at you instead? What would you do then? Purely a hypothetical question.'

Hiyoko is unfazed. If anything her look is pitying. 'I'm not going to give you the gun just yet. Another company member is on the way. Once they're here I'll give you the gun. Then you won't be able to do anything rash.'

'Who's coming?'

Casually, as if it's nothing at all, she says, 'The idiot son. He'll be here soon.'

Suzuki's whole body clenches and his mind goes blank.

Hiyoko switches the gun to her left hand, and with her right she points toward the windshield. Then she taps it once, seeming to affix her finger to the glass. 'He'll come from right over there, across that intersection.'

'Terahara?' There's a crash inside Suzuki's head, like everything he had in there has collapsed. 'Terahara is coming here?'

'Not Mr Terahara. His son. You two haven't officially met yet, have you? Well, you will now. How lucky for you! The idiot son who killed your wife will be here shortly.'

Hiyoko says Terahara's son's name, but Suzuki doesn't process it. He'd rather not acknowledge the man as a flesh-and-blood human being.

'Why is he coming here?'

'I told you, to get a look at you and see what you do. When we test people like this he always comes to watch.'

'Nice hobby.'

'Oh, you didn't know that particular detail?'

He's at a loss for words. Somehow he manages to look out the windshield. The pedestrian crossing of the big eight-way inter-section looms like it's right on top of them. There's a crowd of people waiting for the signal to change. They look like they're gathered on the shore, looking out over the boundless expanse of the sea.

The density of the crowd once again calls to mind what his professor had said. *He was right, it's like a swarm of insects.*

'Oh, there he is. The idiot son,' Hiyoko says cheerfully, point-ing. Suzuki jolts upright and cranes his neck forward to look. Slightly off to the right, at the diagonal crosswalk, is a man in a black coat. He appears to be in his mid-twenties, but his long coat and suit give him an expensive air. He grimaces as he pulls at his cigarette.

Hiyoko grabs the door handle. 'I don't think the idiot has noticed us.' As soon as the words are out of her mouth, she's out of the car, gun still in hand. With her other hand she waves to Terahara's son.

Suzuki also gets out. Terahara's son is just a few meters away.

He recalls what his wife always used to say: *Guess you just have to do it.* No matter the situation, she would clap Suzuki on the

16

shoulder and say that. If you come across a door, you have to open it. If you open it, you have to step through. If you meet a person, you have to talk to them, and if someone puts a meal on the table, you have to give it a try. *When you have a chance, you should always take it.* She was always saying that, so light and bright. It also meant that when she was online she would say, *I just have to click on it*, and she did click on everything, so her computer was always riddled with viruses.

Suzuki gets a good look at Terahara's son. There's a brash aura that seems to clear the way around him. His shoulders are broad and his spine is straight. He's tall, and even handsome, like a Kabuki actor who plays romantic leads. Without realizing it, Suzuki is leaning forward. Now he's got Terahara's son in his sights, he's locked on. His vision seems to be zooming in, giving him a clear view of the man's face.

He sees the thick, rich eyebrows, the flat nostrils on the snub nose. The lips that hold his cigarette. Then the cigarette is done, the butt tossed on the ground, bouncing once off the pavement. He sees the left heel that crushes the cigarette butt with a fastidious twist. In Suzuki's mind the crushed cigarette doubles as his wife. Underneath the black leather coat that is both expensive and tasteless, he sees a red necktie.

Suzuki pictures what will happen next. The light will turn green, and Terahara's son will cross. He'll come right up to Suzuki. As soon as Suzuki gets the gun from Hiyoko, he'll turn it on Terahara's son. It may not work, it may have been doomed from the start, but that's his only choice. *If I have the chance, I have to take it. I just have to do it. Like you always used to say.*

'Wait, what?' It's Hiyoko. The moment the traffic light turns yellow.

Terahara's son steps out into the street. The pedestrian signal is still red, but he seems like he's starting to cross, one step, another.

Then a car slams into him. A black minivan moving at full speed.

Suzuki fixes on the moment of impact, like he's trying to capture it with his eyes. The world around him falls silent. It's like his hearing has shut off so that his vision can sharpen.

The bumper collides with Terahara's son's right thigh, which twists inward, breaking. His legs lift off the ground and his body is swept up onto the hood of the car, sliding him toward the windshield on his right side. He crashes against the glass, his face grinding into the wipers.

Then his body rebounds off the car, tossed onto the street where he lands hard on his left side, then rolls, his left arm wrenching under him. Something small flies off and hits the ground – Suzuki sees that it's a button popping off his suit. The button spins away in an arc.

The body tumbles into a depression in the asphalt, rotating with the head as the fulcrum, the neck bent at an unnatural angle.

The minivan keeps barreling forward after sending the body flying, now running over Terahara's son as he lies on the ground.

The right tire rolls over the right leg, ripping the pants, flattening the thigh. The whole car bumps up onto the chest. Ribs break, organs are crushed. The minivan skids a few more meters before finally coming to a stop.

The spinning button slows, then falls flat.

It's like when the symphony ends, everyone in the hall takes a breath, and silence fills the space for a moment – then explodes into applause. Except instead of applause, people start screaming.

Sound returns to Suzuki. A flood of car horns, shouting, the din of confused voices, like a river bursting its dam.

He's shaken up, but he still keeps staring. He saw someone.

Amid the chaos across the intersection, a man was there, a man who turned around to walk away.

'What just happened?' Hiyoko says, her mouth hanging open. 'He – he got –'

'He got run over.' Suzuki can feel his heart hammering like an alarm.

'But did you see what I saw?' She sounds uncertain.

'Huh?'

'You saw it, didn't you? There was – *somebody* – somebody shady-looking leaving the scene.' Now she's talking quickly, almost breathless. 'You must have seen it. Someone was there. And it looked like the idiot was *pushed*.'

'I –' Suzuki isn't sure how he should answer. But then: '– saw it.' The words are already out. 'I saw it.'

Hiyoko falls silent. She peers at Suzuki's face, then looks down at her feet. She clicks her tongue. Then she looks back across the street. Her eyes say that she's made up her mind. 'Go after him.'

'Go . . . after?'

'You saw a man, right?'

'I –' Suzuki is still trying to wrap his head around what happened.

'Don't get the wrong idea. You're not off the hook yet. But we can't let whoever pushed Terahara's son into the street get away.' It appears to have been a highly unpleasant decision for her. 'And don't think about trying to escape yourself.' Then she brightens up, as if she's had a great idea. 'Actually, if you try to run, I'll kill those two in the car.'

'How does that –'

'Get after him! Go!'

The chaotic turn of events is destabilizing, almost hallucinatory, but before he realizes what he's doing Suzuki is on the move.

'Go get him!' Hiyoko shouts almost hysterically. 'Find the guy who pushed him!'

He runs like a racehorse under the lash. As he runs he looks back over his shoulder. His eyes fall on Hiyoko's black high heels. *She'd never be able to chase anyone in those – I guess she didn't think she'd have to.*

THE WHALE

THE WHALE STEPS BEHIND THE seated man and looks out the window. He had just closed the curtain, but now he slides it open five centimeters or so and peers down at the city below. There's nothing particularly interesting to see, though. The room on the hotel's twenty-fifth floor isn't high enough for him to see above all the other buildings, and the scene of the entertainment district at night is nothing special. Just headlights from the cars passing through the big intersection and the lights from the electric signs. Hemmed in by the surrounding buildings, the sky above looks like a narrow patch of ceiling.

He closes the curtain again and turns back to the room. It's spacious, much more so than he would have guessed for a single. There's an austere dignity to the bed and the mirror stand, the design sleek and reserved. This is one of the higher-class hotels in town.

'You want to look outside?'

He asks the man's back. The man, in his fifties, is seated

facing the table, staring at the wall. His posture is good, like a young student on their first day of school.

'No thank you.' The man shakes his head. His mind must have been wandering, and the Whale's voice pulled him back to reality.

Among the political secretaries the Whale has met in his career, this man seems to be one of the more likeable ones. His hair is parted neatly and he has a fastidious, honest air. He wears a foreign-made suit of good quality, but without any flashy details, which is rare. He must be ten or twelve years older, but he speaks very politely to the Whale.

'You won't get another chance to look outside.' The Whale knows it isn't necessary to tell the man this, but he does anyway.

'Oh?' The man's eyes seem dim.

It'll be the last view you get, because soon you'll be dead. The Whale thinks about spelling it out, but decides against it. They never fully grasp their situation, so there's no point wasting words. Anyway, there's nothing special to look at.

The man turns back to the table. He stares at the stationery and envelope on it. 'Does ... does this sort of thing ...' He doesn't look back at the Whale. 'Does this happen often?'

'Does what happen often?'

'I mean what's happening now – to me.' He seems to be groping for the right words. In his confusion, an English word he thinks he knows pops out. '*Seaside?*' He goes back to Japanese. 'I mean, people being forced to kill themselves. Do you do this often?'

His shoulders are shaking.

It's always the same. At first, they try to look calm. They do their best to appear at ease, even philosophical. They put on a knowing face and say things like *This is what has to happen*. After a little while they get talkative. They probably think that as

22

long as they keep talking they'll stay alive. But it makes no difference how much they talk. It always ends the same way.

The Whale says nothing. He just looks up at the ceiling, where a vinyl rope is tied to a vent. The end is fashioned into a noose. The client hadn't given any instructions that it should be a hanging, but when they don't specify, that's what he usually goes with.

'Don't you think it's a little odd, the idea that my dying would settle anything?' Now the man rotates the chair a bit to peer sideways at the Whale. 'I'm just a secretary. My suicide doesn't change the situation at all. And I'm sure everyone knows that. The real culprits are still out there, but somehow my killing myself will put the issue to rest. Doesn't that strike you as strange?'

There's nothing to be gained from engaging. The Whale knows this from experience.

'It's not like I came up with the plan,' the secretary continues. 'Of course I didn't. I could never have come up with something so involved on my own.'

The man is secretary to a legislator named Kaji. The media had recently found out that Kaji was taking bribes from a communications company, and the last few weeks had been a mess for him. It was a potentially career-ending scandal. Elections in the House of Representatives were coming up, and Kaji was in danger of being ousted from the ruling party.

'Are they really going to stop the investigation because I kill myself?'

'Kaji's a coward. He squawks at the littlest thing. When he's frightened, he lashes out. Am I wrong?' The Whale pictures Kaji. He's a small man, an elder statesman with a babyish face. He lets his whiskers grow in hope of projecting an authority that he lacks, and he's always twitching his thick eyebrows for effect, but he's not fooling anybody.

'Does Kaji often use you for this sort of work?'

'First time.' Another politician the Whale knows had recommended him, and Kaji got in touch three days ago. 'Doesn't strike me as a very likeable man, but a job's a job. So I took it.'

'If we had just taken a bit more time, I'm sure we could have handled this whole thing better.' The man sounds frantic now, speaking quickly, his eyes bloodshot. 'But Kaji, he threw a fit and made a mess of it all, and now there's no fixing it.'

'You're the one who signed on to be his secretary. You have only yourself to blame.'

The man's breath comes in gulps. 'That doesn't make any sense!' he bellows. Then he immediately looks shocked at himself for having raised his voice.

'They'll stop the investigation.'

'What?'

'When someone kills themself and takes the blame, that's how it works out.'

'Even though everyone knows that it doesn't mean anything?' The man looks betrayed.

'I've been doing this for fifteen years.'

'Forcing people to kill themselves?'

'If it didn't work, I'd have had to look for another job a long time ago.' The Whale sits down on the bed. He's a big man, nearly two meters tall, weighing in at ninety kilos, and the bed creaks under him. He reaches into the jacket pocket of his dark gray three-button suit and produces a small paperback. Ignoring the man's pleading eyes, he begins to read.

'Wh-what book is that?' the man asks. He's probably not that interested in the book, he's just afraid of being left alone with his thoughts. Silently, the Whale holds up the cover for the man to see. It's a well-worn paperback. 'Oh, I read that too, when I was a teenager.' The man's eyes light up, as if he's made an important discovery, a common interest they can shake hands over. 'It's a classic. The classics are the best, aren't they?'

'Of all the novels in the world, this is the only one I've ever read.'

The man looks confused, his mouth open slightly.

'That's not something I'm proud of or bragging about or upset about.' It's tiresome to explain, but he's already doing it. 'I've just never read anything else.'

'Have you read it more than once?'

'When my copy gets too beat up to read anymore I buy a new one. This is the fifth one I've had.'

'I imagine you must have it memorized by now.' The man is clearly trying hard to sound cheerful. 'You know if you rearrange the title it makes a pun – *Pun and Crimishment*.' His voice is reedy and desperate, as if his dumb joke were the most important thing in the world he could say.

The Whale looks up from his book slowly. 'Never noticed.'

He suddenly recalls an earlier time in his life. Ten years ago he thought that someone else who was a fan of this book could be a friend. It was a mistake. And it caused him to mess up. There are countless people who have read the same book. That doesn't make a single one of them his ally. But back then, he didn't understand that yet.

The man's temple is twitching. 'Do I really have to kill myself? . . . You must think I'm pretty pathetic.'

'No. Everyone's like this.'

'I just still don't see how a politician's secretary's suicide will change anything.'

'When there's a suicide, it complicates the investigation. That's just how it works.' A secretary claims responsibility for the whole affair, a lie so obvious that not even a schoolboy would try it. But they also hang themselves, which is all it takes to turn down the heat on the politician. It's the same when a giant corporation is under fire for spewing out pollutants and the CEO takes a walk off a skyscraper. Some might say that the suicide is just a dodge, a cowardly way out, but most are content to let the matter rest.

'Once there's a scapegoat, it gets tougher to pursue the investigation, even if the facts don't add up,' the Whale concludes.

The man moans and covers his face, then lowers his head to the table. Just like everyone always does. The Whale sits reading his book, waiting for the man to stop crying. Once the sobbing and trembling cease, he's fairly certain he knows what the man will say next.

Sure enough, it's exactly what he expected.

'I may have to die, but my family will be fine, right?'

This is the signal that the preliminaries have concluded. Things are picking up speed now, like a minecart heading down a mountain. Outside the window the red lights from the signs flash as if they're urging the Whale's work onward.

'You don't have to worry about them.' He slips his bookmark into place and gets up off the bed. Steps over beside the man. Taps his fingers on the stationery on the table. 'Write a note. It can say whatever you want it to.'

The man's expression reverts back to childlike, peering up at the Whale like a boy trying to gauge his parent's mood. *Kill yourself. If you do that, your family will be safe.* Which also conceals a threat: *If you don't kill yourself, your family will be in danger.*

'Does anyone ever refuse?' the man asks.

'Some.'

'What happens to them?'

'They die with their families in fires of unknown causes.'

The glimmer of hope on the man's face evaporates.

'Or a drunk truck driver slams into the family car and kills everyone inside. Or a gang kidnaps the guy's only daughter and has their way with her.' The Whale rattles off examples like he's reading a table of contents. These are all outcomes that he's heard of, and he doesn't know for sure if they're actually true. But in his world, they seem true enough.

The man hesitates, his lips trembling. 'But if I do what you ask, then my family will be safe?'

The Whale nods, though he's never actually checked in to see if any of his targets' families had come out okay, and he doesn't care to. But he has a general sense that it works out that way. Politicians and wealthy folks don't like to incur unnecessary debts, even if it's to a dead man.

The man's shoulders fall, making a slope off which all his hopes have slipped away.

He takes the pen and a piece of paper.

Making them write their suicide notes is part of the job. Some just write a note to their family, some also write to their boss. The Whale lets them write whatever they want, then checks it when they're done. Anything problematic he throws away.

He sits down on the bed again and goes back to his book. All it takes is reading one or two lines to be reabsorbed into the world of the story. He feels more comfortable there than in the real world.

The man writes for nearly thirty minutes. Every so often he tears up a sheet and crumples the shreds into a ball. But he never gets angry or pounds the table. Once he's done he twists around in his chair to face the Whale.

The Whale's breathing is quiet, and he's been turning the pages noiselessly, so the man might have thought that maybe he had left the room. 'Do some people have a hard time writing because their hands are shaking?'

'Maybe a third of them.' The Whale emerges from the world of his book.

'So then I'm doing all right.'

'Yes, you are.' He turns another page.

At this stage it's typical for them to want to know how they did. They might be staring death in the face, but they still worry about their status relative to others.

The Whale inserts his bookmark and softly closes the book, then puts it in his pocket. He stands up and explains to the man what will happen next: he'll move the chair, then put the noose around his neck. He assures him that it will be over quickly.

'All right.' The man's tone is deferential. He's already drifting away into a trance-like state.

You seem to have a strange kind of power. A prominent politician had once said this to the Whale. 'When you look at someone, it's not that they feel physical fear, but somehow they start to lose hope. I'm certain of it. Even a hard old bastard like me feels it – just a little bit, but it's there. The guilt and helplessness that everyone carries around inside, they start to expand, and it's like suddenly falling into a depression. My little sins start to inflate, and it makes me feel like living is nothing but pain.' The Whale had scoffed. The man's sins were more than just little. The politician concluded: 'I think you have the power to drive people to suicide.'

'If that's what you think, then why don't you kill yourself right now?'

The Whale couldn't say for sure what it felt like to look at him, but he knew that people who did so for long enough took on the same dark expression, like they had lost hope. Like they were staring into the void.

'Stand on the chair,' he whispers in the man's ear.

The man's eyes roll around wildly, and his body begins to tremble. He takes off his shoes. Stands on the chair. Lowers the noose over his head. He knows that each instruction he follows brings him one step closer to death, but he keeps going.

It doesn't seem like there will be any need to use the gun. There are some people who won't look into the Whale's eyes, which means they're not falling under his spell, and they try to escape. When that happens he has no choice but to bring out the gun. *If you don't kill yourself, I'll kill you*, he softly says. Bizarre logic, but somehow persuasive. They obey his instructions in order to avoid being killed. No one believes they're actually going to die until the moment it happens.

The man fingers the rope. 'How many people have you done this to?'

'Altogether, thirty-two.'

'And you remember all of them?'

'I keep records. You're number thirty-three. And you're the eighth one to ask that question.'

'Doesn't this line of work make you sad?' The man's face seems older, more lined, his skin like parchment. Settling his affairs before an unexpected death sentence. 'Do you ever feel a sense of guilt?'

The Whale smiles darkly. 'I do see ghosts.'

'Ghosts?'

'The people I've forced to take their own lives. Recently they've started showing up.'

'Do they take turns?'

'All thirty-two of them.'

'So you do feel guilty.' The man sounds a bit like he's feeling bad for an insane person, and at the same time like he's interested in hearing more of this cheap ghost story. 'And that means that sooner or later I'll haunt you too.'

'There's no guarantee of that.'

'When I was at university I listened to a lot of jazz.' A sudden non sequitur. This tells the Whale that the man really knows his life's about to end. 'I loved Charlie Parker.'

The Whale has no intention of following the man's conversation.

'He had a famous song, "Now's the Time." Isn't that a great title?'

29

The Whale has to admit that he does like the ring of it, and without meaning to he says it out loud. 'Now's the time.'

As if the Whale's words are the signal, the man says, 'I guess it is.' Then he kicks the chair out from under his own feet. It topples. His body drops, then the rope catches him and pulls taut. The ceiling creaks. The Whale watches.

The yellow vinyl rope bites into the man's neck. It makes a tight ring just below his chin and behind around his ears. His nostrils flare as they try to suck in air. A gurgling sound escapes his lips.

His legs work back and forth, like swimming practice. The chair lies on its side. First his legs are kicking fast, but before long the pace slackens. Drool spills down, and foam bubbles at the corners of his lips with each strangled croak. His fingers clutch at the noose, trying to find space between the rope and his neck. His nails tear at the skin.

Blood pressure must be spiking now since the man's face and eyes have turned deep red. His neck is swelling and his body starts to spasm. Then his body goes limp. Color drains from his face, turning white by shades. Now the body seems weightless, swaying gently in midair.

The Whale stares at the floating body, then sets to finishing up the job. He wipes for fingerprints and makes sure there are no identifying scraps or bits of trash. He reads through the man's note. As he expected, the man wrote only to his family. Words of encouragement to his wife, expressions of love to his children, advice about life, and a final message: *I'll be watching over all of you.* Nothing especially unique about it. The handwriting is steady enough.

Then a wave of dizziness hits him. He fights to stay on his feet and keep his eyes open.

'Nothing but people and more people, same as always.' The voice comes from behind him.

Someone is standing by the window, gazing down through

the gap in the curtain. The Whale clicks his tongue. It's a member of the House of Councilors who had hanged himself two years ago. Forced into suicide to cover up a bribery scandal.

Jobs from politicians are always about money. Money or pride. Just once, it would be nice to get a contract that had to do with ideological differences, or how to steer the country. But so far that's never happened, not even once.

The supposed-to-be-dead councilor taps the glass of the window, his finger aimed like a gun. Down below is the big intersection with the eight-way crosswalk. The people waiting for the light to change look like a swarm of ants.

The Whale squints. Then something unexpected happens.

A person standing on the corner jumps out of the crowd, into the street like a shot. And is instantly run over. It happens so fast it's almost anticlimactic. Jump out, run down. 'Oooh, that guy is dead!' The shade of the councilor feels solid and real. 'Suicide?'

No, that's not it, the Whale says to himself. He didn't see anything clearly. But he's sure about it.

The people at the intersection burst into a flurry of movement, like a military troop suddenly scattered. People crowding around the man hit by the car, people averting their eyes, people pressing their phones to their ears, people further away who've heard the commotion and come running to see what happened – the Whale can imagine all of it.

But he's watching something else: amid the chaos, there's one person who doesn't seem at all disturbed, walking away from the scene like nothing even happened. A lone ant of a different species.

The Pusher. The words float into the Whale's head.

Memories that he'd thought were buried emerge one after the other. Like muddy water bursting the lid off a pipe. He sees himself, his mistakes, his regrets. Memories from ten years ago come rushing back.

He stuffs it all back down into the deepest recesses of his mind.

The councilor's ghost is gone.

He takes one last look at the dead man hanging from the ceiling. The creaking from the weight of the corpse is blocked out as he shuts the door behind him. On the door is a reminder to take your key with you. He walks away, leaving the key behind.

CICADA

'I REALLY WISH YOU'D SHUT the hell up,' Cicada shouts at the housewife standing in front of him. He picks at his light brown hair and scratches the inside of his ear. 'You're, like, really annoying.'

'But I have no idea why this is happening.' The housewife is over forty. She has makeup caked over the lines on her face and is squeezed into a shirt from a brand that's much too young for her.

Cicada is in her living room, in a two-floor house in a new residential development in Mito City, Ibaraki Prefecture.

Her eyes are red and she's so worked up that she's tripping over her words. 'What is this? *Why?*' She points behind her. Two men are sprawled motionless, covered in blood.

'What it *is* is your husband, face down on the sofa, and your son, face up next to the TV. And both of them're dead.'

'I know that! But why?'

He glances at the clock on the mantle. Iwanishi should be calling any minute. You do it yet or what? he'll ask, all breezy and casual. And then he'll get solemn, like he's reciting the

33

words of a prophet. 'As Jack Crispin says, keepin' track of time is keepin' track of yourself.' Or something like that.

'W-why is this happening to me? Who are you? You said you were with the realtor!'

'Well, yeah, I was lying about that. Sorry.' Cicada shrugs. Now he runs his fingers through his chestnut hair, brushing it behind his ears. 'I can't do my job if you don't let me into the house. I can't, like, ring the doorbell and say, Oh, hello, I've come with my knife to kill you all. You'd never let me in. Or maybe you would have?'

'Of course I wouldn't!'

'Right? So I said I was a real estate guy and you let me in. You all were planning to buy a condo, right? Even though you've got this nice house. I don't get it. Well, whatever, I was told that you're looking at condos and I should say I was a realtor.'

'Told by who?'

'Iwanishi.'

'Who is that? I don't understand any of this!'

'My boss. I mean, it's just him and me. He gets the job, and I do the work. Which is fucked up, right? Don't you think so? I do all the work, he does nothing.'

There's a cabinet running the length of the living-room wall, full of handbags, like it's a show window at a bag store.

'So I came to kill you. That's the job.'

'Why, why would you want to kill us?'

'I dunno.' Cicada takes a step closer to her and she flinches, then loses her balance and props herself up with a hand on the table. 'That's just the assignment. I don't know the details. Iwanishi really doesn't tell me anything. Jack Crispin again.'

'Crisp . . . what?'

'Yeah, I guess you've never heard of him either. Not surprised. I never heard of him. But anytime that jerk wants to tell me anything he just quotes Jack Crispin. Some singer in a band. Nobody knows him. But that's all Iwanishi ever talks about. Loves the guy's lyrics. "As Jack Crispin says, the less a young man knows, the better." C'mon. Gimme a fuckin break. He never tells who the job is coming from, why they want it done, none of that. But in this case I think I at least have some idea. Your son, you think he's like a good kid, right?'

'My son?'

'But didn't he maybe set a homeless guy on fire in Fujisawa Park not too long ago?'

The woman widens her eyes. Cicada doesn't miss a little twitch in her eyelid. *Momma knows.*

'Yeah, this was just recently. An old homeless guy was burned alive in Fujisawa Park. Somebody poured gasoline on him while he was sleeping and lit him up. It was your son, right?'

'N—' No it wasn't, she seems about to say, but the words don't come out.

'Iwanishi never tells me anything, so I did a little poking around myself. Signs pointed to your kid. Lives out here in Mito, but went up to Tokyo to get into some trouble. I can respect that kind of effort. But the other homeless folks weren't happy that their buddy got cooked. And they can make things happen, when they want to. They may be homeless, but they're not hopeless.'

'But the police are looking into it.'

'Yeah, well. The homeless folks aren't so interested in an arrest. They're looking for revenge. I mean, your son's a minor, there wouldn't be much of a legal punishment for him anyhow. So they got together some money and brought the job to Iwanishi. Get rid of that no-good kid, they said. Real touching, right? And that's how I ended up here.' Cicada talks in a stream, barely stopping to breathe. He finally pauses for a moment to gulp some air. 'At least, that's what I figure happened.'

'But even if it was my son, why did my husband have to die too?'

'That was the job.' Cicada scratches at his head again. 'Kill the

35

whole family. We got paid for three people. But, hey, here's another annoying thing – I don't get triple my rate! Makes no sense, right? This is, like . . . what's the word?'

'Exploitation?' For a moment the woman seems to snap back to her normal thinking self.

'Yeah, that's it. Exploitation.'

'You don't think you'll get away with this, do you? When three people are murdered, it's a big deal. They report it on the news, the police launch a whole investigation. You'll get caught in no time. They'll give you the death penalty. The death penalty!'

'Uh, you know, this kind of thing isn't all that rare nowadays. A robber breaks in and kills a whole family for just a couple thousand yen. Happens all the time. You know how many cases like that are left unsolved?'

'The only people who do that are Chinese people.'

She sounds quite convinced. Cicada smiles grimly. 'Wow, don't let any Chinese people hear you say that. You're pretty racist, huh? Japanese people do it too. There are people in every country who will do anything for some cash. Anyway, I'm telling you, there are tons of cases like this, and most of them never get solved. Ha, and also . . .'

'Also what?'

'Here in Japan, the more people you kill the longer it takes for there to be a trial. Weird, right?'

'You'll never get away with this.'

'Sorry to tell you, but I will.' Cicada shrugs. 'Hey, wanna hear a great line?'

'What are you –' The housewife seems more upset about his attitude than the fact that she's in mortal danger.

' "If you told Charlie Parker he could bump off the first ten whites he met in the street, he'd throw his sax in the ocean and never play again." ' Cicada machine-guns the words out so quickly he sends spittle flying. 'It's from a Godard movie.'

'What are you *talking* about?'

'Basically, Charlie Parker played sax to distract himself from wanting to kill white people. But nowadays, you know, there's a lot of folks who don't have saxophones.'

'What's that supposed to mean?'

'Life is tough, is what I'm saying. And they never tell you that in school.'

'You wouldn't hurt a woman, would you?' Her expression doesn't reveal what's going on in her head, but the way she shouts it almost sounds like a challenge.

'I'm a pro.' Cicada fires the words out, once more spraying spit in her direction. 'You'd never hear a surgeon say he doesn't operate on men. Prostitutes service anyone who comes by, no matter how ugly they are. I don't discriminate.'

The housewife screams, no time to form words. The instant her mouth opens Cicada's hand moves, the knife flashing toward her.

The tip of the knife finds her midsection, to the right and above her navel. He pushes and the blade digs in. Cuts through muscle, bursts capillaries, severs nerves. It plunges further, deepening the hole, only stopping when it reaches her liver.

The woman groans, saliva burbling from her mouth.

As the knife comes out it brings gouts of blood from the slashed veins.

The moment it emerges he stabs again, aiming higher, a few centimeters under her left breast.

The blade sinks deep, passing through fat, threading between ribs, finding her heart.

Her eyes are open. Breath escapes her mouth in a rush, like she's expelling steam.

The knife slides out once more. Color fades from her face and she collapses.

*

Cicada watches the woman convulse. He steps closer, avoiding the pooling blood. Then crouches down like he's inspecting a squashed insect. After confirming that she has no pulse, he grabs the gym bag he brought with him and changes clothes. Nondescript, mass-produced shirt and jeans, the kind you might see anywhere.

His phone rings. As expected, it's Iwanishi, asking, 'You do it yet or what?' He's in his forties but he talks like a surly high-schooler.

'Just finished,' Cicada answers.

'Then get outta there. Tomorrow come by and get your money.'

'Yeah, I know. Obviously.'

'It's like Jack Crispin says, "Get it done, and get away." '

'If you couldn't quote him I don't think you'd have anything to say.' He'd like to throw the phone across the room.

'Well, everything I wanna say, Crispin's already written a song about it.'

'Whatever. Hey, listen, how come all my jobs are like this? Killing the whole family? It's a real pain in the ass. And the wife was so annoying, she wouldn't shut up.'

'Cos no one else'll do it.'

'No one will do it?'

'Nobody likes killing innocent women and kids.'

'Come on.' Cicada cocks his head. It makes zero sense to him. 'Why do people have a problem with killing kids? Kids grow up to be adults. How old does someone have to be for it to be okay to kill them? If someone had a problem with killing dogs or cats, that I could understand, but when it comes to people, age and sex have nothing to do with anything.'

'That's what I'm saying. That kind of thing doesn't bother you. That's why we take these jobs. Nobody else wants them. It's how a tiny little operation like ours can earn some cash. You know, look for your chance and grab it.'

Probably another song lyric. 'Well, it's no sweat for you. You don't even have to do anything.'

'With cormorant fishing, it ain't the cormorant who's great, it's the cormorant keeper.'

'Stuff it, you exploitational bastard.'

'Oho, you with the fancy words. Listen, I'm not trying to exploit you.'

'Right.'

'All of Jack Crispin's songs are anti-exploitation. He was very passionate about it.'

Yeah, figured you'd say something like that. Cicada hangs up without responding. He's about to leave when he spots a magazine he's never seen before. He grabs it. It turns out to be a program guide for cable TV. The variety is impressive. *Guess rich people get a lot more shows and channels. Soon they'll make you pay for the news. I wonder what these shows are like.* He reaches for the remote.

SUZUKI

SUZUKI IS OFF RUNNING, DIAGONAL across the intersection and onto the sidewalk. He can see the back of the man up ahead. Most of the pedestrians are walking toward Suzuki, getting in his way. The commotion around the accident has drawn people in and the crowd of spectators is swelling. *But what happened?* As Suzuki picks his way through the onlookers the question rings in his head.

Terahara's son was hit by a car. No doubt about that. But was he actually dead? A minivan slammed into him, leaving him crumpled on the road with his neck wrenched backward, and he wasn't moving at all. *He couldn't still be alive, could he?*

And then there was the glimpse of the man who pushed him. Suzuki was less sure about that, but Hiyoko said she had seen it too. Was it true? Had someone really pushed him? The only thing Suzuki could do was go after the man.

On his right is a line of buildings full of sex shops and massage parlors, their garish signs glowing. The headlights from the steady stream of oncoming traffic shine in his face. Further up the street, high-rise hotels rear into the sky.

A dozen meters ahead is the man he's after. The man who pushed Terahara's son. Who beat Suzuki to his revenge, when it was just across the street. The realization hits him. *What now?* As he chases he angles his body to avoid crashing into pedestrians. The one goal he had was suddenly gone, unceremoniously vanished before his eyes. *What now?*

He urges himself onward. *Just keep going.* If he loses the man, he'll never know what actually happened. Since his wife was killed, revenge has been the only thing keeping him going. If even the chance for vengeance is taken from him, he'll have nothing to live for. Of that much he's certain.

The man up ahead seems unnaturally calm. Keeping up a brisk pace, but in no way giving off the feel of someone fleeing the scene of a crime. Suzuki weaves through the passing people, twisting left and right, bumping shoulders as he struggles onward, while the man seems to flow along like a river.

He's short, wearing a black coat. He carries himself like someone with no extra weight on his frame.

Suzuki is desperate not to lose him. The man keeps slipping in and out of view between the heads of all the people.

Someone's shoe bites into Suzuki's ankle. There's a jolt of pain but he doesn't let himself stop. A motorcycle roars down the street. He keeps moving his legs, not sure if he's reeling or chasing, but always moving forward, forward.

The man goes down the stairs into the subway.

Suzuki speeds up, not wanting to be left behind. Fujisawa Kongocho Station services three lines and has a complicated layout. He knows that if he loses sight of the man, it'll be over.

His phone rings. He answers, his eyes on a humming fluorescent lamp, swirling with tiny insects.

41

'Where are you?' Hiyoko's question stabs out of the phone.

'I'm –' his voice echoes as he runs down the stairs – 'chasing. Going into the subway. Where are you?' He misses a step and nearly tumbles forward. 'How –' he skips another step – 'is he doing?'

'They're taking him to the hospital.'

'Will he make it?' He tries to keep his voice from shaking.

'We'll see.'

No way he'll make it after that, Suzuki thinks, but says nothing. The phone still pressed to his ear, he hurries down the corridor of the station. There's a thicket of circular columns. Here and there are signs leading to the different lines. On his left is a row of closed shops and a bank of vending machines. He heads toward the ticket gate. The man is thirty meters ahead, but nothing is in between them.

'Don't let the killer get away.'

'We're not sure he's the killer.'

'It's him. We both saw it. I just talked to the idiot son's crew, they were there with him and they said it looked like someone pushed him.' An ambulance siren starts blaring on her end of the call.

'Sorry, I can't hear you.'

'The Pusher!' Her voice is shrill, she sounds incredulous.

'Pusher?'

'I don't know, apparently there's someone who does that professionally. I don't really have any information, and it's the first time I've ever heard of anyone like that, but there are some other company employees who have.'

'Does what professionally?'

'Pushes people. Into the street, or onto train tracks. So that they get run over.'

Was she saying that someone else hired that man to kill Terahara's son?

42

'In any case, stick to the man you're after. See where he goes. We don't have any other info on him.' She's almost yelling.

'Why do I have to do this?'

'Because if you prove yourself now, it'll be a good thing for you. It'll clear up any suspicions.'

Seeing the man go through the ticket gate, Suzuki brusquely tells her he'll talk to her later and hangs up, then hurries to the ticket machine. He glances at the price chart and buys the ticket that will take him the farthest. Yanking it out of the machine as it emerges, he rushes through the gate.

There are throngs of men in suits and women in heavy makeup. Suzuki picks his way among them, eyeing the signs overhead. He gets on a long escalator down to the platform. In front of him is a group of five middle-aged women chatting animatedly about a big win in mahjong.

The inbound and outbound trains must have both just pulled away because the platform is mostly empty.

He sees the man.

Standing on the left side, track one, outbound. Suzuki slows his pace and comes to a halt under the train status monitor. He looks back and forth between his watch and the monitor, pretending to check the arrival time, stealing glances at the man.

He appears to be in his mid-thirties. Not a young face, but also no sense of approaching middle age.

The platform begins to fill with people. They seem to accumulate out of nowhere, like mold springing up from a damp floor. Lines form. Men reading weeklies, young people with headphones, company workers chatting. Amid it all the man stands quietly at the front of the line. His calm is almost intimidating.

The train pulls in. The people lean toward the opening doors, entering one after the other. Suzuki follows. *I just have to do it. Like you always used to say.*

THE WHALE

WHEN THE ELEVATOR REACHES THE ground floor, a subdued chime sounds and the door opens. He steps out and crosses the lobby. The front desk is fairly lively, with seven or eight people waiting to check in. The kind of tasteful aura given off by high-class people. A bellboy carrying luggage looks up at the Whale. Only for a moment – he averts his eyes almost instantly. Other than that, no one seems to mark his presence.

Out the automatic doors and along the winding path, then he leaves the hotel grounds. A chill wind encircles his neck. His body tenses to the core. He flexes his fingers against the numbness.

When he reaches the big intersection, there's more of a commotion on the far side than he would normally expect. No doubt on account of the accident he saw from the twenty-fifth floor.

The Pusher. Was it the Pusher?

Onlookers form a half-circle around the ambulance parked by the curb. There are police cars as well. A uniformed officer is standing facing a young woman beside the minivan. She's wearing a neon red coat. It's immediately clear that she was the driver

44

who hit the victim, but she's surprisingly calm. Not perturbed in the least. There's a cigarette in her hand. She stares down the police officer, a look of challenge on her face.

'I didn't hit anyone.'

'You very clearly did.'

'That guy just jumped in front of my car.'

'You *ran* him *over*.'

'Can we just hurry this up? This is, like, really annoying.'

'Are you serious? A man is dead.'

'Well, I'm dying from being annoyed.'

At least, that's what the Whale imagines they're saying.

Traffic starts to back up. The endless flow of cars has to change lanes around the accident, and people start honking their horns. A good portion of the onlookers have their phones pressed to their ears. There's a large digital billboard for a carbonated beverage on a nearby building, intermittently lighting up the faces of the crowd. Every flash shows their excitement, their agitation.

The Whale takes his phone out of the inner pocket of his black leather coat. He enters the number he's memorized. Someone answers right away. 'Who's this?' says the voice on the other end. One more person who thinks they're so important that they don't need to identify themselves when they pick up.

'The Whale,' he says curtly.

'Oh?' The voice sounds vague, as if its owner is taking a moment to check their surroundings. Then after a few moments: 'How did it go?'

'It's done. You can arrange to have him found whenever you want. The note is on the table. It's to his family.' He relays the room number.

At that Kaji exhales, like his marriage proposal has been accepted. 'You really saved my skin.' There isn't a trace of sadness

45

for the death of the secretary who had worked with him for nearly ten years. 'And this'll put the matter to bed, right?'

'I just did what I do. It's up to you how you want to handle the rest.'

'And you're sure he only wrote to his family?'

'What?'

'There's nothing else, maybe something else that you took with you?'

'What exactly are you talking about?'

'Like a letter to the media.'

The Whale is silent a moment. This man Kaji is even more finicky than he had thought. No sooner is his problem solved than he starts seeing another problem, and gets jumpy. He's just that kind of person – foolish, embarrassing, a nuisance. Foolish and embarrassing the Whale can deal with. But nuisance people cause trouble.

'What guarantee do I have that you won't talk about this?' Kaji presses.

'I've been doing this for fifteen years. You'll just have to trust me. Or go ask the guy who introduced us.'

'But how can I be sure you won't screw me on this?'

The Whale hangs up with no answer. *What a pain*, he thinks. Cowards like that are always flailing around, trying to feel safe. They don't plan long term or short term, they just react as things happen, endlessly trying to stamp out uncertainty.

The crossing signal turns green and he steps into the intersection, along with all the other people waiting. They pour into the street, jockeying for position. He crosses and turns to the right. There's a closer subway entrance in the other direction, but he just goes with the flow of the people.

'Did anyone see what happened?' A woman's voice rings out. The Whale looks in the direction it came from. A young woman with short hair, off to his side. She's slim, but her presence is large, and her tone is rough as she accosts passersby. 'Nobody saw anything?' The strobe of streetlights and neon signs and police flashers layers pink and red onto her pale white face.

'Hey, you. You see anything?' She's standing in front of the Whale. Her smile is casual, like they already know each other, but there's something jaded in her eyes under their single lids. Against her white skin her ruby lips wriggle like slugs.

'What would I have seen?'

'The accident that just happened. You didn't see it? One of my coworkers got run over. You didn't see anything?'

'Don't know what you mean by anything.'

'Like maybe somebody who pushed him.'

This jolts the Whale, but he hides it. A name pulses in his head: *the Pusher.*

'No.' His voice is low. He recalls the scene from the hotel window. But he doesn't see any reason to tell her about it. The man lurching into the street, and another man who passed by behind. *So it was the Pusher.* 'I didn't see anything.'

The woman's jaw works back and forth. She stares up at the Whale. 'Yeah, well, if you remember anything, get in touch, okay?' She offers her card, so apparently she means it.

He looks at the card. It says Fräulein, Inc. The Whale's lip curls. He knows the operation. 'Terahara's outfit.'

'You know the boss? So you must know something about the accident. Come on.'

'The Pusher.' He doesn't let it slip carelessly. He's testing her.

She raises an eyebrow. 'So you know about the Pusher, too.' She reaches out to grab hold of him, but he bats her hand away.

As he descends the stairs into the subway, the clamor of the street recedes. Through the ticket gate, down onto the platform. Blending into the flow of other subway riders. Before long the yellow train car rolls in. Lucky timing: the person on the end of the bench gets off and the Whale claims the seat. A drunk woman next to him glares, but when she sees his size she looks away.

He pulls his book out of his suit jacket pocket and opens to his bookmark. He reads a passage that he's read many times before. After a bit the speaker announces the next station stop. In that instant the Whale senses the seats across from him start to shudder. *Not again.* He clicks his tongue. It's not just the seats, the whole scene begins to ripple, all the outlines blurring. It's not an actual physical vibration – it's his own vertigo. It's been happening for the past six months. Always the same. His vision starts to blur, then goes dark. Then when he can see again, one of them has appeared.

One of them meaning the ghost of one of the people he's killed. Looking smug, like they had been there all along.

It's no different this time. When the dizziness passes and he opens his eyes, there's a woman sitting in the seat across from him.

All the other passengers have vanished. They were just there a moment ago – a man reading a newspaper. A girl in a high-school uniform staring at her phone. A company employee dozing while he holds on to a strap. All gone. The only person he sees is the woman across from him, long hair with a spiral perm, well-proportioned eyes and nose, stylish dark gray pantsuit. She waves demurely at the Whale, grinning.

It's a strange feeling, sitting facing someone in an otherwise empty train car.

She's a newscaster whose suicide he had forced, five or six years ago. Even though her job was just to report the news on TV, she had a strong sense of right and wrong, and whenever there was some news item that didn't sit right with her she would do her own investigations, ignoring the warnings of her superiors to stay out of it. She was especially persistent when it came to politicians trying to cover things up. Politicians don't

48

love it when journalists poke into their business, even when they don't have anything to hide, and when they do have something to hide, their natural response is to strike back.

But she wasn't the type to take the hint just because she got roughed up a little. All that did was strengthen her resolve, almost to the point of obsession. She ended up paying for it with her life.

She had crossed the politicians that nobody should ever cross, who then got in touch with the Whale.

'That's the whole point of journalism,' she had told him in the hotel room before killing herself. Her voice was trembling with emotion, but there was conviction in her statement. 'I can't stand to see justice perverted.'

'Justice?'

'I was raised on Japan's old folk tales. The ones on TV. All those stories where the wicked old man gets punished, and the kindly old man gets rewarded – they shaped how I see the world. So I can't stand injustice.'

'Reality is all there is,' the Whale had answered. 'Right now you're sitting here, crying, writing your suicide note. Some double-chinned politician is in a bed with a girl watching TV. That's the only reality that exists. It has nothing to do with what we like or don't like.'

She wouldn't agree with him, but in the end, once she looked into his eyes, she turned grim, put the noose over her own neck, and swung like a pendulum.

Now she's sitting there waving to him. The ghosts that keep appearing to the Whale don't look any different than normal human beings. It confuses him, and he doesn't like being confused.

Go away, he wants to shout.

There's a sudden pain in his gut. He presses his hand to his stomach as his body contorts. It doesn't feel like the kind of pain that comes with any particular physical ailment, more just a vague sense of something wrong, *right here*, but hard to pinpoint where exactly, like a cavernous emptiness inside his body. He knows that there's no need to panic, but he feels panic creeping in. The unexpected pain persists for a few moments, then fades. With each episode like this, the pain lasts longer. And it's been happening more often. He doesn't know the cause. He isn't planning to involve any doctors, but if he did, he has a feeling that they wouldn't know what it was either. Or how to fix it.

'It's your guilty conscience.'

The voice is gentle in his ear. He looks up. The newscaster's face is right beside his. She's attractive, her makeup tasteful. She brings her lips close. 'Don't you think?' He turns back to the front. The seat where she was is now empty. 'You didn't think you could keep forcing people to kill themselves without ever starting to feel guilty, did you?'

The Whale doesn't answer. Answering is exactly what she wants him to do. He knows that she's just an illusion, and that there are other people riding the subway. If he starts talking to ghosts, people will think he has mental issues. He recalls a passage from the book he carries around with him: 'There is nothing in it at all to worry about! It's simply physical derangement.' That was how the young Russian man steadied his nerves before he committed his murder. *That's what I'm experiencing now. Just some physical derangement.*

He feels the woman's breath on his cheek. 'Hey, that accident you saw before. That was the Pusher, wasn't it? It had to be. You know it just as well as I do.'

The Whale almost clicks his tongue. She's really pressing his buttons.

'Sorry to bring up old news, but didn't you lose to the Pusher once, a long time ago?'

He smiles acidly at her wording: *lose to.* It sounds like something a child would say when keeping score. *Don't talk to me about the Pusher,* he replies in his head.

'You were weak, so the Pusher beat you to the punch. You really should just retire. Go ahead, retire.' Now her soft voice is in his other ear, though he didn't see her move.

Shut up. Say one more word and I'll kill you. He stays quiet, glaring.

'I'm already dead,' she replies lightly. She smiles broadly, then brings her face close to his. 'Because of you.' Now her voice is cutting.

There's a sensation in his head like a rush of wind. He shivers. Presses his eyes closed for a few seconds, then opens them again.

The woman is gone. The world is back to normal.

In the seats across from him are a passed-out man in a suit, a girl completely absorbed in her phone, an old woman with a glum look on her face, a man ogling the swimsuit photos in his magazine, a couple talking animatedly. Just like it was before.

CICADA

CICADA IS CLIMBING THE FIRE escape of a shabby nine-story condo building on the south edge of Shinjuku. He winds his way up the spiral stairs, hand on the rusty red railing.

He ended up spending the night in Mito City after finishing the job, then caught the first train on the Joban line back to Tokyo. It's been raining since daybreak. Not heavy rain, but steady enough that it's slick underfoot, and strong enough to rustle the leaves on the stand of trees beside the building. The clouds are deep gray with ripples like muscles. They hang over the city but he can see where they break, far off in the distance.

He heads down the walkway on the sixth floor, hands in the back pockets of his jeans.

The movie he watched last night is still on his mind. He found it on a cable TV channel after he finished the job at the house in Mito.

Oppression, by Gabriel Casseau. He had never heard of the director before, and the title seemed pretty nondescript.

He almost changed the channel as it was starting, but

somehow he kept watching, and before long he was into it. It was about a boy in France who lost both parents in an accident. It told the story of his brief life.

Every day the boy delivers a stack of newspapers all over town, running through a maze of streets.

As he gets older, he upgrades his means of getting around, from running to riding a bicycle, from bicycle to motorbike. There isn't much dialogue, but through all that time it's clear that the thing he likes least in his life is his boss at the newsstand. All the fat shopkeeper ever does is order the boy around, never doing any of the work himself, living a lazy life.

The boy is poor, but he experiences love, and then inevitable heartbreak, living out his days one after the next. The shopkeeper gets worse and worse. He looks down on the boy, gives him unreasonable orders, sometimes even hits the boy. The one thing he doesn't like to give him is his pay. When he does, he throws the bills at the boy's feet. Every time, the boy gets angry, telling the shopkeeper he should hand it over properly.

Finally the boy comes to the shop with a knife to kill the shop-keeper. In that scene, the shopkeeper says to the boy, 'You're my puppet.'

The boy is enraged, but then suddenly there are strings attached to his body. The sort of strings for controlling a marionette.

'A puppet on a string,' the shopkeeper says softly. 'The death of your parents, your love and your heartbreak, even your very birth, I've been pulling the strings the whole time,' he says. 'Do you see now, my puppet?' He mocks the boy, laughing.

The boy smiles at first, then goes pale, then screams. But the scream that comes out of his mouth is a rooster's cry. He under-stands that this is the shopkeeper's doing as well, and he sinks into despair. He swings the knife around, trying desperately to cut the strings from his body, until he's taken to an insane asylum. In the end the boy is in his hospital bed muttering, 'I'll be a good puppet, just let me be free.'

The story was somber and rather dark. Apparently it won some award at a French or Italian film festival. It was mostly in black and white, but from time to time there was blue mixed in, maybe to show the boy's state of mind. The effect left an impression. But when the movie ended, Cicada felt oddly unsettled. He had the unpleasant feeling that he had been shown the story of his own life.

'Nothing like me,' he had said, to hear himself say it. Proof that it had actually touched a nerve.

In the last scene, the shopkeeper is drinking a can of beer while watching the boy in the hospital bed. He takes a sip, then laughs. 'Whereas I am free to do whatever I wish.' In that moment Cicada saw Iwanishi's praying mantis-like face layered over the shopkeeper's.

Now he continues along the open-air passageway of the condo building. The back of the building never gets any sunlight, hemmed in as it is by the trees. There's a relentless dankness, and it smells of mold. Along the edge of the walkway are three dead hornets. *Killed by mold*, Cicada concludes with no proof. Their black-and-yellow stripes give off a sense of threat. *Tigers, hornets – the black-and-yellow color combo says danger*, he muses. Then he recalls having heard about an assassin who goes by the working name Hornet. *Hornet sounds stronger than Cicada.*

He comes to room 603 and rings the bell. There's no answer, but Cicada turns the knob and enters. He knows that the door being unlocked means Iwanishi isn't going to come greet him.

The two-bedroom condo is twenty years old but feels much newer, probably because the fastidious Iwanishi keeps it so clean, from the floors and carpets to the bathroom and toilet to the walls and ceiling. Jack Crispin says, 'Keep your room clean and your body shows it.' *Ridiculous.*

'Yo.' Iwanishi looks up at Cicada and waves.

The room is twelve mats in size, and carpeted. Next to the window is a steel desk that looks like it was stolen from a teacher's staffroom at a primary school. Not much on it besides a phone, a computer, and a map. Iwanishi sits there with his legs kicked up on the desk. For a moment Cicada sees him as the newsstand shopkeeper from *Oppression*, and it startles him. Then he feels miffed. Then he clicks his tongue. A quick progression: startle, miff, click.

There's a long black sofa in front of the desk. Cicada sits down.

'Looks like you did good.' Iwanishi folds the newspaper in half and tosses it in Cicada's general direction. It falls at his feet. He looks down at it but doesn't pick it up.

'Already in the papers?'

'Take a look.'

'Nah. Whatever.' It doesn't make any difference. Family slaughtered, violence in the night, always the same kind of headline and the same kind of article. Same handwringing, same calling out societal ills.

When he started doing this kind of work he would check to see how it would show up on the news or in the papers. He looked forward to it, like an athlete collecting articles about the games where they play well. But that got old quick. The articles never said anything important, and he got bored seeing the descriptions of suspects that were way off the mark.

'Anyway –' Cicada looks up at Iwanishi – 'why don't you go ahead and crunch the numbers on your little computer and gimme my cut? And maybe once in a while you could thank me.'

'Now where do you get off talking so high and mighty like that, huh?' Iwanishi shrugs and shakes his head, his chin tiny and pointed. His wrists look like sticks coming out of his sleeves. 'If you wanna put labels on it, you're the employee and I'm your

55

boss. You're the foot soldier and I'm the commanding officer. You come into my place and talk like that, you're likely to lose your job, or maybe your head. So you'd be unemployed, or you'd be dead.'

'Then go ahead and do it. Not like you even can. Without me you got nothing.'

'And if you didn't have me, you wouldn't have any jobs.'

'I'd be just fine.'

'Moron – just killing people doesn't get you any money. Do you even know how this works?' Iwanishi points his finger at Cicada. 'I get an inquiry from someone, I negotiate, then I do all the research. The most important thing is the prep work. It's like, before you jump outta the tunnel, better watch your step.'

'As Jack Crispin says.'

'Very good.'

Cicada sighs. *All your dumb lines are Jack Crispin.* 'Here's what I wanna know, what kind of music did this fuckin guy even play anyhow? Punk? Free jazz?' Cicada is pretty familiar with most of the old rock bands, but he's never once heard of Jack Crispin. Sometimes he wonders if Jack Crispin is real or made up.

'Crispin was the first one to write about not wanting to live like he's dead. All the other artists stole the idea from him. And he was also the first rock musician to ever throw his guitar pick into the audience.'

'Did he also discover electricity and invent the telephone?'

'He just might have, yeah.'

'You're so full of shit.'

'In any case, these jobs require research. Why don't you just try killing someone based only on what you get from the inquiry? You'd get nabbed for conspiracy to commit murder. That's why you gotta put a lot of attention into things like time and place. Find out everything you can about the target. I do all of that.'

'Target. You don't need to dress it up to make yourself sound

56

cool.' Cicada sticks out his tongue and makes a sour face. 'They're victims. They're just victims.'

A reverberating voice comes in through the window. It's a fervent address from a candidate for the upcoming election in the House of Representatives. It's hard to make out what exactly the voice is saying, but it's clear the speaker is asking for support. Hearing this, Iwanishi's grim look suddenly brightens up and he starts in about the election. 'Who are you voting for?'

'I don't vote.'

'Do you know what people way back when went through so that you could have the right to vote?' Spittle flies out through his crooked teeth.

'Whatever. Gimme my money.'

Iwanishi doesn't answer. Instead he turns to his computer and starts typing.

Cicada looks around the room. It's been three months since he was last here. There are no decorations on the blank white walls. No bookshelves or cabinets either.

'Didn't bring me any nice snacks from Mito?' Iwanishi says, still tapping at the keyboard.

'Stuff it.'

'You could have at least brought me some natto. Nothing, huh?'

'Listen.' Cicada stands up, annoyed. 'I went there for a job. And, like, it was going to someone's house in the middle of the night and killing the whole family, so, kind of a big job. Like asking a mover to move someone out of their apartment in a high-rise with no elevator. And it was late, all the shops were closed anyhow. I didn't have anywhere to spend the night, so I just hung out in a manga cafe by the station. When exactly was I supposed to go shopping for local treats for you?'

'A manga cafe?' Iwanishi's voice has an edge. 'You didn't show them your ID, right?'

'Not my real one. You know, Mito's not that far – if you want natto so bad just go there yourself and get whatever you want.'

Cicada plops back onto the sofa and closes his eyes for a moment. He needs to calm down. He keeps thinking of the French boy from the movie. Raggedy and thin, delivering his newspapers, talking over and over again about wanting to be free. *I'm not like him*, Cicada tells himself. Fatigue hits him and he feels like he's about to fall asleep. Instead he sits up, props his elbows on his knees and rests his chin on his hand. Zones out.

He's a breath away from sleep when he hears a noise. He looks up and sees an envelope on the floor in front of him and a bit off to the left. An open envelope, with cash spilling out.

'Why don't you, like, hand it over properly?' Cicada hauls his body up and collects it. Checks the contents. He doesn't count it out, but he sees there are three bundles of bills. 'You know, I've been thinking for a while, for killing that many people, three million yen doesn't seem right.'

'It's too much money, you feel bad about taking it?'

'I'll fuckin kill *you*,' Cicada spits back. Iwanishi cackles.

'You shouldn't joke about murder, you know.'

'I'm saying that three million feels like not enough.'

'If you've got a problem with it, I can just find someone else to do the work. Plenty of folks who'll happily kill someone for a hundred thousand.'

'Anyone who'd do that, you can't trust. That's why you need me.'

'I don't wanna hear it. You can live off that for a whole year.' Iwanishi takes an ear pick from the desk and starts digging around in his ear.

'And it's not really a big deal but you could at least, like, offer me some tea or something.'

Cicada was sure that Iwanishi would snap at this, but

surprisingly he goes to the kitchen and brings back a cup, which he hands over. 'If black tea works, here you go.'

Cicada mutters his thanks and takes a sip. Then he sighs into the cup, sending up little wavelets of tea. 'Must have been hard work making tea this weak.'

'Not hard at all,' Iwanishi says with smug satisfaction as he sits back down at his desk. 'It's easy when you use the same teabag four or five times.'

'Come on.' Cicada sighs again. 'This is cheap black tea from the supermarket. And you use the same teabag four or five times? You can't even call it tea. It's like an empty shell of tea. Don't be so damn stingy, man. You're already hoarding all the money I earn for you.'

'Man, you really are like a cicada. You don't stop chirping and shrieking.'

'You could at least give me some intel.'

'What do you mean, intel?'

'Like with last night's job. Why did I kill them?' He recalls the middle-aged housewife's face, protesting to the last. 'I mean I'm not stupid. I figured it out. It was that thing with the homeless guy, right? The kid from the family set the homeless guy on fire.'

'Homeless guy? Fire? What are you talking about?' Now Iwanishi looks annoyed, and his voice hardens. 'Does it really matter that much?'

'I mean, no, I'm not like all twisted up over it. But, you know, if someone's at the river every day, fishing and doing laundry and stuff, sooner or later they start to wonder about where the river comes from, right? What's going on upstream, what's the source of the water. They'd wanna go find out. I'd at least like to know who ordered the job.'

'Sometimes you go upriver and you find out that it's all being pumped out of a giant pipe. You'd be sad when you found out.

Wouldn't it be better off to just stay downstream and hang out and be happy not knowing anything? Yeah, it would. The less a young man knows, the better.'

'Yeah, yeah.' Cicada waves away the Crispin lyric.

'Hey,' Iwanishi says, a sudden shift in his tone, 'I've been wondering. What do you think about, when you do your thing? When you kill someone?'

'What kind of a question is that?'

'When you're killing, do you think about excuses for what you're doing? Justifications? Do you pray?'

'Why would I do any of that?'

'So – you just kill without thinking of anything?'

Now he asks me this? It feels like a catcher asking a pitcher what kinds of pitches he can throw after being teammates for years. Cicada feels thrown off, but he looks for an answer. 'I'm not that smart so I've always been good at running away from tough questions. Like in school, all the math equations, English grammar. Even when my teachers would write it all out on the blackboard, I didn't get any of it. So I would just, like, switch my brain off. Which I guess is what I do now. I don't think about whether it's right or wrong to kill someone. It's my job, so I do it. That's all. It's like, I dunno, when the light's changing.'

'What light?'

'Like you're driving, right, and the light's yellow and about to turn red. You don't think about it, you just hit the gas and go.'

'Yeah. And sometimes, the car behind you makes it in time too, which always surprises me.'

'Sure. And maybe once in a while you time it wrong and stop right in the middle of the intersection. Then you block all the other cars. And you feel a little bad about it, right?'

'Yeah, I guess that's happened.'

'So it's like that.'

'Huh?'

'When you block the road, you feel a little bad. But it's not that big of a deal. You're like, my bad, okay? So that's how I feel about killing. And anyway, everyone who I've had to kill, it turns out they're all pretty annoying people. They're loud, and dumb, and selfish. No need to feel bad about killing people like them.'

'You know, you've got a real talent.' Iwanishi shrieks with laughter, like a drunk.

SUZUKI

SUZUKI STRAIGHTENS THE LAPEL ON his jacket. 'Your lapel is always rumpled,' his wife used to say while tugging at his suit jacket. He pictures her face. Takes a deep breath in and out, then looks at his watch. It's 11 a.m., roughly twelve hours since he saw Terahara's son get run over. The sky is blanketed with clouds. A steady rain is falling, which may be why there are so few people out and about despite it being Saturday. He's in a residential neighborhood on the southern edge of Tokyo. Signs here and there identify it as Netozawa Parktown.

Trash bags are piled at the collection area next to the sidewalk. Rain hits the plastic with a popping sound. There's a damp odor in his nostrils, maybe the smell of the rain, or the waft of the garbage seeping out from the bags.

He exhales slow and long. *I just have to do it. Like you always say.*

Hiyoko had called him at one in the morning.

'Where are you?'

'I just got back to my apartment.'

'It's not a good idea to lie to me,' she shot back. 'I'm right out-side your apartment now. So where are you actually?'

He was in a business hotel in town. A five-story building, old, cheap, much to be desired from both the service and the cleanliness.

'What do you think you're up to? Where are you? You found where the guy is, right? It's kind of crazy over here.'

'Crazy?'

'Terahara flipped his shit. He got all the employees together, shouting at them, find the man who did this already! I mean, his son died. Hey, you didn't lose the guy, did you?'

He hesitated a moment, thinking how to answer. 'I found where he lives. I took the subway from Fujisawa Kongocho to Shinjuku. Then I transferred. Then I rode the train to the end of the line.'

'The end of what line?' Hiyoko asked questions like she was shooting arrows. 'What station?'

Suzuki almost answered reflexively, but he stopped himself. 'Not yet.'

'Not yet?'

'I can't tell you yet.'

'What the hell does that mean?' Her voice hardened. 'Are you making fun of me?'

'I'm still not sure if the man I followed is actually the culprit.'

'So tell me the place. We'll find out in no time if he's the cul-prit or not.'

'How?'

'Some Fräulein employees will go to his house and ask him all about it.'

Right away Suzuki insisted, 'That's no good. They'll just force a confession out of him.'

'Not if he comes right out and says that he did it, but other-wise, yeah, I imagine they'll rough him up a little.'

63

He got the sense that 'a little' was more than just a little. 'No. That doesn't work for me.'

'Do you understand your position here? If you don't tell me where the Pusher is right now, you'll regret it.'

'But we're not even sure that he *is* the Pusher. It could have just been an accident.' It could even have been a suicide, though the chances were admittedly slim.

'The guys who were with him say no way it was an accident. Somebody pushed him. And it was the work of a pro. Which means that it had to be the Pusher. Hey – you don't think you can get away from us, do you?'

'What I don't think is that a pro would let themselves be spotted so easily.'

'Maybe he just messed up.'

'Well, now I –' Suzuki said, feeling frantic – 'now I could get away. I'm not in your car anymore. You don't have a gun on me. No one knows where I am.'

'If you don't tell me, someone from the organization will find the guy eventually. We've got a serious information network. The Pusher? We'll find him, easy.'

'Then why don't you just do that?'

'Because I'd rather get it over with now.' She sounded like she was talking about a one-night stand.

'No.'

'Okay then.' Her voice brightened noticeably. 'Understood.' The cheerful tone made Suzuki even more uneasy. 'If that's your decision, I'll just kill these two.'

'Who?'

'You know, the guy and girl we put in the back of the car. They looked so cute back there sleeping, didn't they? Young guy and girl, their whole lives ahead of them.'

Suzuki immediately pictured the face of his former student. 'See, Mr Suzuki, I can do good too –' His smile, his hand scratching his head. Somehow similar to the pair in the back seat.

'What,' Suzuki began, trying not to let his voice show how much this affected him, 'what about them?'

'Like I said, if you don't cooperate, I'll kill them.' She said it as lightly as if she had been talking about finishing a meal.

'They have nothing to do with me.'

'So you're fine just letting it happen to them?' The way she said it seemed to lay all the blame on Suzuki, not just for this, but for all the unhappiness in the world.

'I'm not letting anything happen.' As he said it, deep in his head a voice reverberated, *Thanks for not giving up on me, teach.*

Now he's standing in front of the house. Back in Netozawa Parktown. It doesn't appear that anyone has followed him.

A standalone house, two-story, light brown walls. The roof is flat, like a large board laid down atop the structure. The curtains are closed so he can't see in. A concrete block wall surrounds the yard, wet from the rain, overhung with zelkova branches, bind-weed vines twisting around the post beside the entryway. There's a mailbox built into the wall, blackened with rust or dirt. The rain is loud, spattering on the roof, overflowing from the gutters.

Through the gate he can see steppingstones crossing the small garden, leading to the front door. He tilts his umbrella back and squints, but can't find any nameplate.

Attached to the gate is a call button. He stares at it. Extends his finger. His legs feel unsteady.

Up above on the balcony, there's a kid-size shirt hanging. *Why wouldn't they have brought that in from the rain?* Then he sees the roof extending out over the balcony, far enough to keep the shirt dry.

There's a child in the house. The man who lives here is the Pusher. The Pusher has a child. A family.

65

This is too much.

The scene from the intersection in Fujisawa Kongocho last night replays in his mind, like a film in slow motion. He pictures the slim man who brushed by behind Terahara's son.

Now the rain has mostly stopped. He extends his palm, feels no droplets, closes his umbrella. Then he stares at the house once more.

'What are you doing here?'

He almost leaps out of his skin at the sudden voice. There's a boy next to him. He must have been too focused on closing his umbrella to notice the boy show up. The boy's blue umbrella and close-cropped hair make him look like a schoolkid who dreams of being in the Navy. It's cute the way the tip of his nose angles upward.

'This is my house.'

'Oh –'

'I'm Kentaro,' the boy announces.

Suzuki looks at him carefully. He must be in his third or fourth year of primary school.

'You looking for my dad?'

After a flash of doubt and a momentary stammer, Suzuki answers, 'That's right. Is he home?' He's made up his mind now. There's no time to lose. *I just have to do it. Like you always used to say.*

'Dad says not to trust people who don't tell you their names when you tell them yours.'

'Oh, I'm Suzuki.'

'Who named you that?'

'What?'

'Who gave you the name Suzuki? My mom picked my name, Kentaro.'

'Well, it's my family name.' The boy's misunderstanding is throwing him off.

'Dad doesn't like it when people smile like that.'

Now Suzuki is getting frustrated. Confused, even. He came looking for a man who committed a murder, but instead he's going back and forth idly with a young boy. The incongruity is disorienting.

The boy opens the gate and heads toward the house. 'Don't worry about it, I'll go get my dad.'

Suzuki looks down at the path in front of him, then closes his eyes. *Could I have made a mistake?* His confidence is shaken, and doubts start to bubble up one after another. *Maybe I should leave. Maybe I should just run away.*

He hears something and looks back up.

His heart lurches in his chest. The man is standing right in front of him, holding the gate open. The same man he saw the night before at the intersection, no mistaking it. Every hair on Suzuki's body stands on end. The man is wearing a black turtleneck and brown corduroys. His cheeks are sunken and the air he gives off is sharp-edged. Suzuki swallows hard. He wants to blink but can't. The man's hair is long and unruly, his eyes wide and penetrating.

'I'm Suzuki.'

The man doesn't react. He could easily say I don't know you and you're not welcome here, and wave Suzuki away, or get aggressive and demand to know how Suzuki knows where he lives. But he just stares quietly.

Then: 'Asagao,' he replies, giving his own name. *Morning glory?* Suzuki asks what characters he uses for the name, and the man mimes writing the kanji for a different flower.

'Isn't that the kanji for hibiscus?'

The man just shrugs. 'What do you want?'

Suzuki looks over the man's shoulder at the steppingstones. He doesn't mean to avoid the man's gaze, and he realizes it probably makes him seem unsure of himself. 'Well,' he begins, but can't continue. *You're the Pusher, aren't you?* He had intended to come right out and ask, but now that he's facing the man he just can't do it. Are you the Pusher? Oh, yes, I am, how can I help you? Well, last night you pushed Terahara's son into the street, correct? Why, yes, I did. You did do it, I knew it! Thanks, have a nice day! . . . It doesn't seem likely the conversation would go that way. The man in front of him, Asagao, is staring as if looking right through him. Suzuki's legs are stuck, his face frozen, his lips paralyzed.

'If you don't have any business with me, maybe you should leave. My son told me you were here to see me, though.' Asagao's words are brusque, but his tone isn't especially cold. He seems relaxed. Maybe he can see through Suzuki, or maybe he's just sizing him up.

Suzuki feels a sudden rush of urgency, like he doesn't have a moment to spare, so his head starts working, and before he even realizes what he's doing, he says: 'Have you ever considered a private tutor for your son?'

What the hell did I just do?

THE WHALE

BEFORE HE'S PROCESSED THE FACT that it's morning, the Whale registers that it's raining. He opens his eyes. Still lying down, he watches the droplets fall from the edge of the tarp stretched overhead.

He's in a park on the eastern outskirts of Shinjuku. The section facing the main street has a fountain and a broad grassy lawn, well taken care of, but the Whale is further into the park, down a flight of stairs. Hidden in the beautiful park, a decidedly un-beautiful spot. A world away from the fountain that catches the light on sunny days, from the vivid shadow on the grass of a ball a father throws to his son, from anything wholesome. A damp hollow.

The park administrative office used to be there, but it had been demolished, leaving an empty depression thirty meters square. Sunken below the main area of the park with the fountain and the lawn, the sun barely reaches it.

It's now crowded with tarps, tents and cardboard boxes. The Whale had heard that the first homeless folks who took up residence had pretended that they were there to look at the cherry blossoms. When the park attendant told them to move along they insisted that they were just having a blossom-viewing party, but of course after the blossoms fell they were still there. In no time others showed up, more and more of them, and before long a whole little shanty town had sprung up.

The Whale has been there since the end of the summer. Which means he's been sleeping under a tarp for nearly two months.

'We're not living here, we're just surviving,' the middle-aged man who slept in the next tent had once yelled. It was in reply to the ward office worker who came by, face a mask of pity, saying they couldn't live there.

We're not living here, we're just surviving. It had a certain power to it. The Whale was dozing when the man shouted it, but it made him open his eyes.

No tent for the Whale. All he uses is some cardboard for a floor and tarp for a roof. With no walls the wind can get chilly, but it's not so bad he can't handle it.

He sits up slowly. Several men are already up and about. Tending to their tents, doing some stretches. If the rain picks up then people will start to wash their hair, but no one is doing that yet.

Two men have a fire going beside the stairs. They're using a piece of cardboard to shield it from the rain, and they're heating up some food in a hotpot. He checks his phone, there on the ground beside him, and sees that it's past eleven.

Bruise-black clouds float overhead, looking like he could touch them. The wind is strong enough to make them swirl visibly, a fluid spiraling pattern. The rain will probably let up in the afternoon.

'Say hey, say hey,' comes a voice from right next to him.

The Whale stands up, swivels around and shoots his hands

out toward the voice, grabbing its owner by the collar and hauling upward before he even sees who it is.

'Sorry!' the man squeaks, his face pale. His tongue sticks out and he can't properly form words, probably because the Whale has him by the neck. 'Sorrysorrysorry!'

It's an older man who sleeps nearby. He always looks like he's got a cold. Even in summertime he wears a heavy coat. Always just hanging around. The Whale lets him go and the man rubs his throat, coughing. There are what look like food scraps in his graying beard. Flecks of dried milk, too. A sour odor assaults the Whale's nostrils, maybe from the food scraps, maybe from the man's greasy hair.

'Anyway anyway,' the man says, flakes coming from his white hair as he points behind the Whale. 'Mr Tanaka, Mr Tanaka, he wants you to come over, wants you.'

The Whale turns to look. Two men stand over the hotpot, looking back at him uneasily. One of them must be Tanaka.

Not once since he started staying in the park has the Whale had a conversation with anyone else here. He hasn't even nodded a greeting. The other residents must have been curious, seeing this sturdy-looking guy with no tent who never talks to anyone, but none of them have tried to engage. They just keep their distance and watch. The Whale doesn't want to be a member of this oddball gang, but he follows the man over.

'Ah, look, he's here,' says a short man swishing chopsticks around in the hotpot. His front teeth are missing. Looks to be over retirement age.

Next to him is a skinny man with glasses. Everyone who stays here is on the skinny side, but this guy really has no meat on him. He must be in his forties. The bags under his eyes make him seem older. His cap has a picture of a magnifying glass, a childish-looking detail that doesn't fit with the rest of him. He has a broken plastic umbrella over his head.

71

'What do you want?' The Whale's voice is dark and low.

'Mr Tanaka wants to talk to you,' says the one with the missing teeth, looking over at the other man.

Meaning that this skin-and-bones guy with the magnifying glass hat is Tanaka. He's got a stick in his right hand that he's leaning on like a cane. Must have a bad leg.

Mr Magnifying Glass scratches his hairline, then points at the Whale. 'You've been moaning. In your sleep.'

The Whale narrows his eyes. He tries to remember if he's been having any nightmares but comes up blank.

'Something's troubling you. This past little while. Seems to me.' As Tanaka talks, the other two watch the Whale carefully, gingerly, like they're watching to make sure their coworker hasn't offended an important client.

'Something troubling me.'

'All around you. All the time. I see them. Strange things.' Tanaka strings together snippets of language, then agitatedly scratches his hairline again.

'Strange?' The Whale looks hard at him.

'Mr Tanaka, Mr Tanaka, he sees 'em. Ghosts and spirits, ghosties and spirits,' mumbles the white-haired man. Every word from his mouth brings a rotting waft.

'Spirits of the dead. Always floating around you. Even right now. A man in a nice suit.' Tanaka proceeds to describe the spirit's appearance, or more like the ghost's outline.

There's no doubt about it: the man Tanaka's describing is the politician's secretary that the Whale forced into suicide in the hotel room the night before.

'He's moaning, what about Kaji?'

'Kaji. His boss,' explains the Whale.

'You're all wrapped up in it. That's why you don't sleep well. Right?' Spittle bubbles at Tanaka's lips. 'You keep doing it. You won't stop.'

'Mr Tanaka, maybe take it easy, take it down a notch,' puts in the man with the missing teeth, like he's interceding in negotiations. Probably something he used to do back when he was a salaryman.

'What are you talking about?' the Whale asks softly.

'All the spirits around you. They're there because of the work you do. Isn't that right? And that's why you should stop doing that kind of work.' Tanaka's way of speaking is shifting away from disjointed snippets into more fluent speech. Just as the Whale notes this, he sees that behind Tanaka's glasses the man's eyes are suddenly unclouded, and his skin seems to almost glow. The buildup of spittle around the edges of his mouth is gone. There's suddenly something almost imposing about him. Even threatening, like he might leap forward and attack with his cane.

What is going on? Am I still asleep? Am I hallucinating? The Whale can't make sense of it. Tanaka has transformed from a homeless man into a venerable teacher, a respected master.

'Mr Tanaka used to be a therapist. He almost always hits the nail on the head,' says the toothless man.

'You should give up the work you're doing. If you do, you'll be released from all this.' Tanaka's words feel like a blessing.

'If I stop, I'll be okay?' The Whale is surprised at his own voice. Like a troubled teenager seeking advice at church. He sounds sincere.

'That's right.'

'How?'

'Simplify things for yourself. All the questions that swirl around you, all the people, deal with them one by one. Clear away all the unnecessary static so that you're left only with what matters. Remove the complications from your life. Settle your accounts.'

'Settle my accounts?'

'Every last one of them. Settle your accounts.'

The Whale doesn't know how to respond. He's silent for a few moments. 'And if I do that, the pain will go away?'

'Yes. Do you have any work left unfinished? If not, your suffering should disappear.'

At that the Whale thinks back to all the jobs he's done. As he winds his way back through his memories, Tanaka watches silently.

After some time, Tanaka speaks up again, with the quiet dignity of a psychiatrist. 'As long as no work is left unfinished –'

But the Whale cuts him off. 'No. I have a score to settle.'

'Do you?'

'From ten years back. The one time I failed at a job.'

He remembers it clearly. Ten years ago, in a hotel in Shinjuku. The scene has been floating up inside his head since last night.

A single room in the hotel. A politician. She's an advocate for the people. Inexpensive suit, low heels, face white as a sheet. 'Why do I have to kill myself?' Asking the same question that they all ask. Trembling.

'And this failure is still bothering you?' Tanaka probes.

After finishing her last letter, the politician turned to face the Whale, having to look up at him due to the height difference, but nonetheless keeping her voice steady.

'Go to the crossroads, bow down to the people, kiss the earth, for you have sinned against it too, and say aloud to the whole world, "I am a murderer."'

He recoiled, blinking hard. It was not the meaning of what she said that rattled him. It was his shock at the fact that it was a line from his book, from the only book in his life.

'I made a mistake. I thought that she and I were allies. Just because we had both read the same book. So I didn't finish the job. I let her go.'

She had been bewildered that she was getting out of the hotel with her life, but she left nonetheless.

'And what happened because of it?' asks Tanaka.

'Someone else got to her.'

The next day, at an intersection in Hibiya, she found herself in front of a black four-wheel drive that ran her over and killed her. The politician who had hired the Whale had also hired the Pusher. Or at least that's the rumor the Whale heard after the fact.

'So you feel regret.'

'Because I made a stupid mistake and didn't finish the job.'

'Regret is the root of misfortune. It leads to all sorts of disasters. If that's how you're feeling, then even if you were to retire your troubles might not subside.'

'I see.' The Whale pulls his chin back and looks hard at Tanaka, a full head shorter than him. 'What should I do?'

'Settle the score.'

It sounds a bit silly to the Whale. But he sees how it tastes in his mouth: 'Settle the score.' As he says it, he feels a sensation like pressure escaping from the whorl of hair at the back of his head. 'Settle the score, huh?'

'Here, have some.' The toothless man's voice brings him back to reality.

He blinks several times. In front of him are three homeless men, same as before. Tanaka looks like he first did, an undernourished man, dark and sickly. Not even a glimmer of psychiatrist. Just a grimy, unhealthy man. *Did that conversation even happen? Did I just imagine it?* Doubt grips the Whale like tightly wound chains.

The man with the missing teeth pokes his chopsticks at something in the hotpot.

'Here you go. Eat.'

The Whale leans in for a look and sees that it's some kind of fish. They must have caught it in the park pond.

'You did it, didn't you?' Toothless sounds excited. 'I read about

75

it in the paper this morning.' He points at the fire below the pot. The newspaper must have been the kindling. 'Last night, a family in Mito was killed.'

'And?'

'That was you, right? You got him for us?'

The Whale isn't following.

'The kid in that family, he's the one who set one of our friends on fire. All the homeless people know about it. Now he's dead. And some of us, well, we were thinking that maybe you did it. Right? It was you, right?'

'You've got me figured wrong.'

'Sure you did. You're on our side, aren't you? I mean, you are, right?' The man is almost supplicating, like a catcher pleading with the umpire to change a call.

'I only do jobs I get hired for. Unless someone asks and I agree, I don't work.'

With that, the Whale turns and leaves them behind. The three men mumble their farewells. He goes back to his residence, that is, to his cardboard and tarp. He waves his hand like he's warding off mosquitoes, when he's actually trying to banish the spirits that even now seem to swirl around him.

His phone vibrates.

Settle the score. The words ring in his ears. *Settle the score, then retire. Doesn't sound bad. Settle the score. Close my accounts.*

He looks back over his shoulder toward the three men, but they've vanished. He's rattled. *It really was just some messed-up hallucination.* But the hotpot is still there, steaming away.

They probably just went to go get some more water.

He answers his phone and hears Kaji, sounding unnaturally cheerful.

CICADA

AFTER LEAVING IWANISHI'S CONDO, CICADA walks along the river to the station where he finds a bicycle that looks like it'll ride smoothly, so he steals it. The rain has mostly eased up. He straddles the bike and pedals off. Stops at a supermarket to pick up some things, then heads back to his apartment. It's an old building with a small gate. It looks like a block of jellied konnyaku stood on its side.

He goes to the last apartment on the second floor, retrieves his key from its hiding place behind the gas meter, unlocks the door. His place is two rooms, each six tatami in size, with wood flooring. The room on the west side has a single bed and a cabinet stuffed with CDs that takes up much of the space. The square clock on the middle of the cabinet reads 11 a.m.

He steps into the kitchen and puts the freshwater clams he just bought in a bowl of water to get the sand out. Getting them ready for dinner.

Gazing down into the bowl, he sees bubbles floating up to the surface where they pop, pop. It's the clams breathing. Silently opening their shells and breathing. It fascinates Cicada. *They're alive. Kind of amazing.*

The times when he's rinsing the sand out of clams, just watching them, are the happiest times for him. He doesn't know if it does anything for other people, but he never feels quite so calm as when he's watching the clams breathing.

People too, he thinks, not for the first time. *If you could really see people breathing, like when they exhale bubbles or smoke, you could probably get more of a sense that they're actually alive. If all the people walking around sent out little bubbles when they breathed, it might be harder to hurt them. It'd definitely be harder . . . Although I do still eat the clams.*

For a while he stands there staring, lost in the clams' peaceful proof of life. *I'm going to kill them and eat them*, he thinks. For him, this is critical. He can't help but feel that people should be more aware of the fact that they survive by killing and eating other living things.

The cold ringtone of his phone starts up and he goes into his room to get it out of the pocket of his suede jacket. There's only one person who ever calls him.

'Sending someone home and then calling them right back in is not cool.' Cicada lowers himself into the sturdy chair against the wall and glares at Iwanishi, who is sitting with his elbows propped on the steel desk. It's the first time he's ever been to Iwanishi's place twice in one day. 'Didn't your precious Jason Crispin have anything to say about that?'

'It's Jack Crispin.' Iwanishi sounds annoyed. 'Not like you were doing anything important anyway, right? Probably just hanging around your apartment, watching TV.'

'Clams.'

'Is there a clam channel now?'

What an idiot, Cicada thinks with a sigh. 'You've got a lot of nerve trying to get me on a job as soon as I just finished one, no break or anything.'

'Save it. A job came in. I'm not just gonna ignore it. Anyway, Jack Crispin says: "I'll only forgive you the first time." Meaning, you gotta forgive me at least once. Right?'

'Wrong.'

'This isn't just any job. It's from a politician.' Iwanishi lifts the cup on his desk and takes a sip. He's trying to disguise his excitement, which comes off as a little creepy.

'What kind of an asshole gets so pumped up by a call from a politician? I'm surprised you'd be so easily impressed. Don't make me think even less of you than I already do.'

'It's not like that.'

'Then what is it? Who's this politician anyway?'

'You know who Kaji is? From the House of Reps. The ruling party. He's always shouting on TV.'

'Kaji? Never heard of him.'

'Do you have any appreciation for how people once suffered so that you could have the right to vote?'

'Not that again. Listen, I'm doing the best I can with my own life. I have zero interest in politics.'

'Sooner or later the apathetic get swallowed by the flood. Understand? Get wise about politics, or they'll be writing cautionary songs about you.'

'More lyrics from Johnson.'

'Crispin sang about how the real rulers of the country don't look like politicians. Pretty sharp. Fascism never looks like fascism. He said that too. Pretty sharp indeed.'

'Politicians are all the same. Doesn't matter who they are.'

'You're a moron.' Iwanishi puffs out his chest. 'Leave something where it is for too long and it starts to go bad, you ever heard that? If the same people hold power forever, they get corrupt, every time. If they're all the same, that's even more reason to switch them out on a regular basis. It's like if you leave water standing too long, it grows algae, which then rots. And it's pretty rare for any country to have the same party in power for so long.'

Cicada snorts. *You're the one who got all hot and bothered about a politician in the ruling party.* 'So what's this Kaji want?'

'Most people go to a bookstore looking for books. They come to the killers to get someone killed. Obviously.'

'You know, I fuckin hate politicians.' Cicada scratches his ear. 'All they think about is themselves. Themselves, and the people in their district. Shouldn't politicians care about what's good for the whole country?'

'Nah.' Iwanishi's lip curls. 'This particular fellow isn't that kind of noble guy.'

'Then what kind of guy is he?'

'The kind who uses his money and power to kill people. Who comes to me and says, this afternoon there'll be a man at the Tower Hotel by Tokyo Station. A big man, well built, almost two meters tall. I need you to take him out . . . That kind of guy.'

'And his name is Kaji.'

'Yep. A real-deal politician.'

'The target's a big guy, huh.' The prospect isn't exciting. 'Not my area of expertise.'

'And what exactly is your area of expertise?'

'Like you said before. Killing families, doing jobs that no one else wants to do, that kind of stuff is my specialty, right? This job isn't a family, it's not a woman, it's not a kid. It's a big guy.'

'Don't be so picky. It's a job. And the money's good. This is a politician we're talking about.'

'How come the big guy needs to die?'

'Would you ask someone buying a porno mag why they're buying it? Who cares why?'

'It's not like Kaji's gonna get mad if you ask him.'

'Of course he'll get mad. I didn't even wanna take the job. Partly because I'm well aware that you just finished a job and I knew you'd bitch and moan about another one so soon. I was planning to turn it down.'

Bullshit, thinks Cicada. He's only half listening.

'But since yesterday our whole world has been a royal mess.'

Cicada notices through the door to the balcony over Iwanishi's shoulder that the rain clouds are all but scattered. White rays of sun are starting to beam through.

'What do you mean, our whole world?'

'I mean our professional world. People who do work like we do.'

'Are you serious right now?' Cicada knits his eyebrows. 'Talking about murder like it's a profession?'

'Shut it. I have a close info network. I hear all kinds of things. When somebody new shows up on the scene, I hear about it. It's business, after all. I hear all the rumors. You do it too, right? You get info from that porno shop.'

He means Momo, an adult magazine shop. It's on a back alley not far from Tokyo Station. The woman who runs the place is also called Momo – maybe it's just convenient for her to go by the name of the shop, or maybe she named the shop after herself. 'What do you know about it? I just like that shop is all.'

'Because of the porno mags?'

'I mean, it's like an entire wall of covers with naked girls. Gorgeous. I dunno, I just like it.'

'You're a little perv.'

'No, it's not like that. I'm saying, rather than a girl who's all decked out trying to look fancy, I think it's more impressive to pose nude like that. Nothing hidden, no tricks. It's like, clean. Feels honest.'

'You really are a moron.'

'Fuck you. Lots of people feel the same way I do. That's how all those rumors end up at Momo.'

'Momo's part of our professional world. It's a market for rumors and gossip.'

'Speaking of which, you ever heard of someone called the Hornet?' Cicada pictures the insect corpses on the condo building walkway. He'd heard about the Hornet from Momo.

'The guy who kills with poison? Haven't heard much about him recently. Hornets can only sting once before they die. What's there to be afraid of?'

'That's bees. Hornets can sting as many times as they want.'

'There's also the Whale.'

'In the ocean?'

'A guy who specializes in making people commit suicide. Gets his contracts from the rich and powerful and makes his victims kill themselves.'

'Sounds unsatisfying. If you're gonna kill someone you should do it yourself, come at them head-on, stick the knife in. Millions of people kill themselves every year on their own anyway. Suicide's not a way to kill someone, it's just something that happens.'

'You sure like to chatter.'

'Well, yeah, that's why they call me Cicada.'

'Anyway. I'm sure you know about Terahara's outfit too, yeah?'

'Oh, Fräulein?' He's heard of it. It's a whole company. A guy named Terahara is in charge. They're into drugs, human trafficking, black-market organ sales. He's never had any direct contact with them but he's heard some wild rumors. One that actually upset him was about a woman they kept locked up and forced her to keep having babies, which they then shipped overseas for organ harvesting. He doesn't know if it's true or not, but even if it's just a rumor it's pretty twisted.

'Well, last night Mr Terahara's son died.' Iwanishi's nostrils flare, like he's proud of himself for knowing.

'That's good news.' It's how he really feels. Cicada has never met Terahara's son, but he's heard stories, and they're all bad. The guy took advantage of his dad's reputation so that he could run wild. 'Someone kill him?'

'He got hit by a car. A minivan.'

'Divine retribution. I heard he was always drunk driving and running people over. Or egging his friends on and they'd run over kids on their way to school.'

'So they're saying that it wasn't just a normal accident that killed him.'

'No, it was getting run over that killed him.'

'What I mean is, he was probably pushed in front of the car.'

'Pushed? Come on.'

'There's a guy who does jobs that way.' Iwanishi mumbles it, which is rare for him. Maybe he doesn't want to have to explain it.

'What do you mean, does jobs that way? And who would have hired someone to do that?'

'Lots of people hate Terahara.' Iwanishi stretches his arms overhead. 'Anyway, Mr Terahara's furious. He's got all his own people looking for whoever killed his son, his eyes are peeled, he's hiring people left and right to search.'

'He doesn't think we did it, does he?'

'Probably not.' A self-deprecating smile appears on Iwanishi's face. He knows they're small-time. 'But we did get this other job come in.'

'The Kaji thing.'

'Everyone else in the business is running around with Terahara's thing. Looking for the guy who did it. We must have been the only ones available to take the job. This is a big chance for us. While everyone else is at the parade, we get a new client.'

'I'm not really interested. Didn't you just say a couple of hours ago that it's dangerous to do back-to-back jobs?'

'It's fine. You'll do it.'

The finality in Iwanishi's tone really gets to Cicada. He tries not to let it show as he swallows hard. It felt like he was being told, *After all, you are my puppet.* The scene from the movie replays in his head. He sees himself tied down in the hospital bed. *No way.* He forces himself to think of the clams breathing.

SUZUKI

HE'D BE HARD-PRESSED TO EXPLAIN why he hit on the idea of posing as a private tutor. But thinking about it, he reasons that if it works out then he'd have a reason to visit on a regular basis, maybe even a few times a week. That would give him more opportunities to find proof that the man of the house is the Pusher.

Asagao looks momentarily taken aback. 'Huh.'

Suzuki isn't sure what that's supposed to mean and he flashes a lame smile, but then Asagao continues: 'You want to come in?'

'Oh! Er, are you sure?'

'You have a problem with coming in?'

'No, no, no problem at all.'

What happens next is a blur. Suzuki does not process crossing the threshold, or register whether the door opens inward or outward. The next thing he's aware of is looking down at his feet. His shoes are off.

He's shown into the living room where he sits on a beige couch. He crosses his legs then uncrosses them. His right thumb and index finger rub his left index finger, then move on to rub his left thumb. He looks over into the adjoining room. There's a dining table and a built-in kitchen.

'So, are you?'

The question snaps him back to attention. Asagao is sitting on another couch facing him.

'Er, am I what?'

'Are you in sales?'

'Yes, I am,' he answers automatically, but then hastily corrects himself. 'I mean I find new clients, but I also do tutoring.' If he doesn't establish that, this won't work.

'Sounds like a lot to handle.'

'Oh, I'm used to it.' *Or I would be if it were true.*

'So you would be the one tutoring Kentaro?'

'That's right.' Convincing himself that he's ready to go through with this, Suzuki looks directly at Asagao.

The man's hair has a slightly wild look, as if he only ever combs it with his fingers. But he doesn't look at all grimy, or even that old. His eyes are sharp and his brow well defined. There's no extra flesh on his cheeks or chin. The lines between his eyebrows and at the corners of his mouth look less like wrinkles or signs of fatigue and more like scars, or etchings.

'I'm calling on houses in the area with children in primary and middle school.' Suzuki starts spinning a story, not sure how specific he should be. It's one thing to go with your gut, but this was already absurd.

'You're in sales but you don't have a card?'

'Oh –' Suzuki's vision blacks out for a moment. He feels like they sat down to play shogi and he lost on the first move. 'I actually gave out my last one at the last house. Sorry about that.' His heart is hammering. He launches into his pitch. Which is of course all completely fake.

He makes up a name for the private tutoring company, gives a

86

location for the office, talks about the number of tutors and their level of experience and their teaching method, invents his own career history as a tutor, conjuring one detail after the next. He fabricates a reason why he's making sales rounds with no pamphlets or materials, comes up with an excuse as to why he's wearing rumpled daily wear instead of a suit. It turns out his tutoring company has operations across the country, and last month Suzuki was given responsibility for Netozawa Parktown.

It's a tightrope act. But the month he's spent as a contractor for Fräulein seems to be coming in handy, what with all the nonsense sales presentations pushing diet products.

When he finishes his performance, he takes a deep breath and exhales through his nose. *Pretty decent, for having made it up entirely on the spot.* 'So, what do you think? Shall we enroll Kentaro for private tutoring?'

'Well now.' Asagao sounds calmer than Suzuki was expecting. 'How much does it cost?'

'Oh!' Suzuki's voice pitches upward. He had forgotten that detail. 'I guess I left that to the end, didn't I?' He scratches his head with an exaggerated gesture. He has no idea what the going rate is for home tutoring. 'Let's talk about it.' He raises his eyebrows. 'To the extent that I can, I'd like to offer you a price that works for you.'

'A price that works for me, huh?' Asagao smiles. There's a ripple of interest, like a breeze rustling through forest leaves.

Suzuki's phone rings. Monotonous, insistent.

'You have a call,' Asagao points out.

'Yes, probably the office.' Suzuki starts to get up. 'Do you mind?' It'll be Hiyoko calling. The phone is the one that Fräulein gave him.

'Sure,' Asagao says with a wave. 'No problem.'

Suzuki stands, takes out his phone, quickly presses the accept button and holds it to his ear. He turns to face the wall, his back to Asagao.

'Well?' asks the no-nonsense female voice.

'I'm just in the middle of the presentation.' Conscious of Asagao behind him, Suzuki plays up the salesman act.

'What presentation? Did you go to the guy's house or not?'

'That's correct. I'm giving the presentation now.'

'Why are you talking like that?'

I can't explain right now. He steals a glance toward the couch to get a read on Asagao but the man isn't there.

At the same moment he hears a voice over his other shoulder: 'I'm going to go get Kentaro.' His hair stands on end. He turns toward the voice to find Asagao standing right beside him. He hadn't felt the man approach at all. No sense whatsoever of when he stepped up next to him.

Suzuki nods his head enthusiastically. His grin stretches his cheeks to the maximum.

'I'm talking to him now – just lay off me, will you?' He keeps his voice low, suppressing his urge to shout into the phone.

'You sure are taking your sweet time.' Hiyoko sounds rather relaxed herself. 'Tell me where you are.'

'Are they safe?'

'They?'

'The couple from the back of the car.' Those two trusting, not-so-smart kids.

'Oh, yes, they're fine.' Her tone isn't exactly reassuring. 'There's no upside to me just killing them. But if you don't tell me exactly where you are soon, they won't be fine much longer.'

'Listen –' He explains what's going on, speaking flat and quick. In one breath he tells her that he's not yet sure if the man is actually the culprit, that he's made it into the man's house and it turns out the man has a family, and that he's trying to become the son's tutor.

The whole time he's talking he has his eyes on the entrance to the room. He's terrified that Asagao will materialize behind him

88

and give him a push. Then a subway train will speed through the room to crush him under its wheels, even though they're in a residential neighborhood with no nearby station, even though he's inside someone's house. He can see the front car of the subway train bursting through the wall, obliterating concrete and wood. It rears up like a wild horse, floating for a moment in space, then crashes down on him. There's no driver. No tracks. Just a long rectangular mass, grinding him into pulp.

'Are you stupid? Tutor the kid? What the hell are you thinking?'

'It's to get close to the guy!' He's still keeping his voice low. 'I think it's a good idea.'

'I can't tell if you're being serious or not. You really think doing that'll tell you whether or not this guy is the Pusher?'

'Does the Pusher sound to you like the kind of person who has a cute little kid?'

'Anybody can have a wife and kids. Terahara had a son.'

The name makes Suzuki's temple throb. 'Well, anyway, I'll find out if he's the guy. It won't take long. Just hang on a bit.'

'Oh, I'm fine waiting. But Terahara's not. I'd hurry if I were you. And if you're not careful, you might get killed yourself.'

'What?'

'Say this guy is the killer, you really think he'd let some random man into his house? Or tutor his kid? If he would, then he's the sloppiest criminal of all time, and if it's not that, then he's seen right through you and he's just toying with you before he kills you. Those are the two possibilities. But if you think about it, it's probably the second one. Right?'

He doesn't know how to answer. He tries to put the pieces together in his head but it's all a jumble.

'Are you even listening to me?'

He isn't. He hears footsteps and people talking. Coming closer. He hastily turns his back toward the entrance and in a pinched voice says, 'I'll call you later,' then hangs up.

89

'Done your phone call?' Asagao enters the living room.

Suzuki nods, trying to relax the muscles in his face.

'Perfect timing, my wife just got home.' Asagao gestures toward the front door. 'With our younger son.'

Suzuki doesn't know if he should keep up the tutor act. But he doesn't know what else he would do if he dropped it.

THE WHALE

SITTING IN THE TAXI, THE vertigo starts again. He grimaces and leans back in the seat, looking out the window without really looking. It feels like his head is being sloshed around. At first he thought that the taxi was just driving over a rough patch of road, but then his stomach clenches and he knows what's going on. The skin around his brow tightens, and there's pain behind his eyes. The lids slide shut.

'A taxi ride in the middle of the day? Aren't you fancy?'

He looks up at the sound of the voice from the front seat. His eyes find the driver's eyes in the rearview mirror.

But it's not the driver. When the Whale got in the taxi, the person in the driver's seat was a middle-aged man with glasses, frowzy hair and a Tohoku accent. Now the Whale is looking at a long-haired woman. She's in her forties, well put together. 'It's been a long time.'

The Whale doesn't answer. He just looks out the window. A tidy little camera shop with green branding flows by. There's a round clock on the sign. He doesn't get a clear look at it, but the hands appear to be showing that it's just before noon.

As soon as they merge onto the inter-prefectural route headed in the direction of Tokyo Station traffic slows to a crawl.

He thought it had stopped raining, but droplets keep bouncing off the windshield. Must be dripping from the trees lining the street. The car in front of them stops and starts and stops again as it inches forward, brake lights glowing red. The swirl of cloud overhead stretches and thins off into the distance. 'Looks like it'll clear up soon,' the woman says gently. 'May I ask you a question? Why did I have to die? I was just an admin worker at a private university.'

Three years earlier, he had forced her to jump off the roof of a condo building. He remembers the contract coming from a quiet-seeming government official, but he can't recall what ministry they worked for.

'Why was I killed?'

'You killed yourself.'

She smiles sadly. 'That's just a technicality. I jumped off the roof myself, but you forced me to. Like a forced double suicide, only it was just me.'

'Somebody wanted you dead.'

He heard the basic gist of it from the client. The bureaucrat was having an affair with this university office worker. At a certain point he realized he was sleeping with her far more than he was with his wife, and got spooked. 'I don't just mean over the course of a year,' the man had said with genuine surprise, 'I mean it's more than the total number of times I've ever been with my wife.' He started to worry that this woman was trying to take his wife's place.

'But that's no reason to kill me!'

'You weren't being reasonable. You came on too strong.'

Traffic is still barely moving. The driver in front of them must

92

be getting aggravated because they honk the horn. Like dogs hearing other dogs barking, other horns start blaring. Finally the brake lights in front wink off and the car starts to ease forward. The Whale's taxi starts rolling too, but the driver doesn't come back. It's still the woman.

'Are you really going to this hotel?' She glances back at him through long eyelashes. 'That politician who called before, what's his name, Kaji, I'm not sure you should trust him.'

Kaji had called an hour ago.

'This about the thing from yesterday?' The Whale pictured the secretary hanging from the hotel-room ceiling. But Kaji said, 'Oh no, that's fine, fine, all taken care of,' sounding notably easygoing. 'I have a different job for you now.'

'It was weird, right?' The woman in the driver's seat puts her hand to her mouth and chuckles. 'I mean, yesterday he was so jumpy, and then suddenly today he's acting completely calm.'

'Acting?'

'If that wasn't an act, I don't know what it was. He's normally so frightened and paranoid.'

The Whale is both annoyed and confused about how solid she appears to be. *Aren't ghosts and spirits supposed to be more see-through? What kind of a ghost are you anyhow?* 'He sees threats everywhere. He liked my work. He has another job for me. That's all.'

'Do you really think he's trying to become a repeat customer? Just yesterday he was pressing you, "You're not going to tell anybody about this, right?" And then today, he's back again, "I'll have another contract kill, please." It's too fishy.'

'All politicians are fishy.'

Kaji had asked him to come to the lobby of Tower Hotel next to Tokyo Station shortly after one. When the Whale asked why, Kaji said it was to discuss the next job.

The Whale insisted that Kaji be there himself. He was firm on that point. 'If you don't show up, doesn't matter what the reason, I'll take it as you trying to pull something.'

'And what does that mean, if you decide I'm trying to pull something?'

'Then I'll come pay you a visit.' It wouldn't be hard for the Whale to find Kaji's home address. Kaji didn't need to ask what would happen if the Whale paid him a visit.

'Understood. Of course I'll be there myself.' The Whale thought he had heard a slight quaver in Kaji's voice at the end.

'Whose suicide are you looking for?'

'My secretary.'

'Your secretary hanged himself yesterday.'

'This is a different secretary.'

'Sounds like you could win an election with only votes from your secretaries.'

'Well, anyway,' Kaji went on, 'I need you to handle this man the same way you did the fellow from yesterday.' With that he rattled off the secretary's name, age, address, how many people in his family.

'He was absolutely lying to you,' says the woman. 'Having two of his secretaries die by suicide two days in a row would be far too suspicious. It doesn't matter how stupid or cowardly he is, no politician would go that far. It's a setup.'

I'm thinking the same thing myself.

'He's trying to take you down.'

I'm thinking the same thing myself.

'He's playing you for a fool.'

I'm thinking the same thing myself. Then he realizes: *Of course I'm thinking the same things as this woman. She's all in my mind.*

The flow of traffic has finally smoothed out. At the moment the taxi pulls into the passing lane, the Whale's head pulses with pain. He presses his hand to his temple and shuts his eyes, trying to push past it.

'Sir? Are you all right?'

He opens his eyes at the voice. There's a man in the driver's seat. In the rearview mirror, the Whale can see the man's face is taut.

'Was I saying something?'

'Well . . .' The driver doesn't seem to want to answer.

'What was I saying?'

The driver opens his mouth, hesitates, and then seems to decide that he has to reply. With a pained expression he says, 'Upsetting things. About killing . . . and suicide . . .'

'Did I say anything else?'

'Anything else . . .' The driver is clearly unsure whether or not he should be sharing any of this. For several moments his mouth opens and closes without making any noise, like a goldfish. 'Something about a repeat customer.'

CICADA

IWANISHI TOLD HIM TO BE there at one in the afternoon. He leaves Iwanishi's, heads to the closest station, and gets on the subway. It doesn't stop at Tokyo Station, but he can get off nearby. He knows where the Tower Hotel is, he'll have no problem getting there on time. *Looking out for the time is like looking out for yourself.*

In his head he hears the song lyric Iwanishi's always quoting. He's seized by the sense that all his own thoughts and movements, the way he scratches his nose, the corny jokes he cracks, all of it is just copied from Iwanishi. He has the nervous urge to check if there aren't actually strings attached to his body.

He gets off the subway and starts toward Tokyo Station. Down a few side streets, across a large intersection, past a boarded-up sushi place, into a back alley. It's a narrow passage hemmed in by mortar walls. The shortcut should take him straight to the station.

It feels less like an alley and more of a crack between the buildings.

The ground is littered with empty cans, magazines, flyers for strip clubs and massage parlors. He picks his way around a plastic trash bin and a dead air-conditioner unit. Twenty meters in, he hears a voice.

'Dead end,' it growls.

There are three men. Two in suits on their feet, looking down at a third man in a squat. One of the two standing suits is the one who had spoken. Broad shoulders, close-cropped hair like an athlete. 'Beat it,' the man barks at Cicada, waving him off like he's waving away a dog. *This guy's the dog. Got hair like a Shiba inu.* Cicada steps closer.

These men are obviously not having a friendly chat.

The suits are each gripping rocks roughly the size of a fist. They look to be in their early thirties. They might be wearing suits, but the crisscross of scars on their faces says that they're rough customers. The squatting man has his hands tied behind his back and duct tape over his mouth.

'Hey, kid, get the fuck outta here,' snaps the other suit.

Now Cicada's annoyed. 'What are you guys doing?'

'Nothing to do with you. Get lost.' This guy has long hair, a flat nose and a round face. He's wearing leather gloves and instead of a belt there's some kind of chain wrapped around his waist. It reminds Cicada of the rope a champion sumo or fighting dog would wear. *Oh, and this guy's a Tosa mastiff. The one guy's a Shiba, and the other's a Tosa*, he decides, satisfied.

'Two dogs picking on a human, huh?' Cicada thrusts his chin at the squatting man, whose eyes are puffy and his hair a mess. There's a weird thin patch on his hair – looks like maybe a clump was pulled out.

'Who're you calling a dog?' Shiba's brow knits.

Wow, when he scrunches up his eyes like that he looks even more like a Shiba inu! Cicada is delighted.

'We'll fuck you up like this guy,' says Tosa, his jaw working back and forth. Must be chewing gum.

'What is this, anyway, hazing?' Cicada shrugs.

Shiba and Tosa don't lose their tempers or make any moves toward Cicada. 'We don't have time to mess around with you, kid. If you're trying to get past, then go already. Just keep your mouth shut about what you saw here.' With that they turn their attention back to the man at their feet.

'You ready to talk yet?' Shiba lightly slaps the squatting man's face a few times. The man's mouth is still taped shut. Tears well up as he shakes his head from side to side.

'We know you know about the Pusher!' Tosa winds up a kick and stops just before contact, the top of his shoe hovering right at the man's ear.

The Pusher? The unfamiliar word piques Cicada's interest. 'What's the Pusher?' Then he realizes why it's sticking out to him: the word *push*. It had already been rattling around in his head from the conversation with Iwanishi an hour ago. *Terahara's son was probably pushed in front of a car.* Iwanishi had definitely said that. 'Yo, what's this Pusher you just mentioned?'

'You still here? Get gone already!' Tosa scowls. 'You might just be a kid, but kids get killed too.'

'People who don't tell me what the Pusher is all about could also get killed.' Cicada sounds more serious than he means to, which surprises him.

Shiba and Tosa exchange looks. They seem to wordlessly agree that they shouldn't get involved with some young lunatic, and they turn back to the crouching man. 'If you don't talk now, Mr Terahara's crew will come for you. You're much better off just dealing with us.'

Cicada almost shouts when he hears the name Terahara. *Jackpot.*

Shiba leans over and takes hold of the edge of the duct tape. Then he yanks it off. The man screams, blood spilling out of his mouth at the corners. Then he starts spitting out little chunks of something. At first they look like pebbles, but after a few moments Cicada realizes that it's shards of a shattered beer bottle. Shards soaked in blood. They must have shoved a broken bottle into his mouth.

The man lets out a sound that's not quite talking, not quite panting. Then: 'I don't know!' His pleading voice comes out with a spray of blood and saliva. 'I don't know anything about any Pusher!'

'If he's still saying that after everything we've put him through, maybe he's telling the truth.' Tosa looks at Shiba. 'What do you think?'

'I mean, we broke some fingers. Broke some toes. Crushed his earlobes. Cut up the inside of his mouth. That's all we've done so far.' Shiba counts off the items on his fingers. 'But he does look like he's just about had it.'

'Yes – Yes!' The man nods his head, begging. 'I've had it! I really don't know anything!'

'Hey. What's the Pusher, anyway?'

'You're *still* here?' Shiba and Tosa both say it at the same time. They sidle up to him. 'You sure are stubborn.'

'What's the Pusher?'

'Nothing to do with you.'

'But maybe it has something to do with Terahara's dumbass son getting run over?'

As soon as the words are out of his mouth the dogs' expressions change, hardening around the temples and between the eyes. 'What the fuck do you know?' one of them snarls. Suddenly Tosa has a switchblade in his right hand.

Oh, you wanna knife fight with me? Cicada is getting a little excited. *Let's see if you're any good.*

Tosa takes a step closer, then another. His movements aren't slow, but they aren't fast either. *I can see exactly what he's gonna do.* Cicada smirks, fully at ease.

He takes a step back and rotates, letting the blade pass by. Tosa pitches forward with the momentum of his strike, then immediately tries to shift his center of gravity backward to steady himself. With perfect timing Cicada darts in and smashes his right hand into the man's stomach, making a fist at the moment of impact and putting his hips into it.

In the next instant his knife is in his left hand. The glittering tip makes an arc through the air as he slashes forward.

He aims for Tosa's face. It bites into the right cheek. Must have hit a tooth because it stops in mid-slash. He pulls it right back. Tosa's eyes widen and he drops his own knife. *Nah, you're not any good at all.* Cicada's disappointed.

'You little fucker.' Tosa presses his hand against his cheek, eyes wild. Then he looks at his bloody hand. *No time for touchy-face, buddy.* Cicada takes a step to the left but switches his knife to his right hand. Tosa just stands there dumbly. Cicada drops down and drives the blade hard into the top of Tosa's shoe, aiming for the man's right instep. The knife passes through leather, through skin, right into the bones. Cicada can feel the impact run up his arm. The weird sensation of cutting into the foot bones with barely any meat on them gives him a thrill.

Tosa lets out a wordless scream. Shiba, meanwhile, is up on his toes, clearly agitated. He doesn't seem to be able to comprehend the situation.

Cicada pulls out the knife. *Guess now I have to kill all three. Shiba and Tosa and Mr Crouch.* But then he remembers something important: the time.

He checks his wristwatch. Less than ten minutes to one. Suddenly in a hurry, he kicks off into a run. The Tosa mastiff clutching his foot and groaning, the Shiba inu standing there in a daze, the weeping hunched-over man, they were all secondary.

He's late for a job. *No good, I'll never hear the end of it from Iwanishi.* He runs faster. But after a minute his pace slackens. *Wait a sec. Think about it. What does it really matter if I'm late?*

SUZUKI

THE WOMAN ENTERS AND GREETS them brightly. She looks quite young, less like a housewife than an upbeat university student. If Asagao hadn't said she was his wife Suzuki would never have guessed.

Asagao introduces Suzuki and explains what he's doing there, and she seems surprised. 'My name's Sumire. I'm just taken aback is all – my husband almost never has any guests.' Her voice has bounce to it, making her seem even more like a student.

Her black-framed glasses also give her an intellectual air. Short hair, highlighted chestnut. There's a little boy hugging her legs, half hiding behind her.

'That's my younger son,' Asagao offers. 'Kojiro.'

Must be a shy kid. He looks like a woodland creature peeking its head out of its burrow. In his right arm he clutches what appears to be a photo album.

'Very nice to meet you,' Suzuki says with an awkward bob of his head to the boy, who darts back behind his mother.

'So, private tutoring,' Sumire says, thinking about it. 'Our

Kentaro's still only in primary school – doesn't it feel a bit too early for that kind of thing?'

'Ah, well, I suppose you could be right,' Suzuki answers.

Not missing a beat, Asagao calls out from where he sits on the couch, 'Funny that a salesman would give in so easily.'

Suzuki turns hastily to look at Asagao. He wasn't just poking at Suzuki's sales pitch; his tone seemed to say that he sees right through the tutor story.

'But, but actually,' Suzuki gropes for words, 'studying is a habit that it's never too early to develop.' Even when he was a teacher he had never once said something so cheesy.

Kentaro walks over to Kojiro. 'How was it?' he asks.

'It was just a normal cold,' Sumire says, looking down at the little boy clinging to her legs like a koala. 'Right, Kojiro?'

'Cold,' Kojiro responds in the barest of peeps, maybe because there's a stranger in the house, or maybe he's always like that.

'I bet the doctor was scary, huh?' Kentaro is playing the older brother.

Kojiro brings his hand up to whisper, 'Yeah, scary. But Mommy bought me stickers.'

Suzuki doesn't know why this would be a secret conversation, but maybe that's just how he likes to talk.

Kentaro makes a jealous noise and then snatches the album from under Kojiro's arm. Ignoring his little brother's squeak of protest, he flips through it. 'Nice collection you got here,' he says, sounding like a pint-sized criminal.

Suzuki peers over at it as well. There are rows of insect stickers. Luridly colored poisonous-looking ones, creepy winged ones, all sorts. He recognizes the stickers as the kind that come as a prize in a box of candy, but it feels like most kids nowadays aren't this into insects.

'Today I got a treehopper!' Kojiro's voice is tiny but he's

obviously proud. He points to the upper right-hand corner of the page his brother has open.

'This is a treehopper? Coooool.' Kentaro is clearly excited, sounding both astonished and impressed. Suzuki looks too and finds himself surprised. The bug is green and oddly shaped, looking almost exactly like a thorny protrusion from a tree. It's even a little cute. *Is there really a bug like that?*

Human beings are like insects.

He can picture his old teacher saying it. *No, I still think humans and insects aren't alike at all.*

Kojiro takes back his prized sticker collection album.

'Hey, what can you do?' Kentaro looks up at Suzuki.

'Sorry?'

'What can a private tutor do?'

'What can . . .' In a certain sense, this question cuts right to the heart of things. Suzuki smiles sheepishly. *What good are you contributing to this world? Go ahead, answer.*

'I'll just tell you right now,' Kentaro declares, 'I hate studying.'

Sumire bursts out laughing. Asagao's expression doesn't change.

'Well, actually,' she says, talking to her husband, 'I do have to head to Kyoto for work from the day after tomorrow.'

'Oh, really?' He cocks his head.

'It might be good to have someone else around to help look after Kentaro.'

'What you're talking about,' he says, getting smoothly to his feet, 'isn't a tutor, it's a babysitter.'

A tiny voice pipes up inside Suzuki, but he ignores it. 'That's no problem at all,' he quickly says. 'I'm a teacher, but when children are young there's plenty for them to learn besides what they can get at a desk.' He makes himself sound cheerful. 'Broadly speaking, a private tutor isn't much different from a babysitter.'

Which is totally untrue, he tells himself.

'So you're gonna play with me?' Kentaro asks.

'Would that make you happy?' Asagao looks at Kentaro. Suzuki thinks he detects a certain chilliness. Rather than indulging his son Asagao seems to be observing an animal.

'Well, *you* never play with me, Dad,' Kentaro shoots back, then turns again to Suzuki. 'But you'll play with me, right?' He goes on, sounding like he's trying out an unfamiliar magic spell: 'You look like you'll do whatever anyone tells you.'

Suzuki knows that now isn't the right time to take offense at the remark. He just nods like a bobblehead. 'Yes, I'm sure we could play together.'

'Can we play soccer?'

'I bet we could play soccer.' He folds his arms and nods some more. 'When I was in high school I went out for the national team.'

'Really?'

At that Kentaro becomes serious, like he's about to make a pronouncement on world peace. 'Dad, I think we should hire this guy.'

The suggestion to hire someone sounds funny coming from a primary-schooler, but Suzuki can't deny that the boy has suddenly become a powerful ally.

'How about it? On a trial basis?' Looking to clinch the deal, Suzuki presses on. 'Your wife said she'd be traveling – would you be interested in a trial period for the few days that she's gone?'

He tries to gauge the balance of push and pull.

Asagao sits deliberating, arms folded. Sumire asks him, 'What do you think?' While they wait for an answer, Suzuki swallows hard.

'How about this?' Kentaro pipes up. 'How about you play with me now? Then Mom and Dad can talk about it. Okay, Mom and Dad? Decide whether or not you're going to hire him.'

Then he tugs on Suzuki's arm. 'C'mon, let's go.' He strides toward the front door. 'You come too, Kojiro.'

Kojiro brings his hand up to his mouth like he's telling another secret. 'I'll stay. I have a cold.'

'Okay then, just you and me, big bro,' Kentaro says, dragging Suzuki along. Suzuki grabs his coat but Kentaro says, 'You don't need that for soccer! Leave it here, let's go.'

So Suzuki puts it back down and heads toward the door, taking only his phone with him. In the vestibule he puts his shoes back on.

He finds himself confused by what's happening. He's supposed to be here finding out who the Pusher is. *So what am I doing right now?* He shakes his head gently. *Who's playing this prank on me? What's even going on? . . . Guess I just have to do it. Like you always used to say. Right?*

The rain has stopped and gaps are opening up in the clouds, light shining through. The water in the gutters, the drops on the concrete block walls around the garden, they seem to be evaporating before his eyes.

'Let's go.' Kentaro grabs a soccer ball from the garden and tugs on Suzuki's sleeve, pointing off to the right. 'The riverbank is this way. We can play soccer there.'

They walk through the neighborhood, all the houses looking the same. Past the nondescript residences, then a bit further along, and they come to the riverbank. It's not too far. There's a soccer pitch, apparently with good drainage because it isn't that wet. Pebbles are scattered around too, keeping it from getting too muddy. Goals at either end. No one else is using it at the moment.

They space out about twenty meters apart and start kicking the ball back and forth.

At first Suzuki aims for the boy's feet, gently, more of a roll than a kick. Before long they're kicking harder, sending the ball through the air, making each other run a bit.

Kentaro clearly knows what he's doing with a soccer ball. Kicks with the inside of his foot, kicks with the laces, good power, good control. His form is correct, the toes on his pivot leg are always pointing in the direction of his kicks. He must practice a lot.

Plant foot, shift center of gravity, rotate body, bite down, swing leg.

Kentaro receives the ball and launches it back. It flies off to the right, but that was probably on purpose, since it's close enough that Suzuki can just get to it at a run. He extends his leg and manages to stop the ball.

If that's how we're playing, Suzuki thinks, and he aims the ball off to Kentaro's right. *Run or you'll miss it!* Kentaro is just as quick as expected. He dashes to where the ball is headed and almost instantly sends it back again.

Cheeky! Suzuki chases the ball and only just catches it. He fires it right back.

He's starting to forget that he's playing with a primary-schooler. No matter where he kicks it, Kentaro neatly contains the ball and returns it, and Suzuki finds himself starting to get more and more in the zone. His head feels like it's been emptied out. There's no room for thoughts about anything else. Just the ball, where he should aim it, what he should do with it to impress Kentaro. It's almost funny how everything else is fading from his mind.

With every pass of the ball Hiyoko's voice recedes further and further. The sight of Terahara's son mangled by the car becomes more indistinct. The pressure on his chest lifts. *If you don't report in soon those two are done for* – even that threat has vanished. *Which two was I even thinking of?* He stops the incoming ball with the inside of his left foot.

'Anxiety and anger, those are animal responses,' his wife used to say. 'Looking for the underlying reason, or searching for a solution, that's something only humans do.'

'So are you saying that's what makes humans special?' Suzuki had asked. 'Or that's what makes humans bad?'

'If you could ask an animal how they survive, I guarantee the answer would be, "It just happens." '

What she was saying, he thinks, is that worrying about plans and strategies and getting all worked up is a human defect. Meanwhile, just kicking the ball back and forth seems like he's getting closer to solving his problems. Even though of course not a single thing is getting solved.

His instep makes contact with the surface of the ball, grabbing it like a hand. When his leg completes its arc, the ball takes flight. Even as it hurtles away from him it somehow feels like it's a part of his body. A projectile part of him, describing a graceful arc, until it lands right at the boy's feet, like it was glued there.

No more thoughts of Hiyoko, or the Pusher. The back and forth of the ball is everything. It feels deeply good. A sense of rapture suffuses him.

Up until Kentaro calls for a timeout, no surrounding sounds reached Suzuki's ears, and he didn't even notice that the ring on his ring finger is gone.

My ring. He blanches white, then looks frantically at the ground around his feet.

'You didn't lose it, did you?' He's sure he can hear his wife's voice. *Of course not*, he answers from somewhere inside his chest. *I'd never lose it.*

His wife was always afraid that she'd be forgotten, once she was gone.

She was always there for him when things went wrong, laughing off his little frustrations, like when the electric bill went up, or when the futons they'd had drying outside all day got soaked from a sudden evening shower, or when he questioned his worth as a teacher; she would say, 'Don't worry, it's not that serious.' But every so often she would sigh, 'People will forget about me, eventually. There's no proof that I was ever even here.' She always said it lightly, playacting the drama, but Suzuki knew that she was actually worried. A big part of it is that they never had any children. 'If we had children, they would remember me. They'd never forget.' She had said that more than once.

'You don't have anything to worry about. It's not like I'm going to just forget about you.' But when he said that she started in with her silly argument about Brian Jones.

'Nobody remembers that Brian Jones was in the Rolling Stones.'

'Of course people remember that.'

'Oh really? Even though there's no proof of it?'

'There are records and CDs.' And there's that footage of him that Godard shot. Although in that footage he's looking rather forlorn.

'I wonder,' she said dubiously. 'I just don't think anyone remembers that Brian Jones was in the Rolling Stones. Because there isn't any proof of it.'

'I think you're the only one who forgot about him.' Poor Brian.

He had an idea that he proposed, exactly two months before she died. He had been racking his brains to find something that would put her mind at ease, and then he hit on it. Nothing that special, a very simple idea, but its simplicity gave it power. 'How about this?' he said, showing her the ring on his left hand. 'This ring. Any time I look at this ring, I'll think of you. It's a promise. That'll make it pretty hard for me to forget you.'

'Hard to forget me? What's that supposed to mean, hard to forget me? How about "I will absolutely never forget you"?' She was laughing.

'There are no absolute guarantees in life.'

'You're just not trying hard enough.' She jabbed her finger at him. 'You need to try as hard as you can not to forget me.'

'I'm trying, I'm trying!'

'What are you talking about? I'm the one who's always trying. I do all the cleaning and the cooking, I'm always working overtime.'

'I'm not sure that's the trying we're talking about here.'

She started counting on her fingers as she rattled off other examples. She put more effort into cheering for their baseball team, she did more of the work when they were having sex, she spent more time finding the good cake shops. Their life rode on the wave of her effort. She was obviously pleased with herself.

The overwhelming force of her onslaught made Suzuki sure that he could never possibly forget her. But thinking about it later, he realized that her enthusiasm was just a cover for her anxiety.

And now he's missing the ring. *If I actually lost it . . .* He bends over to get a closer look at the ground. *Maybe it flew off when I kicked.* Trying to picture the trajectory of the ball, he crawls around searching, straining his eyes.

Luckily, he finds it on the ground about a meter away. He snatches it up, wipes off the dirt, puts his finger through it. *Do you really remember me?* He feels his wife's disapproving gaze. *Of course I do. It's exactly because I remember you that I'm in this mess right now.*

Kentaro dribbles the ball over toward him and the two of them sit down on a bench. 'You're good at soccer, big bro.'

'You're very good too. Do you play in school?'

Kentaro looks down at his feet and purses his lips, suddenly sulky.

'I guess not?'

'Yeah,' the boy mutters. 'Guess not.'

'Even though you're so good.'

It's not just an empty compliment. The boy could really be flourishing on the school team. He's just about to say what a shame it is, when it hits him: *Maybe this has something to do with his father being the Pusher?* The Pusher needs to keep a low profile. That much seems obvious. It might also mean that he never stays in the same neighborhood very long.

'So . . . does your family move around a lot?' Suzuki probes gently.

Kentaro looks at him for a moment. He opens his little mouth, seemingly about to say something, but then presses his lips together in a frown. 'You really are good at soccer, big bro.'

'Guess maybe there's a little more to me than just doing whatever anyone tells me to do, huh?'

'Yeah!' Kentaro's eyes shine like a dog recognizing its master, or like a stray cat leveling up to a housecat. 'Hey, since you're so good at soccer, can you tell me what P K means? I'm not so good at English.'

'Oh!' The question makes Suzuki think of his wife again.

'Do you know what P K means?' she had once asked him. 'If we have a son he might ask you one day.' Although it seemed like something it was way too early to be worrying about.

'Well, it's not an English word, it's initials,' he says to Kentaro, and then tells him the same nonsense he told his wife: 'It's the first letters of Pooh and Kick, for when Winnie-the-Pooh takes a shot at the goal.'

'That's ridiculous,' his wife had said, clearly not satisfied. But she eased off when he said that he wouldn't feel right explaining the idea of 'penalty' to a child.

'Really?' Kentaro looks surprised by the unexpected answer, but almost immediately he groans, 'That's so stupid!' He says this in a monotone, making it sound like it's not Japanese.

'Pooh took the world's first ever P K. And the goalie was the tiger. I forget his name, but you know, the one who's always bouncing all around.'

'Tigger?'

'Yeah, that's the one.'

'That's sooo stoooopid!'

This feels like . . . Suzuki can't help but think that this is what it would be like to joke around with his own son. He smiles, thinking of his wife. *If we'd had kids, it'd be like this.*

Suzuki tries imitating Kentaro. 'That's soooooo stooooopid!'

THE WHALE

HE GETS OUT OF THE taxi across the street from the Tower Hotel. Climbs the stairs to the pedestrian bridge and makes his way over. It connects directly to the second-floor entrance of the hotel.

The tower is forty stories high. He has to tilt his head way back to take it all in. The automatic door opens and he rides the escalator down to the spacious lobby, staring at the ornate chandelier that hangs down over the atrium. The carpet in the lobby is springy underfoot, as if it's signaling to his legs how expensive it is. He takes a seat on one of the sofas and checks his watch. 1.15 p.m. No sign of Kaji. He crosses his legs, takes his book out of his leather overcoat and looks down at it. The instant he does, he's absorbed into the world of a young Russian man and all his worries.

'Thanks for coming,' says a voice about ten minutes later. A small-framed man is standing in front of him. White hair, deeply etched lines around his eyes. A wispy moustache floating there like it's been glued onto his face. The same face from the

113

TV screen. Always posturing and making cheap threats, but never projecting any real depth. The Whale closes his book and puts it away.

'Another job so soon?' he says.

'Let's go to a room. I'd rather not have anyone see me talking to you out here. It'd be hard to explain.'

'You don't have to explain it.'

'Being a politician means having to explain things.'

As if any of you has ever given a satisfying explanation for anything, the Whale almost says. *All you ever do is beat around the bush.* 'All I need is your secretary's name, photo and address.'

'It's complicated. I wouldn't expect you to understand.' Kaji starts walking toward the elevator. The Whale follows. *He's trying to take you down*, echoes the voice of the ghostly woman. *He's playing you for a fool . . .* She's probably right.

Kaji leads him to an expansive room. Twenty-fourth floor, number 2409. The closet is spacious, and there's a luxurious oversize bed in the center of the room. A long desk in front of the mirror, with a whole array of cosmetic amenities laid out. The room is sparklingly clean, so much so that a politician looking to bring a girl there for a good time might feel like it didn't match his dirty intentions. There's a round table and a chair by the window, where the Whale takes a seat. Kaji stays standing and looks around the room.

'What's wrong?' asks the Whale.

'Oh –' Kaji answers, but doesn't say anything else. All at once he wheels around and heads back toward the entrance. *What's he doing?* the Whale wonders, getting up to follow. Kaji opens a side door in the entryway. The Whale peers in behind him. There's a sink and a toilet, and next to that a glass-paneled shower. The fan must be on because he can hear a propeller whirring. Kaji closes the door again, as if he were scared of his reflection in the mirror.

'What are you hiding?' The Whale's quiet question from behind seems to startle Kaji terribly. If the citizens of Japan were going hungry in the streets he probably wouldn't be as upset as he appears to be now.

A weapon, or a person, the Whale guesses. Those are the two possible reasons why Kaji brought him there. Somewhere in the room is a gun or a knife or maybe some kind of sedative that Kaji is planning to use to take him out, or else there's someone hiding in the room who's supposed to do the dirty work.

'Tell me about the job.' Acting as if he doesn't suspect anything, the Whale goes back to the window. The sun is finally starting to shine. 'Give me the details on the secretary I'm supposed to have kill himself. I can get right to work on it.'

'Well, there isn't much in the way of details,' Kaji says, opening his large briefcase and producing a single sheet of paper. He hands it to the Whale. It's a résumé. A photo is attached, and there's writing on it in a feminine hand.

'One of the old-guard members of my staff.'

'You're killing your old guard?'

'I'm not killing him. He's killing himself. Right?' Kaji is speaking smoothly enough, but it feels forced. The Whale stares intently into Kaji's eyes. The pupils are quavering.

Without a word, the Whale goes into the bathroom. Above the smooth pink toilet seat is a rack with folded towels and a bathrobe on a hook.

He grabs the bathrobe and pulls out the belt. Holding it in both hands, he tugs the ends in opposite directions. It's sturdy. Certainly sturdy enough to make a noose that could choke off someone's carotid artery.

Bathrobe belt in hand, he returns to the room. Kaji has his phone pressed to his ear but hastily hangs up.

'Phone call?'

'There was no answer.' Kaji sounds forlorn.

'Who did you hire?' the Whale demands to know, stepping closer.

'What?'

'You hired someone to take me out. Isn't that right? But they didn't show up. Even though you brought me to the agreed location.'

'What are you talking about?'

'I feel sorry for you.'

'What are you talking about?!'

'You hired me for a job. Now that it's over, you decided you can't trust me, so you hired someone to get rid of me. Didn't you? But on the off chance that it goes as planned, next you'll start to worry about whether you can trust the person you hired to kill me. Am I wrong? You'll just have to keep hiring the next person to kill the last person, on and on. After all, there are more than a hundred million people in the country. You could keep it going for quite a long time. But it's not a smart way of doing things.'

'Are you calling me stupid?' Now Kaji looks genuinely upset.

He actually thinks he's not stupid.

'I can tell you're very anxious. There's an easy way to solve this.'

Kaji stands a bit straighter, a pulse visible at his temples, and looks up at the Whale. His pupils have already dilated and his eyes seem to take on a different color. He's being pulled along by the Whale's words, matching his breathing to the rhythm of the Whale's breath.

'All you have to do is die.'

'That's stupid.'

'You seem to think you're not stupid.' This time the Whale says it out loud.

'Where will dying get me?'

'At the very least you won't have to worry anymore.' The

116

Whale's tone is matter-of-fact. At first Kaji was tensing the muscles of his body, like he was standing in front of a hypnotist but determined not to be hypnotized. But before long his shoulders relax. A placid look comes over his face, as if his fever had broken.

It's too easy. All humans want to die. *Right now. Now is his time.* Kaji sinks into the sofa. The tension and fear seem to have drained all his strength.

'I'm closing the curtains,' the Whale intones.

CICADA

HE ARRIVES AT TOKYO STATION and weaves through the flood of humanity, heading for the east entrance. Just to cut through, not to get on a train, unlike the group of young people hauling their luggage who cross by in front of him, blocking his path. He feels a spike of rage. *Why do they need to be walking right here in front of me?* His hand almost reaches for his knife. He glances at the station clock. Twenty minutes after one. Twenty minutes late.

Part of him wants to blow off the meetup and piss off the politician client. Then watch Iwanishi scramble when 'Mr Kaji' gets mad. 'Cicada, do you have any idea what you've done to us?!' He can just picture Iwanishi's face cycling through different colors.

But he decides that even though he's late, he'll still go through with it. Being late might not be professional, but he's not quite ready to ditch a job entirely.

The job is pretty straightforward. The client, Kaji the politician, was supposed to meet with a big man in the hotel lobby at one. At first the client was saying he wanted the hit to go down right there, but of course Iwanishi put the brakes on that. Too many people in a hotel lobby. He suggested bringing the target to a hotel room.

'And then I go to the room too, right?' Cicada had asked.

'Just like in the movies,' Iwanishi replied. 'When the killer pretends they're room service and goes into the room and takes the cover off the tray and there's a gun.'

'Yeah, very realistic. How about I attack as soon as the door opens? It's gotta be a lightning assault. So how am I supposed to get into the room?'

'He said you should get there first and lie in wait.'

'Um, lie in wait?'

'Mr Kaji doesn't want to be in the room alone with the guy. He wants it to happen as soon as they come in.'

'He's afraid of being alone just the two of them? Sounds like something a hot girl would say.'

'There's no hot girls nowadays. You ever seen one?'

'Nah, but they must exist.'

'You're a moron. Anyway, politicians are allowed to say they're afraid to be alone with someone.'

'Yeah, yeah.' Cicada dug around in his ear. 'No matter what politicians do, they can get away with it.'

'So this hotel has two keys for each room. They use keycards. You go to the front desk, get one of the cards, go into the room and hide.'

'I don't like hiding.'

'Sure you do. Cicadas hide out underground for seven years.'

'They're not hiding. They're waiting for their moment.'

'Whatever. Just get to the hotel room and kill the guy when he comes in. And don't mess it up – your target is the big guy. The short one with the moustache is Mr Kaji. Do not fuck that up.' Then Iwanishi told him the room number.

'What's the big guy's deal?'

'Does that have anything to do with your job? You saying you can't kill someone who's big and strong?'

'Not what I'm saying at all.' Cicada's voice was forceful. 'Big guys usually only just look tough. I just want a little bit more information is all.'

'Well, I don't know anything about him either. What's more important is that we do a good job and earn Mr Kaji's trust. You got me? This could be huge. Do it right.'

'Oh, you mean like, if you wanna get in good, you gotta do the thing right.' Cicada tried saying it as if he were quoting a certain someone.

Just as he hoped, Iwanishi sat there silently for a moment, looking slightly lost. 'Is ... is that a Jack Crispin lyric?' He clearly didn't like not knowing.

'Yup.'

'Oh. Ha. Oh.'

Man, this guy lives his whole life according to Crispin, Cicada marveled.

Now out of the corner of his eye he sees waves of families coming from the Keiyo Line platform, back from a day at the theme park, carrying bags with that famous white-gloved cartoon mouse. He hurries onward.

He arrives at the Tower Hotel lobby at thirty minutes past one. Striding across the springy carpet, he makes for the front desk. He can feel the three hotel staffers lined up at reception looking at him with distaste, but when he asks the man on the left for the key to room 2409, he gets it with no questions asked. It looks like a bank card. Key in hand, he heads to the elevator. The door opens right when he approaches. He steps in and hits the close-door button. Multiple times, as if that could speed it up. Urgent, insistent.

The elevator comes to a stop and he exits. One glance at the room guidance sign and he strides off to the right. Now he's in front of room 2409. Looks left, right. No one around. No guests, no staff. *If this were a Kubrick movie there'd be a tidal wave of blood right about now*, he muses. He likes that scene.

He puts his right hand in his jacket pocket and readies his knife. Then realizes that he didn't bring a change of clothes. Very often his jobs end up with him splattered in blood. That's why he always goes to a job in clothes he buys just for that episode and then throws out. It completely slipped his mind this time. He's not feeling out of it or anything. He's ready for what needs to be done. But he doesn't have his change of clothes. *I'm off my game.*

He checks his watch. Way past the agreed-on time. At least he's sure of that much.

He inserts the keycard into the slot under the doorknob, then pulls it back out again. A little light blinks and he hears the lock release. Knife in his right hand, left hand on the doorknob. Then he shoulders the door open and bursts in.

He spots someone, head higher than his own. *That's the guy.* He instantly locks in. *The big guy.* He springs forward into the room, blade held out in front of him. Rotates his body. Raises the blade to strike.

Then stops himself. It's not the big guy. The person in the room only looks tall because they're hanging from the ceiling. There's a towel or something tied to a vent on the ceiling, and the other end is a noose with a body dangling from it.

What the fuck is this?

Bubbles of spit cake the hanged man's lips under his moustache. His body rotates slowly. There's a puddle underneath him. Probably pissed himself. *Nasty. That's gonna stain the carpet.* An odor assaults Cicada, like sweat and rotting vegetables.

He stands there blankly for a moment. Then he thinks, *Maybe Kaji was so sad I didn't show up that he hanged himself?* He even feels a little bad about it. *I think I messed this one up.*

SUZUKI

WHEN THEY GET BACK TO the house, Kentaro tosses the soccer ball back into the garden. 'When you've used something, put it back where it's supposed to go,' Suzuki says, not even really meaning to. It was something his wife used to say all the time. Kentaro stands there sulking for a moment, then puts the ball back on the rack.

'I don't know where it's supposed to go,' he complains, which strikes Suzuki as odd.

The moment they step onto the concrete of the entryway the aroma of cheese pricks their nostrils. A particularly funky cheese smell, so ripe that it's almost threatening. A reminder that cheese is a natural thing on its way to rotting. The smell has notes of sweat and saliva. But broadly speaking, it's the smell of life in action.

'Pasta!' Kentaro exclaims, scrambling to get his shoes off. 'Mom's pasta is really good. You'll have some too, big bro.'

The soccer field by the riverbank wasn't at all waterlogged, but there's still mud on Suzuki's shoes. He steps back outside for a moment to clean them, wiping away clumps and finding more stuck on the soles.

His phone rings in his pocket. Hiyoko. He walks away from the house as far as the gate and answers. She keeps calling him. The frequency gives him an idea of just how frantic they must all be, and how much their efforts are coming up dry. Keeping one eye on the open front door, he brings the phone up to his ear.

'Well?'

'Nothing yet.'

'Tell me where you are.'

'I still don't know if it's him.' He hasn't gotten any closer to finding out if this man is the Pusher. Which makes sense, since he's spent the last hour playing soccer with the man's son.

'What are you even doing?'

Playing a little soccer. 'I'm still filling in the outer moat.'

'You're not laying siege to a castle. There's no moat. We're running out of patience.'

'I'm doing the best I can.'

'Two of our people are already dead.'

'What?' *Is that just an oh by the way?*

'Two of our employees were taking too long. Ten minutes ago Terahara shot them.'

'Why?'

'They weren't doing their jobs. He got mad.'

Who ever heard of a company like that? he wants to say, but stops himself. A company like that does in fact exist, and that's why he's where he is at this very moment. His wife was killed, he swore vengeance, and now he's on the trail of the Pusher.

They're looking for Suzuki. But they haven't found him yet. They're probably stamping their feet and grinding their teeth in frustration, but they have no way to reach him other than by phone. They could probably find out where he is by tracing his phone, but as far as he can tell that hasn't happened yet.

123

'What would you do if I just ran?'

'What do you mean, just ran?'

'It just occurred to me is all. If I were to run now, I'd probably get away. I mean, you don't know where I am.'

'We know where you live.' She recites his apartment address.

'I don't need to go back there.'

'And you think we'd just let you get away?' For the first time there's some tension in her voice.

'I'm not saying that. But you haven't found me yet.'

'And you haven't gotten away yet. You can't. And if you try, that young couple is going to die. Plus what happens to you will be awful. Worse than dying.'

I've already been through something worse than dying. He's surprised at the cold detachment of this thought. Cold as a metal spoon. *My wife is dead. Killed by a thoughtless, self-absorbed man. That was worse than dying.*

'Just go up to this guy and ask him, are you the Pusher, then go on home. That's all you have to do.'

'I'm hanging up.' Suzuki has had it with her. At this point the only connection he has to Hiyoko is over the phone. 'I'm about to go back into his house.'

Asagao is sitting on the sofa, legs crossed, reading a newspaper. He doesn't look up at Suzuki.

'It was really fun,' Kentaro says excitedly. 'Big bro's good at soccer.' Then he goes off into the Japanese-style room next to the living room, like he has something important to do in there.

'Well, that's good,' says Asagao, in a voice that sounds like he knows all too well there's nothing good in this life.

Not knowing quite where to put himself, Suzuki meanders between the living room and the dining room. He's debating whether he should have a seat on the sofa or go to Kentaro and ask him for an endorsement to get the job as private tutor.

He realizes with a start that Kojiro is standing at his feet. He doesn't quite jump, but he is surprised. The boy looks up at him, delicate hair flopping back. 'You wanna sit?' he asks in a whisper.

'Oh, um. Sure.' He takes a seat on the sofa facing Asagao. 'How's your cold?' he tries asking the boy.

'My cold?' Kojiro looks momentarily frightened, but then his face sets in a serious expression, his chin drawn back. 'I'm okay,' he squeaks. 'I'm doing the best I can.'

It's not something most kids would say, and Suzuki finds himself smiling. At the same time, it reminds him of when his wife would say that he wasn't trying hard enough. The tension in his head from his conversation with Hiyoko releases like knots untying. 'Oh yeah? Are you trying hard?'

'Hey.' Kojiro leans in to whisper, standing right at Suzuki's seated eye level. 'What will you teach me?'

'What will I . . . ?' He feels like he doesn't have a single thing he could teach young children. 'Well, I wonder.'

He catches sight of a clock. It's just before two in the afternoon. Asagao is looking his way, with those eyes that seem to see through him. 'We're having a late lunch. Pasta, apparently. You want to join us?'

Suzuki feels a flash of complication. By inviting him to the family table, does that mean that Asagao is accepting him? Or testing him?

'Are you sure?'

'There should be plenty of food. The best thing about her food is that she makes a whole lot.' Asagao doesn't smile. He's already turned back to his newspaper.

'That's right. This is mass-produced pasta.' The voice comes from the dining room, where Sumire is now standing. She has plates loaded with pasta in each hand.

Suzuki politely accepts one. Kentaro comes barreling in, as if summoned by the smell, his hands full of forks that he brings to the table. Kojiro is a moment behind him.

Once all the pasta is laid out on the table, everyone takes their seats and digs in. The aroma of gorgonzola cheese fills the room like steam. 'Delicious,' Suzuki says reverently. 'Told ya,' says Kentaro proudly, stretching out the words. Then he looks at Kojiro sitting next to him. 'Hey, what're you doing?'

Kojiro is looking through his insect sticker album. Suzuki catches a glimpse of beetles with shells of uncanny colors and butterfly larvae with venomous-looking bellies. He almost wants to ask the boy to put the album away during mealtime.

Kojiro pushes his pasta plate aside, takes out a pen, and starts writing on a postcard. He brings his face right up to the card, as if he's going to lick it.

'What *are* you doing?' Suzuki asks.

Kojiro pops his head up. 'I'm winning a rhinoceros beetle.' He looks quite serious. His voice is as quiet as ever, like a bug rubbing its wings together.

'He says that if you send in ten of the same sticker you win a rhinoceros beetle,' explains Sumire. 'A rare, gross one.'

'A Hercules rhinoceros beetle,' Kojiro says, whispering as usual. He turns back to the postcard, but then glances at Suzuki and points to the back cover of his album. 'What does this say?'

It appears to be the address where he should send his postcard. 'Kurozuka Design, Prize Fulfillment Center,' says the dubious-sounding name. Suzuki reads the rest of the address: 'Tokyo, Bunkyo Ward, Tsujioka.'

'T-o-k-y-o,' Kojiro sounds out as he writes, looking adorable. 'B-u-n-k-y-o, w-a-r-d.' His handwriting isn't exactly neat, but the letters do communicate a sincere effort.

'What do you think, Mr Suzuki? Will you be able to help look after my boys?' Sumire wipes some sauce from her lip and smiles. 'Looks like gross insects will be part of the deal too.'

'Sure . . .' Suzuki's response lacks confidence or enthusiasm, sounding rather feeble. Asagao seems to take note of this and exhales sharply, unimpressed.

'Hey, Kojiro,' Kentaro says, putting his hand on top of the postcard to block his brother's writing. 'Do you know what PK stands for?'

'No, what?' Kojiro dutifully looks at his brother.

'Pooh kick! P for Pooh and K for kick. That's what big bro told me. Pretty corny, huh?'

Not seeming to understand any of it, Kojiro just stares at Kentaro quizzically. Sumire smiles politely.

'Of course, there are all sorts of other things I can teach you.' Now Suzuki puts at least a little oomph into it.

'Okay, okay, how about this, big bro, have you ever eaten that cheese from TV?' Kentaro steers the conversation in an unexpected direction. Suzuki tries to connect the dots in his head. 'You know, the kind you see in cartoons, that mice like to eat. Triangle-shaped cheese with holes in it.' He eagerly traces a triangle on the palm of his hand. 'It looks really good. Have you ever had any?'

'Um . . .'

'I asked Dad too, but he won't answer. Where do you get cheese like that?'

The boy seems to have extrapolated a universe of cheese from comics and cartoons. Suzuki decides to play along. 'Oh, yes, that cheese really is delicious.'

Kentaro and Kojiro look at each other with excitement. 'I knew it! I knew that cheese would be good! Okay, okay, moles really wear sunglasses, right? And is it okay to eat woolly mammoth meat raw?'

Suzuki can't tell quite how much Kentaro believes all of this. He answers the questions one after the other, trying to maintain a balance between seeming too overeager and too flat. It feels to him like an honest effort.

'What about those – are they delicious too?' Kojiro leans in to whisper, hand to his mouth.

'What about what?' Suzuki asks. Everyone pays attention, trying to make out Kojiro's tiny voice.

'Those doggies that save you when you get lost in the snow in the mountains.'

'St Bernards?' Suzuki pictures the shaggy rescue dogs.

'Yes, yes, those big doggies!'

'You can't eat them!'

Kojiro shakes his head. 'Not the doggies. The barrels around their necks. What's inside.'

'Whiskey?'

'Yes, that.'

Suzuki and Sumire both burst out laughing at Kojiro's earnestness. Asagao stays quiet, but his eyes crinkle at the corners. Kentaro gets excited. 'Yeah, I wanna try whiskey!'

Now Suzuki finds himself curious about the contents of the rescue dogs' barrels. He imagines it must be extremely tasty.

'Let's get lost in the mountains,' Kojiro says in his miniature voice, everyone else beaming at him.

When the laughter dies down, Suzuki suddenly feels dizzy. The wholesome family meal is disorienting. He finds it tough to square this peaceful household with the possibility that Asagao might be some shadowy assassin, let alone the fact that Suzuki himself is on the trail of the Pusher and is now investigating this family. None of it seems real.

He twists his fork in the pasta. Watching the noodles and mushrooms and sauce swirl around his plate he has the sensation that he's being pulled into a vortex. His eyes are open, but it's like he's stumbled into a dream.

He sees an unsettling scene.

Cars, lots of cars. Black, fancy-looking cars, speeding into a residential neighborhood one after the other. Stopping in front of this house.

Ten or more men in suits get out of the cars and enter the garden. Tough guys, and some young guys in glasses with a more intellectual look. Terahara's men. Employees of Fräulein. They step up to the door and enter. In the middle of the group is Hiyoko, giving orders. He sees the living-room table. Kentaro huddled underneath. Kojiro squatting next to him, looking left and right. 'What's happening?' he whispers to his brother. They're both scared, but they have no idea how dire the situation actually is. Sumire is in the kitchen, white as a sheet, frozen. Two men she's never seen before are shoving guns in her face. A flash of a nervous smile, then it clicks that this disturbance is not a prank or a skit, and her lip begins to tremble.

Switch to a different scene.

A dimly lit warehouse. The two boys are tied up on the ground. Sumire is screaming and tearing at her own hair. Terrible things are happening. Interrogation. Torture.

'Are you all right?' Asagao's voice brings Suzuki back.

He had been holding a forkful of twirled pasta in front of his mouth, motionless.

'It was like somebody pulled the plug on you, big bro,' Kentaro says.

'I was just . . . lost in thought.' *I was just thinking about something awful happening to all of you,* but he keeps that to himself. It felt like he was seeing a vision of the future. His heart clangs like an alarm bell.

'What's lost in thought?' Kentaro asks through a mouthful of pasta, his chewing action on full display.

Sumire looks at Suzuki, clearly wondering what was on his mind, but she says nothing. She still gives off the impression of being a college student, curious about everything.

He finishes his pasta and sets his fork down. It seems a shame to leave all that cheesy sauce on his plate, but he's not about to lick it clean. 'I was wondering,' he ventures, turning to Asagao. *Now's the time. I just have to do it. Like you always said.* 'What do you do for a living, Mr Asagao?'

He tries not to blink. He's watching to see if there's any hesitation, or if Asagao will even answer at all.

'He's an engineer.' The answer comes from Sumire. 'A systems engineer? I don't really know what that is, but that's what he says he does.'

'Is that right?'

'He doesn't really tell me about what goes on at the job.'

There's no change to Asagao's expression. It doesn't harden or soften.

'So does that mean you work with computer programs, things like that?'

'Yeah, things like that.' Asagao's reply seems purposely vague, as if he's trying to provoke.

Suzuki searches for what to say next. He wishes he could ask a question that only a real systems engineer would be able to answer, but he doesn't know what that question is.

'What do you know about locusts?' Asagao's sudden question takes him off guard.

'Huh?' Suzuki tries to make his mind catch up. 'You mean the insect?'

Kentaro leans in with interest. At the same time, Kojiro, apparently activated by the word *insect*, starts excitedly flipping through his album.

'Sometimes he says the strangest things,' Sumire puts in, chuckling.

'They start as grasshoppers.'

'The green ones, right?'

'Green, yes, they can be,' Asagao says quietly. 'But there are others that aren't green.'

'There are?'

'When they live together in high numbers, they undergo a metamorphosis. Into the swarming locust.'

'Live together in high numbers – you mean like population density?'

'Yes. That kind is darker in color, with longer wings. And they're aggressive.'

'Darker?'

From across the table, Kojiro points to an open page in his album. 'Here.' He taps at a sticker showing an earth-colored locust. 'Like this one.'

'Locusts behave differently from grasshoppers. Logically speaking, when lots of them live together in one place, there's less food to go around, so they need to fly off somewhere else, and they become stronger flyers.'

'That makes sense.' Insects have all sorts of clever survival mechanisms.

'But you know,' and here Asagao pauses for a moment, slides his plate away and props his elbows on the table. He folds his hands, then stares directly at Suzuki. His eyes are as black as wells. Too dark to see the bottom. Echoing. 'I think it's not just grasshoppers.'

'What isn't?'

'Any animal that lives in a high-density situation will change its behavior. They turn dark, they rush, they get aggressive. Before they know it, they've become swarming locusts.'

'Aggressive swarming locusts, huh?'

'They move in massive groups and fly around eating everything. They even eat their own dead. Totally different from the green, solitary grasshopper. And it's the same with human beings.'

'How so?' Suzuki has the feeling that he's just been called out by name.

'When humans live on top of each other, they start to go crazy. People living their lives all packed into one place. Rush-hour traffic, crowds at tourist sites. It's actually fascinating, how it works.'

Suzuki finds himself nodding vigorously, without even meaning to. He repeats the words of his old teacher: 'In some ways humans are less like mammals and closer to insects.'

'Exactly. That's absolutely right.'

It feels good to be told he's absolutely right. *Although this is probably not a good time to ask if penguins are also like insects.*

'Any grasshopper can turn dark, become a locust. Then they can spread their wings and move on. Humans can't do that, but they do become more aggressive.'

'Do people always behave like that? Like a swarm?'

'Especially in big cities.' Asagao's gaze is sharp, but not quite threatening. 'It's much harder to live a peaceful life.'

Suzuki pictures a slim tree standing quiet and firm amid the throng. At the same time, he feels a strong suspicion welling up inside. They're just talking about locusts, but more and more it sounds like Asagao confessing to being the Pusher.

Asagao's face is impassive. But deep in his eyes there's a light. Suzuki feels it testing him.

He tries not to swallow. There's the strong sense that if his throat makes a single sound then Asagao will reveal himself as the Pusher and pounce.

'Do you think if there were fewer people that things would be more peaceful?' he asks.

'Most likely,' Asagao answers without hesitation.

Suzuki leans right in: 'And since you want to lower the overall number of people in order to help those that have become swarming locusts return to normal, you're pushing people in front of cars and trains.' Or at least that's what he wants to say.

After a moment he notices that next to him, Kojiro has his phone. He had left it sitting out on the table. Now Kojiro is pushing buttons.

No, he thinks, and snatches it back from the boy. He doesn't want there to be any accidental calls to Hiyoko. He must have been a bit too aggressive though, because Kojiro's eyes widen.

'This thing breaks very easily, don't touch it.' It's a lame excuse, totally unconvincing.

'No way,' says Kentaro pointedly. 'He's lying, you can tell from how he said it. He just doesn't want you touching his phone.' Kentaro whispers loudly in his little brother's ear.

Kojiro nods in agreement, then turns glumly back to his postcard. 'T-o-k-y-o, B-u-n-k-y-o, w-a-r-d.'

THE WHALE

HE RETURNS TO THE PARK and cuts across the grounds, finding that the fountain is merrily spouting. The water makes an elegant curve through the air as it descends into the pond. The impact on the surface causes the reflections of the zelkova trees to ripple. The image of the bare branches on the pond looks like a complex network of blood vessels, pulsing vividly. All at once the stream from the fountain cuts out.

Shoulders hunched as he heads toward his sleeping area, the Whale thinks about his interaction with Kaji an hour back.

'Why should I kill myself?' Kaji had asked at the beginning, indignant, but in the course of talking to the Whale he came to understand. The Whale thought he might have to mention Kaji's three daughters, or else take out his gun and threaten to shoot if Kaji didn't kill himself, but it didn't come to that.

The Whale asked if the episode was a setup, and Kaji immediately owned up to it. 'I hired someone to eliminate you,' he confessed. Eliminate sounded so old-fashioned that the

Whale made a face. *Whales are for conservation, not elimination,* he thought.

'He was supposed to be waiting in here for us,' Kaji moaned.

'Too bad for you.'

Very quickly any fight went out of Kaji and he meekly submitted.

The Whale could sense that Kaji knew on some level his day in politics was done, that he was becoming a useless old relic. He was probably looking for a way out. He seemed to even get the romantic idea that taking his own life would throw the political world for a loop.

'Dying will give me new life,' he muttered eagerly, sitting down at the desk with his fountain pen to dive into a long letter. 'I can already see the faces on those journalists when they read *this*,' he said, sending flecks of spittle flying.

At the end, the Whale asked, 'Why did you become a politician?'

By that point Kaji's expression was distant, almost blissed out. He looked down at the Whale. 'Well . . . who wouldn't want to be a politician?'

The Whale nodded once at the completely predictable answer.

Watching Kaji's body stiffen out of the corner of his eye, he picked up the envelope from the desk. It was addressed 'To all those I have left behind,' in an absurdly showy hand. *So typical.*

He left the room and took the elevator down, then exited the hotel. On the way to Tokyo Station he passed a department store with a trashcan outside. He tore up the letter and tossed it in.

'How did it go?'

Someone calls out to the Whale from behind and he stops. He's at a spot in the middle of all the tents. A crossroads of sorts.

When he turns around he sees a man wearing a baseball cap with the image of a magnifying glass on it. Glasses, sunken cheeks. It's Tanaka. He's leaning on the cane in his right hand. Must have bad hips. His posture is all crooked.

'You just came back from doing a job, yes?'

The Whale is confused all over again. Unsure if this is reality or if he's just seeing things. But if it is a hallucination, it's not coming with the normal dizziness. And there's also the fact that this Tanaka is not one of the Whale's past suicide victims. Or at least not that he can remember. 'A job?'

'Your expression seems to say that you just got off work, so I drew my conclusion. Were you able to settle the regrets that you spoke about this morning?'

'No.' The word *Pusher* flashes in his mind. 'This wasn't that.'

'Then you must have dealt with something else that was bothering you. You look quite relieved.'

'Kaji.'

'Kaji?' It's not clear if Tanaka knows what the Whale is referring to. 'Well, I suggest you do what you can to take care of whatever's causing you to hold on to that regret. Then you can retire. If you keep going like this . . .'

'If I keep going like this what?'

'You will become one of the dead.'

'Like you?'

'What do you mean by that?'

'Are you alive?'

'Can't you tell just by looking at me?'

'Does it sound like I can tell?' The Whale's voice hardens.

'You'll be absorbed into your illusions,' Tanaka says.

'What?'

'Your life will become part of the illusions you see. You must be careful. You won't be able to tell what's false and what's real.'

'I already can't.'

'There are signs you can look for. Signs that it's an illusion. For example, if you're on the street and the lights keep flashing, or if you're going up or down stairs and they never seem to end. Or say you're at the station and the train just keeps going by, seemingly forever, and you think to yourself, my, this train is awfully long, then that's a definite sign. These are all signals that you're hallucinating. Traffic lights and trains are common triggers. Lights being typical at the onset of the vision, and trains just before you come out of it.'

'Sounds like pretty much anyone can end up seeing things that aren't there.'

'Yes, that's right,' Tanaka answers levelly. 'On a different note, I read something recently that stuck with me: the future unfolds according to God's recipe.'

'The future? Recipe?'

'Basically, what's going to happen is beyond our ability to influence, it's all already decided. A talking scarecrow says that in this book.'

'And you take a talking scarecrow seriously?'

'What is the novel, and what is reality – people must exist in one or the other, but it's impossible for them to tell which is which. But more importantly, what do you plan to do about your regrets?' Tanaka presses him. 'The future is already decided. You may as well let nature run its course. You've put in a day of work. I imagine that will serve as a catalyst. From this point, things will start to come together, unfolding like the gentle flow of a river.'

'Rivers eventually reach the sea.'

'In finishing this work with Kaji, did you come across anything that might point to the next step?'

'Next step?' This sketchy lecture is irritating to the Whale, but he can't quite ignore it.

'A new clue.'

'Actually.' The Whale puts his hand into his coat pocket. There's a number he jotted down in the hotel. The last number

Kaji called when they were in the room together. Most likely the other professional Kaji hired. The one who was supposed to kill the Whale. He wasn't quite sure why he was taking down the number, but before he knew what he was doing the pen was in his hand.

'That's part of the recipe.' Tanaka looks like he's peering right through him.

Settle the score.

It was Tanaka's voice. But the Whale can't tell whether he said it out loud. *Close out your accounts.* Then again, the Whale might have said it himself.

CICADA

WHAT DO I TELL IWANISHI? Cicada racks his brains. The body dangling in the hotel room, rope around its neck, looking like a textbook illustration of a hanging, had to have been this guy Kaji.

'The target is a big man, right? The short one with the moustache is Mr Kaji. Don't fuck it up, huh?' Iwanishi had been insistent. *That wasn't the big guy. No doubt about it. This guy was short, and I guess that mess around his mouth was some kind of moustache.*

He starts for the subway, but he doesn't feel like getting on quite yet, so he kills some time in the department store. It would be a total drag to get Iwanishi's call, asking if it's done, all upbeat, so he turns off his phone.

The fastest way to gain your freedom is to kill your parents. Cicada read that in a novel once. Nowadays, though, the best way to be free is to turn off your phone. *So simple it's stupid.*

'This is all your fault.' He can already hear Iwanishi yelling at him. 'This only happened because you were late. How are we

139

supposed to report to our client with you bungling the job on account of being late?'

'Yeah but,' Cicada imagines himself arguing back, 'our client, this guy Kaji, he went and killed himself, so there's no one to report to. No prob.'

'What about our fee? The money we were supposed to get for this? Don't you feel at all responsible?'

'Why would I be responsible for that?'

'Cos you were late!'

Well, yeah, when you put it that way . . .

He has a coffee at a cafe, wanders around the shopping arcade. Time passes.

'Hey, Cicada. Fancy meeting you here.' There's a tap on his shoulder that makes him jump. He turns. A plump woman stands before him, wearing something that he's not sure is a one-piece or lingerie.

'Oh, hey, Momo. Isn't it, uh, a little cold for you to be wearing that?'

He can see right through it. Breasts and everything. But it doesn't really turn him on.

'I've been looking for you. Well, not me, it's Iwanishi who's looking for you. If you're hanging around here, can I assume you were planning on coming to my shop?'

'Probably.' He wasn't actually aware of where he was going, but it does seem that his feet had been carrying him in the direction of her shop. Most times he's nearby Tokyo Station he stops by Momo's porno mag shop, so he must have just been walking that way out of habit.

He can't really tell how old Momo is. Last year she had said it was her Chinese zodiac year, but that didn't clear up much – she could easily be twenty-four, or thirty-six, or forty-eight. At least he was sure that she wasn't twelve.

'Iwanishi's looking for me? What's he want? If he wants

something, he should just call me. I mean, we are blessed with the conveniences of modern life. Maybe he doesn't know, nowadays there are phones you can take with you wherever you go.'

'Come on. You turned your phone off.'

'Oh, well, actually, now that you mention it.'

'He just called me. Man, was he pushy. "Cicada's at your place, I know it, he's not answering his phone, if you see him tell him he better call me back." He was kind of a mess, like a guy whose girlfriend won't answer his calls.'

Cicada feels like he's just bitten down on a stinkbug. The news is infuriating. So much so that his whole body starts to itch. 'He thinks he owns me. If he can't get in touch he freaks out.'

'But doesn't he own you?'

'What?' Momo has poked at his most sensitive spot, and it shocks him.

'I said, are you just messing with him?' She looks mildly irritated. Seems that was what she said all along. *Did I just hear her wrong?*

'It's not like there's a law that says you have to keep your phone turned on.'

'People have to be able to get in touch with you, honey. The world runs on information. This city, it's not made up of buildings and streets and pedestrians, it's made of information. You ever hear about that thing in the American major leagues, maybe twenty years ago, that white guy who batted over 400?'

'Is it in the baseball almanac?'

'Know how he got so many hits? Because he knew all the signs. He had a guy in the stands who used binoculars to watch all the signs and then signaled them to him.'

'So?'

'I'm saying the ones who have all the information are the ones that survive.'

'Isn't that just cheating?'

'In our industry, information is a weapon.'

'Our industry. Iwanishi calls it the same fuckin thing. It's so stupid. An industry for killing people?'

'You really don't like Iwanishi, huh?'

'I hate him. I hate him so much.'

'Amid the stillness, the cries of the cicada seep into the rocks. That's a Basho haiku.'

'What's that got to do with anything?'

'I mean, it's got a cicada for you and the rocks for the *iwa* in Iwanishi. Whatever you say, the two of you are a set.'

'Hilarious joke. Anyway, what else did Iwanishi say?'

'Let's see. He wanted to find out how the job went, naturally. And he was trying to find out if you were at my place. And, I mean, you do come to see me quite a bit, even if you never buy anything.'

'Not sure what that's supposed to mean. Okay. So I guess I'll call Iwanishi.' Aggravated, Cicada starts to leave. But then – 'Hey, by the way. You heard anything about this Terahara thing?'

Her immediate discomfort is plain to see. 'How could I not hear about it? Everyone's on this one.'

'What do you mean, everyone?'

'Everyone in the whole industry.'

'The industry again . . . I did see two shady dudes roughing someone up,' he says, thinking back to his knife fight in the alley. The two dogs, Shiba and Tosa. 'Who or what is the Pusher? I tried asking these guys and they got all violent.'

'Well, yeah, that's not surprising.' She raises one finger. 'That's the guy who did Terahara's son, which is what caused this whole mess.'

'There's really someone called the Pusher?'

'I don't know for certain myself, but supposedly he kills people by pushing them from behind. But there's barely any info on him. I never hear much about him.'

'Really?' He's surprised to learn there's something Momo doesn't know about.

'Little things, here and there, but never any solid details. To be honest, I thought he was just an urban legend, or something someone made up.'

'What do you mean?'

'Like, hmm, okay, say there's a guy like you. Somebody who gets hired to kill. And this guy messes up a job, so he says, "The Pusher beat me to it," or "The Pusher got in the way." Excuses like that. They blame it all on some made-up character named the Pusher. That's what it sounds like to me, anyhow. Or you'll hear people say it to scold someone – "Hurry up and finish the job or the Pusher'll get there first."'

'You mean, like, if you tell a lie King Enma will rip out your tongue?'

'Yeah, just like that.' Her face is deadly serious. 'That's how little I actually know about the Pusher. Even though I hear about so many things.'

'You know about the Whale?' Cicada brings up the name he just heard about.

'The suicide guy. He's famous.'

'Oh yeah? Famous?'

'He's scary, and big. You know, like a whale. I've seen him once, from far away.' She sounds like she's talking about the time she spotted an actual whale in the ocean.

'. . . Do you think Terahara's kid really got it from the Pusher?'

'Who knows. Too many possibilities. There're all kinds of rumors. That boy didn't know how to behave, all kinds of people had it in for him.'

'Yeah, I bet.'

'Some outfit somewhere got jumped by Terahara's son and wants payback, that kind of thing, that's all I'm hearing about.'

'Sounds likely enough.'

'But apparently, one of Terahara's employees tracked someone down.' Momo's on a roll now. 'Only he won't report in to tell where the Pusher is!'

'Seriously?' Cicada's brows wrinkle together. 'They should just go get the guy and make him spit it out. He works for them, right?'

'They can't do that because they don't know where the employee is either. They can only call him on the phone. They're not finding him. Know why?'

'No, why?'

'Because Tokyo's *big*.'

'Wow, what insight,' Cicada says archly.

'And nowadays you can take your phone with you.'

'Amazing.' But even as he's poking fun at her, he can't help cock his head in puzzlement. *Why's that employee going to all the trouble to jam things up?*

'This guy must be the type who likes to rebel against his superiors.'

'I mean, I know how he feels.' The employee must want to get the better of Terahara. 'But he's being pretty dumb.'

'He really is. There's no way he gets out of this in one piece.'

'So what's Terahara gonna do?'

'He's gathering up any bit of information he can. They came to see me. I'm sure they must have called Iwanishi too.'

'Nah, nobody wants his help.' As he says this, it occurs to Cicada that on this one thing he's a step ahead of Iwanishi. His face creases into a broad smile. A feeling of expectation wells up in him, pulsing gently, making the hairs on the surface of his skin quiver, tickling the pit of his stomach. 'Hey. You think if I find out where the Pusher is, there'll be some glory in it for me?'

'*Glory?* What year are you from, honey?'

'Everyone's looking for the Pusher, right? And nobody knows where he is. So, first one there's the winner.'

'Well, I just heard,' Momo continues, 'that somehow they're going to call this employee back to base.'

'They're calling him in? But he's not gonna come. This employee for sure knows that he won't get off easy if they get their hands on him. They'll make him scream until he talks. If he's willing to just come along when they call, he would have talked from the get-go.'

'You'd think.' Momo spreads her hands. 'But you know, I bet none of it feels real to this guy.'

'What do you mean, none of it feels real?'

'This employee, it's not like he's got a bunch of guns shoved in his face. He's just going about his normal business. Everyone in the city might be going crazy trying to find him, but it hasn't clicked. I'm sure he knows he's in danger, but he isn't truly *feeling* the danger.'

'You think that's how it is, huh?'

'Say for example –' Momo raises one finger – 'a giant typhoon is coming. People hear about it on the news, and they say, oh, it's dangerous out, and they stay inside. But these days buildings are much sturdier than they used to be, so they can't really feel what's going on outside their walls. They don't hear the wind, maybe they don't even see the rain. They turn on the TV and it tells about all the damage. And you know what they do then?'

'Nope.'

'They look outside.' Momo says it slowly, for emphasis. 'They open the window, or the door, they see what's going on outside. "Is it really that bad," they want to know. Anyone would do that. Then a gust of wind blows a tree branch right into their face. So they slam the window shut, and *then* they're convinced. "Oh, this is one bad typhoon!" they say.'

'Huh.' What she's saying makes sense. 'So then this Terahara employee knows that it's dangerous but still might show up, is what you're saying.'

'Until people actually get hurt, they never believe it's going to happen.'

'Too bad once it happens, it's too late.'

Cicada feels an idea bubbling up inside of him.

'Hey,' he says to Momo. 'You know where this torture interrogation is supposed to happen?'

'What's it to you?'

'I'm gonna nab this employee.'

'Don't be stupid.' Momo clearly isn't taking him seriously. 'You want Terahara to be looking for you?'

'I'm gonna find out from this guy where the Pusher is, and then I'll track down the Pusher and take him out myself.'

'What are you even talking about?'

'While the Fräulein crew is dicking around I'll get their revenge for them. Terahara wouldn't be mad at that.'

'Hm. He might actually appreciate it.'

'Right?' Cicada is clearly feeling pleased with himself. 'And then my being late to the last job will be wiped off the books.'

Momo's mouth hangs open at Cicada, who is suddenly brimming with confidence. 'Guess you really are looking to win some glory.'

'Glory? What year are you even from?'

SUZUKI

THE PLATES ARE CLEARED FROM the table. Sumire's movements are quick and efficient as she washes the dishes. Suzuki is conscious of Asagao's gaze on him the whole time. When she finishes at the sink, Sumire asks, 'How about some coffee?'

Across the table, Kojiro has produced another postcard that he leans over. 'B-u-n-k-y-o, w-a-r-d,' he sounds out the address, half singing it. 'T-s-u-j-i-o-k-a, 3, 2.' It's adorable. He must want to send more than one. *If we'd had kids, this would be what it felt like*, Suzuki thinks, and then he pictures his wife. Crushed between a car and an electric pole, her neck bent all wrong.

It was immediately clear that the person driving the car that hit his wife was a dangerous character. Suzuki wasn't satisfied having it written up as a standard traffic accident, so he used his savings to hire a private detective.

'Mr Suzuki, I think you'd better leave this one alone,' the detective told him after looking into it. It was less of a report and more of a warning.

'That's it? I'm just supposed to forget about it?'

'The car involved in the accident is associated with somebody other than the name on file.' He went on to explain that the crash was one of Terahara's son's joyrides. The detective didn't want to say any more than that, but Suzuki pressed him and eventually got him to reveal what he knew about Fräulein.

'So there's this whole other criminal world?' At the time Suzuki was just a teacher, and was innocently amazed to hear this. Terahara, Fräulein, it all seemed like some fantasy. Perhaps because he was so angry, he didn't think to be scared. He was just angry, and amazed.

'There are all kinds of worlds,' said the detective. 'For instance, do you know how many types of insects there are?'

Guess we were talking about insects then, too, Suzuki remembers now.

'There are a million species. A million. And every day they're discovering more. Some people say that if we include the species we haven't yet discovered, there might be as many as ten million.'

'More than ten times what we know now,' Suzuki replied hazily.

'It's the same for all the worlds that we can't normally see.'

'Lost in thought?' Asagao peers at Suzuki's face.

'Are you that concerned about whether or not we'll hire you?' Sumire sounds sympathetic.

'Oh, no, it's not that.' Suzuki then tells them honestly, 'I was just thinking about my wife.'

'You're married, Mr Suzuki?' Sumire leans forward mischievously, exactly like a college student getting the gossip on someone's love life. Her eyes fall on his ring and her smile widens.

'Yes . . .' Suzuki's voice trails off. He twists the ring around his finger. It's loose and feels like it could fall right off.

'How'd you meet, how'd you meet?' Sumire is clearly very interested.

'At a buffet.'

He first met his wife when he was on a solo trip to Hiroshima, five years back. He was staying at a slightly fancy hotel a short trolley ride from the center of town.

Breakfast was in the restaurant on the top floor, served buffet-style. There was a woman holding a plate loaded with food. The woman he would marry. She was in front of him in the buffet line.

An omelet, chicken karaage, meatballs, green-bean sesame salad, fried whitefish, sausage – her plate was piled high with a mixed feast, Japanese foods and Western foods, showing no consistency of theme or program. He was impressed that nothing was falling off. It was so fascinating that he forgot to take his own breakfast.

At some point she must have felt him staring because she shot him a look. 'Is there a problem?' her face seemed to say.

Once she put her plate down at a table, he watched her get right back in line, this time taking a bowl of curry and loading up a plate of cakes, among other things.

He was interested, but not to the point where he was ready to request an explanation of her breakfast. But he did sit down at the table next to her. He decided he would just politely point to her plate and say, 'That's impressive,' the same way he might say to someone with a bandage around their forehead, 'That looks serious.'

It didn't seem to annoy her. 'Well,' she began, 'I suppose I'd say I'm in a one-on-one contest.'

'A . . . one-on-one contest?'

'I'm not just trying to see how much I can eat or anything silly like that.'

'I mean, I don't think that's so very silly.'

'When I stand in front of each food, I ask, "Do I want to eat this?"'

'Ask who?'

'Myself, obviously. Then if the answer is yes, I put it on my plate. That's all. It's just me versus me. How much food ends up on my plate doesn't really have anything to do with it.'

'Um, I would say that it has a lot to do with it. But hey, everyone's different.'

'What about your food selection? Pretty lame if you ask me.' She pointed at Suzuki's table.

He only had two plates, one with a bread roll and the other with some yogurt.

'If that's all you're going to take, you might as well stay at some business hotel. You're not taking the buffet seriously.'

'I never eat much for breakfast.'

'You're missing out.' There was almost something accusatory in her eyes, like she was looking at a criminal. 'When there are this many food options, you can't hold back, you have to eat and eat. You just have to do it.'

You just have to do it. Now that he thinks about it, she said that in their very first meeting.

By the time he was ready to get up and leave his table, her face was pale and she was holding her stomach. Her plate was still more than half full, looking like a mountain with a chunk taken out of it. 'Hey, you want any of this?' she asked Suzuki. Her voice had none of its earlier bombast.

'Reevaluating your choices?'

'I thought I was in a contest with myself, but it turns out it was me versus a crowd. I was outnumbered.'

'Guess so.'

'I do feel like if I could eat all of this, then I could swallow anything bad that life throws at me.'

'Digestion of food and digestion of life's problems are a little different.'

They started dating a month later, and after a year and a half they were married. For their honeymoon they went to Spain. She did the exact same thing at the breakfast buffet then too. 'I'm engaged in a one-on-one contest.'

'Buffet? You mean like at a hotel, for breakfast?'

'Yes, exactly. A hotel restaurant buffet.'

'You hit on your wife while she was taking food?'

'I wouldn't say that I hit on her.'

'If you get the job today, I bet your wife will be proud of you.' Sumire's manner is quite forward, not really worried if she's possibly touching on a sensitive subject, but it doesn't bother him. He would feel bad about dashing her excitement by telling her that his wife is dead.

That's when the phone rings. His stomach clenches.

'Sorry, phone call.' He takes his phone out of his pocket and stands. 'They'll probably yell at me for enjoying some pasta and tell me to come back,' he says, trying to sound unconcerned.

He walks over toward the entryway and brings the phone to his ear.

'Come to me. Now.' Hiyoko's voice is cutting.

'You sound like you're summoning your lover.'

'If you're feeling confident enough to joke around, I suggest you come back here now. Did you find anything out? Is your man the Pusher? How many more times am I going to have to ask you this? Whatever. Come back here and tell me where he is.'

'Not yet.' All he can do is delay.

'I don't know what you think you're doing, but you don't have unlimited time. At this point we can just assume that this man is the Pusher. You know, we're not the police, we're not the courts. If we suspect someone, we punish them. If there's a possibility someone's guilty, then they're guilty. So come back, now. Then you can tell us what you've found out so far.'

'If I do you'll just force a confession out of me.'

'You think we'd get violent with you?'

'Am I wrong?' Suzuki is incredulous.

'Of course we won't. There'd be no benefit in that.'

'What about those two kids? Are they okay?'

'Who's that now?'

Who's that. 'The two you drugged yesterday. The guy and the girl we put in the back seat of the car.' *The one who looked like my student.*

'Oh, them. Sure, they're fine, just fine.'

'That doesn't exactly sound like the truth.'

'It's true, promise. We're holding them at the office.'

'Holding them?'

'Watching them. They're not chained up or anything. They're pretty out of it, probably from the drugs. But they're alive, at the office. They're actually good at following orders. We might hire them. They seem to be interested.'

'This is ridiculous.'

'Why don't we meet up and talk about it? Hey, where'd you say you are again?'

'I —' She slipped the question in so naturally that he almost answered. 'I can't tell you where I am.'

'Didn't fall for it, huh?' She laughs. 'Okay. I'll give you an hour. Be at Shinagawa Station at four. By the old hotel. I'll pick you up. We'll go to the office and you can tell me what you've found out.' She gives the exact location.

'I'd rather not wait for you there.' He can easily picture standing there waiting and then suddenly being forced into a car.

'You have a problem with the place? Well, where should we meet, then?'

'No, the place is fine, I just –'

'If you're even one minute late, you'll be sorry. I might forgive you, but Terahara will lose his mind. He'll probably kill someone else in your place.'

'Who?'

'Like someone with the same name as you. Maybe a bunch of them.'

'There are lots of people named Suzuki.'

'All the more reason.'

'Come on.' He wants to laugh it off but he can't quite. It does seem like something they would do.

He finds himself checking the time on his watch, which surprises him.

Am I really going to go meet her?

Even though it's probably a trap?

But then again, they probably wouldn't go too far with me. I'm not worth it. The feeling settles in. Sensing his hesitation, Hiyoko presses. 'By the way. Oh, but this probably isn't of much interest to you.'

'Then don't tell me.'

'The idiot son is still breathing.'

'What?'

'Terahara's dummy of a son. Guess the bad ones don't die easy. They fixed him up at the hospital and he's regained consciousness.'

'No way. There's no way that's possible.'

'I'll tell you all about it when we meet. Well? Does that pique your interest? You still haven't gotten revenge for your wife. Which means you still have a chance. You wouldn't want to miss out on that, would you?'

'There's no way he survived that.'

'I bet you're wondering. Come back.'

'There's just no way. That's just –'

'The idiot gets special treatment from his father, from politicians,' Hiyoko goes on. 'But, lucky us, looks like he gets special treatment from God, too.'

THE WHALE

HE GETS OFF THE TRAIN and heads straight to the riverbank. Although the river isn't his destination – it's just the shortest route to where he's going. Gusts of wind whip in sideways and lash his face. Raising his eyes, he can see a bird flying overhead, wings like splayed fingers. He can't tell if it's a kite or a kestrel. He'd be able to distinguish if he could hear its cry, but it calls just when the wind blows and he can't get a clear read: is it *pii-hyoro-hyoro* or *kih-kih*?

It's four in the afternoon. The sun hasn't set yet but it's low in the sky, perched right on the rim of the buildings he can see to the left in the distance.

Then he notices: the river is swaying. Its meandering flow warps toward him, looking like it's going to spill over its banks. The ground at his feet bulges up and the whole scene starts to tremble. Then the usual vertigo sets in.

'Why did you call Iwanishi?' asks a voice.

He looks around with annoyance, wondering who the ghost

155

will be this time, but he doesn't see anyone. He shakes his head. Still no one there.

'Do you really need to know who that politician hired?' the voice goes on. Still no one around.

So now these ghosts don't even show themselves. The Whale looks up again. The bird is still flying. Although actually it's more floating. *Is that thing talking to me? Can't tell if it's a kite or a kestrel but I can hear it talk?*

'Why did you go out of your way to call him?' it presses. 'Don't tell me you believed anything you heard from that Tanaka guy.'

There's not another soul around him. There's no car noise either. He's not sure if that's just a coincidence or if it's because he's in the middle of one of his hallucinations.

Thirty minutes earlier, the Whale called the number he had written down. The number Kaji was trying to reach.

The circling bird speaks again. 'This Iwanishi told you right away where his condo is. That doesn't seem odd to you?'

'He was scrambling.' It occurs to the Whale that he's having a conversation with a bird. 'Probably not a deep thinker. Kind of guy who just says things to get through the moment.'

He recalls the phone conversation with Iwanishi. The man had picked up before the phone even rang once and started talking immediately, his voice shrill. 'Cicada? Why was your phone off?'

'Cicada?'

'Oh, not him, huh. Sorry. Who're you?'

Are you the one Kaji hired? The Whale considered it. *Are you supposed to kill me? If so, where are you and what are you doing? Why didn't you come to the hotel? Kaji's dead. You failed your job. How can you be so casual?*

Then he realized that this person might not be the one who was actually supposed to do the job. He didn't detect in this man's voice any of that particular gravity or wariness that killers have. Could be that he's admin or management. So the Whale

156

answered: 'Your man is down. Unconscious. At the hotel.' He was just making things up, looking for an opening. He wasn't at the hotel, and there was no one unconscious.

'Cicada?' The voice on the phone answered reflexively, all keyed up. 'Who's down? Is it Cicada?'

'Yes. Cicada.' The Whale went along.

'The fuck did he do, that moron? I been trying to get in touch with him forever. I can't believe this. Hey, where are you right now?'

'Tell me where you are and I'll bring him to you.' The Whale spoke smoothly.

'Put Cicada on.'

'I told you, he's unconscious.' The only answer he could give. 'Do you want me to take him to the hospital? Or the police?' He guessed the man wouldn't want either of those, and he was right.

'No, no, no need to go that far. Just bring him here.'

'Where's here?'

'Who are you?'

'I work for Kaji.' It was a reasonable lie. The Whale figured that naming the client would make the man drop his guard.

'Oh, ah, I see. For Mr Kaji, right?'

It must have added up for him, explaining why the Whale had his phone number. He gave the location of his condo. The Whale memorized it, musing to himself that this man's trusting nature was really something else.

'It's fine if I just leave him at the entrance to the building, right?' the Whale said, sounding bored. The man took the bait.

'Better to bring him to my place. Number 603. I'm Iwanishi.'

'I'm heading over now.' The Whale was about to hang up when Iwanishi got one last thing in.

'Hey, wait. Did Cicada do the job? The thing Mr Kaji wanted done?'

'He did.' Another lie. 'See you soon.' He hung up. Thinking about timing and location, he calculated that taking a train would be faster than a taxi through traffic. He went straight into the JR station he was standing in front of, stepping up to the platform just as the train pulled in.

'That man on the phone was ridiculously careless,' says the bird. At this point it doesn't look like a kite or kestrel, just an indistinct silhouette.

'This Cicada must be the one who actually does the work.'

'What do you plan to do when you go see Iwanishi?'

'Have a conversation.' As he says it, the Whale thinks about it. *Is that true? Am I just going there for conversation?*

'You know it's not just for conversation.' The bird circles high against the sky. 'Once he talks to you, the Iwanishi guy will die. You're the suicide specialist. He'll end up dead. Your plan is for him to kill himself. Right? But let me ask you – why?'

'Because I'm sick of it. All of it. I want to wipe the slate clean. Everything around me, I just want it cleared away. I'm settling my accounts.'

'Tanaka's words,' the bird says mockingly. 'You're just doing what he told you to.'

He feels a shimmer in his head. Closes his eyes tightly, then opens them again. The scenery seems more vivid. There's no bird overhead. He does spot a crow on a telephone pole off to the right, but it may have been there all along.

The sound of happy voices comes from further down the embankment. He looks and sees a fenced-in tennis court, four people playing doubles, dressed for much warmer weather, swinging away with their rackets.

Looks like I'm back to reality, he thinks, but then shakes his head. *This could be a hallucination too. Who could say for certain? Not me.*

He could still be in the world of ghosts and phantoms, disconnected from even a fragment of reality. It wasn't impossible. What unsettles him the most is the fact that, if he were still in that other realm, it wouldn't bother him.

The condo building is easy to find. Nine stories, dull gray, emanating an aura of moldy damp even though there's no more rain.

He crosses the threshold, gets into the elevator and hits the button for the sixth floor. Did Iwanishi really take him at his word? Is he just waiting there obediently? The Whale is dubious. It could very well be that Iwanishi is in unit 603 with a gun at the ready.

That'd be fine. The Whale believes this. Clearing up all these complications doesn't require any schemes or second-guesses. He doesn't need a convoluted plan to settle his accounts.

Standing in front of unit 603, he rings the bell, no hesitation. No answer. He tries again. Still nothing.

So it's a setup after all, he thinks, but he doesn't think about retreating. He places his hand on the doorknob. Slowly turns, pulls. It's unlocked. He steps into the vestibule. From further into the unit a voice calls, 'Took you long enough.' Footsteps approaching. 'Keepin' track of time is keepin' track of yourself, you know.'

The moment he hears the man's tone, the Whale knows that he doesn't suspect anything. He's not lying in wait with his weapon drawn, and he hasn't called reinforcements. He honestly believes that one of Kaji's underlings is bringing Cicada to him.

A skinny man appears in the doorway at the end of the hall. He wears glasses but doesn't give off an intellectual vibe. His face is pinched and his jaw pointed.

'Yeah, it took you a while. And where's Cicada? You brought him, right? All he does is cause fuckin problems. He hasn't been in touch once, I had no idea what was going on. I haven't heard from Mr Kaji, either.' He speaks in a rush of words as he walks. 'Hey, what the fuck, man, you're in my place with your shoes on?'

'You Iwanishi?' The Whale starts closing the distance.

'Whoa, wait, what's going on here?' Iwanishi backpedals a step, then another. 'You haven't told me your name or said hello or anything. Ever heard of manners? *Courtesy*, man. Not something you ever learned? For a life worth living, courtesy's the key – know who said that? Anyway, did Cicada do the job or what? Did he take out the big guy?' He's spitting left and right as he speaks, until suddenly he freezes, mouth open.

It's dawning on him that this man closing in is the big guy. 'It's you,' he murmurs. His body seems to crumple. Now he's on all fours, crawling back toward the main room.

The Whale follows. Stepping into the room, his shoes track dirt on the wood flooring. There's a black sofa to the left and a steel desk straight ahead.

Iwanishi is around the side of the desk, fumbling at a drawer.

The Whale advances silently. Plants his left foot and aims a savage kick with his right, just as Iwanishi's hand goes into the drawer. Iwanishi tumbles over backward. The gun he had grabbed clatters to the floor.

Ignoring the gun, the Whale looms over Iwanishi, then bends slightly and launches his hand out to grab the man by the jaw. Iwanishi mewls with pain, so the Whale squeezes harder, grinding his cheeks like crushing an apple in his hand, until Iwanishi falls silent. The Whale lifts him into the air. His feet dangle in space, pedaling feebly.

His teeth must have cut into his cheek because a mix of blood and drool spills out of his mouth, dripping onto the floor, bubbling from his lips. Like he had a mouthful of strawberries and bit into all of them at once.

The Whale lowers his arm and lets go. Iwanishi collapses. He paws his cheek and sees the blood on his fingers, then wails. 'What the fuck do you think you're doing, asshole?'

Saying nothing, the Whale scans the room. He looks for something that will work for a hanging, but finds nothing. He considers looking in the bathroom for a towel, but sees that there's no column or vent he could hang the man from. He examines the window. It's wide enough for someone to fit through.

'So it's a jump,' the Whale murmurs, looking down at Iwanishi as he slowly gets to his knees.

'What's your beef with me?'

'Kaji hired you. You were trying to kill me.'

'Is that wrong? When I get an inquiry, I make the job happen.' Iwanishi seems to have forgotten their difference in size, his overwhelming disadvantage in physical power. 'It's not like you're any more respectable. You do the same thing.'

'The same thing?'

'You kill people!'

'You're wrong.' The Whale surprises himself with how firmly he corrects Iwanishi. 'People who meet me just end up killing themselves.'

'*You're* the suicide guy?' Iwanishi's face freezes.

'You've heard of me?'

'Of course I've heard of you! So you're the Whale. Yeah, you're *big*.'

'Did you think a whale would be small?'

At that moment, Iwanishi finally pieces together why the Whale is visiting him at his home, and blocking any route of escape. 'Wait, wait, wait. Me? Are you here for me?'

'There's no one else here.'

'Wait – honestly – why do you want me to kill myself? Are you that burned that I took the job from Kaji?'

'No.'

'Then why?'

'I'm settling my accounts. All of them.'

'What the fuck is that supposed to mean?' Iwanishi blinks several times. 'So then what happened to Cicada? Guess you got him too, huh?'

The Whale steps in and reaches with both hands to take hold of Iwanishi's shoulders. He fixes him with a glare and speaks in a low voice. 'Ready to jump?'

Iwanishi's eyes widen, quavering slightly. The pupils seem to blend into the whites. The lines on his forehead and around his mouth go slack. *Same as everyone else,* thinks the Whale. Whenever someone is about to kill themselves, their expression goes deeply quiet. Like they've moved past any doubts or fears. Almost serene. Like they're dreaming. Content.

It's like they've wanted to die.

They might have protested, screamed, wet themselves or tried to run, they might claw at the rope biting into their neck, but in the end they all seem happy to be ending their lives.

'It's just back there.' The Whale gestures with his chin over Iwanishi's shoulder.

Iwanishi turns around, his eyes a mix of emptiness and ecstasy.

'Your last look at the world.'

Iwanishi steps toward the window like he's being pulled.

The Whale watches this, certain that he won't have to do anything else. Iwanishi's going to jump.

That's when a wave of dizziness hits. *Not now.* No sooner does he click his tongue in aggravation than he feels a crushing pressure in his head, like someone is squeezing his brain into jelly.

The pain subsides. He blinks several times. As he expected, he's no longer seeing Iwanishi in front of him. Instead, standing just off to the right, there's a middle-aged woman.

'You must be really annoyed that I showed up now, of all times,' she says, mischievous glee showing on the full cheeks and double chin of her ghostly face. The Whale says nothing, making a point of not meeting her eye. *None of this is real*, he reminds himself. *Iwanishi is standing in front of me. I can't see him, but I know he's there.*

'So you're planning to force this feeble bespectacled man to kill himself,' the woman says bluntly, pointing to the place where Iwanishi was standing. 'You're going to make him jump, just like you made me. Right?'

The Whale squints, tries with everything he has to see Iwanishi, but there's just nothing there. He's still locked in his vision.

'But I'll tell you one thing,' says the woman, speaking in a continuous stream, like she must have done when she was alive. 'This man has looked into your eyes and is acting like he's going to kill himself, but it's just an act.'

'What?' The Whale responds despite himself, turning to look at the ghost of the politician's wife.

'He's a clever one. He's just playacting. He's leading you on.'

The Whale slowly faces forward again. All he can see is the window. Beyond the dingy lace curtains is the sinking sun. The lights on the buildings of varied height, the ivy climbing up the telephone poles, the scattered strips of cloud. He can see all of these things quite clearly, but no Iwanishi.

'Let your guard down and he'll get that gun and shoot you dead. But maybe that's for the best. People want to die after all, right? You're no exception.'

When she says this, the Whale feels an unfamiliar sensation seep up from his feet through his body, like blood welling up from an old wound. *What is this?* he wonders, as he feels his hair stand on end. A moment later he realizes.

It's fear.

Fear has overtaken him.

He opens his eyes wider. Still no sign of Iwanishi. *Where's the real world?* His eyes dart left and right, searching for reality.

A phone rings.

A high-pitched electronic trill. Through the first long ring his body is frozen. On the second ring he feels a slight shock, like a pop inside his head. He shakes his head vigorously and blinks several times.

The room brightens. The garrulous housewife is gone, replaced by the sudden sight of Iwanishi.

Before he was standing in front of the Whale, staring out the window, but at some point he had moved off to the right. He's on all fours, reaching for something.

There on the floor, just beyond Iwanishi's outstretched fingers, is the gun. The Whale starts for it too. Behind him the phone on the desk is still ringing, monotonous and piercing. He cocks his right leg and kicks Iwanishi in the face. Iwanishi topples over and crashes into the wastebasket, scattering scraps of paper and instant-ramen packaging.

The Whale takes the gun. 'Don't move.'

The phone doesn't seem like it's going to stop ringing.

'You left yourself open, dummy.'

'Open?'

'Just standing there muttering to yourself. You crazy or what?' Iwanishi's eyes reflect his dire situation, but his face wears a forced grin. 'So much for the suicide guy.'

Saying nothing, the Whale aims the gun. Releases the safety. He has his own gun in his jacket pocket, but it's not loaded. It's only for scaring people into killing themselves.

'Yeah, some suicide guy. You're not such a big a deal.' Iwanishi cackles. 'I bet Cicada's not even dead. I doubt someone like you could take him out.'

The phone keeps ringing.

'Mind if I take that?' Iwanishi has both hands up in a gesture of surrender.

'Why would you think I would let you do that?'

'C'mon, don't I get a phone call before I die?' It doesn't seem like Iwanishi is actually serious. Rather he's making what he thinks is a joke.

Still aiming the gun, the Whale says, 'Do what you want.' He's not showing mercy. Iwanishi's life is over either way. 'Take your call. Then you jump.'

'So I gotta jump, huh?' Iwanishi's lips twist into a rueful smile. Then he speaks in a low voice, not clearly to the Whale and not clearly to himself. 'Just like Crispin says, "If you wanna get away from this life just go jump off a building."'

The Whale is about to ask who would say such a stupid thing, when Iwanishi picks up the phone.

CICADA

'WHERE'S THIS EMPLOYEE BEING TAKEN?' Cicada asks. He's got Momo by the shoulders, shaking her.

'I said I'd tell you, no need to be so rough,' she says, as if she's soothing a child. 'So, as you'd expect, nasty business calls for a nasty venue.'

She tells him about a building that's a fifteen-minute drive from Shinagawa Station, taking out a notebook and sketching a simple map. 'It used to be a car factory, but that closed a while back, and nothing else ever opened up there. It's in the middle of this big grove of cedars, which you don't see too often in Tokyo. And you know, I'd guess that no one wanted to deal with the hay fever.'

'The pollen kept people away, huh?'

'All the places in the area are garages and old buildings, one of which belongs to Terahara's outfit. It's so obviously sketchy when you see it, I had to laugh. The white walls are all stained with soot, basically black, and all the windows are broken too.'

'You've been there?'

'For work.'

'Porno mag delivery?'

'Yeah, that too, but you know I've also got a side gig, honey.'

'I'm never sure which one's the side gig.'

'Anyway, I've done some subcontracted work at that location for Terahara's company.'

'Oh yeah? Subcontracted?'

'Big operations are always farming out work. What's the English word for it, outsourcing? I did that. Calling random numbers in the phonebook, and when an old person answered, we'd threaten them. We'll hurt your grandson, that kinda thing. If you don't want anything to happen to him, send money. It worked surprisingly well. There were ten of us in a room, everyone with their cell phones, dialing away.'

'Sounds like a nice easy job.' Cicada thinks about the work he gets from Iwanishi and sighs. 'It's like zero risk.'

'Yep. We had some plants, you know, actors. They call themselves the Performers, they're good at acting. They'd scream and act like they were being hurt.'

'So this employee is gonna be taken to this building.'

'The employee who's after the Pusher but won't spill? Yeah, I'd imagine so. When the Terahara group has any nasty business to handle they generally do it there.'

They were sure to work this guy over. – Tell us where the Pusher is. – No, I'd rather not. – Then there's nothing we can do. Please let us know if you change your mind ... That's not how it'll go. Whether or not they call it torture, torture is what it'll be.

'When?' Cicada asks.

'Can't say for sure, but I hear they just hired some people on it, so I imagine they'll start today.'

'Who are these people?'

'I guess you'd call them torture specialists. The kind of people who like hurting other people. They're good at getting information.'

'Sounds like a bunch of creeps.'

'Well, I mean, Terahara's son was killed. He's not playing around. But hey, are you really thinking about snatching this guy?'

'Everyone'd know how awesome I am.'

'I'm not sure it's a good idea for you to get involved.'

'So you're saying I should just be a good boy and follow Iwanishi's orders?'

'No, that's not what I'm saying. I'm just saying Terahara's outfit is no joke. They're really dangerous.'

'I'm free to do what I want.'

'What's that supposed to mean?'

'It means I'm nobody's puppet.'

With that, Cicada snatches the map she drew from out of her hand and walks off. Getting to the outskirts of Shinagawa will be quicker in a car. He turns it over in his mind as he wanders the streets.

After walking for a bit, he turns off an avenue lined with office buildings into a narrow side street, where he finds a parked SUV. It's gray and white with a rack on top for skis or snowboards. The engine appears to be running. The body of the car vibrates ostentatiously, as if showing off that it's on. It's not locked either. The keys dangle from the ignition. He guesses that the owner likes to keep it cold and didn't want to turn the AC off. Whoever it was figured they'd be right back, so it was okay to leave it running. Their mistake.

Most excellent, he says to himself, sliding into the driver's seat and pulling the door shut. He puts it into gear. *This*, Cicada thinks, ecstatic, *finding this car is like, the will of the gods.*

He gets on the broad inter-prefectural road but has a bad feeling about the traffic clogging up the intersections and quickly turns onto a side street. The clock reads 4 p.m.

The secondary streets aren't as clear as he'd like though, and before long he starts to see cars slowing down. He clicks his tongue and pulls to a stop behind them. He looks further up the gentle curve of the street and spots some roadwork about a hundred meters ahead. A man with a red baton is directing traffic.

On a whim he decides to make a phone call. Sitting there with his foot on the brake is boring. He switches his phone on and calls the number he has saved. Iwanishi's number.

He scratches his head, listening to the ringtone.

Iwanishi'll never guess that I'm after the Pusher. He wants to hear the surprise in Iwanishi's voice and laugh at him.

The phone just keeps ringing. 'The fuck is he off doing?' Cicada grumbles.

The car at the head of the backup finally starts to move. Cicada is about to hang up the phone when he hears, 'What?' He immediately pictures Iwanishi's haughty sneer.

'It's me. Took you long enough to answer.'

'Fuck you. I'm busy.'

'You're never busy with anything. All you ever do is watch TV or sleep.'

There's a brief pause, like Iwanishi is swallowing hard. 'So you're alive after all, huh.'

'Of course I'm alive. What kinda stupid question is that?' Cicada presses the phone up to his ear. One by one, the brake lights on the cars in front of him wink off.

'Listen, Cicada, you'd be surprised at the stuff that I do.'

'That feels like it's my line.' Cicada's voice gets louder. 'In fact I think you'll be very surprised when you hear where I'm headed right now.'

'Where?'

'Shinagawa.' Cicada can't keep the laughter out of his voice. *I'm not a little pet who just waits by your side.* 'Shinagawa outskirts. To a building.'

'There're lots of buildings in Shinagawa.'

'This building is owned by Terahara.'

'Mr Terahara? What are you even talking about?' Iwanishi sounds distracted.

'Oh, you wanna know what I'm going there for?' Cicada pauses for a moment to savor the thrill he feels in his chest. 'I'm going to take out the Pusher.'

'What?' The sound of surprise in Iwanishi's voice is delightful. Cicada almost whoops with joy.

'It's like this. There's this guy who knows where the Pusher is. Seems this guy got called in by the Fräulein crew. But I'm gonna get him first.'

'Get him? What the fuck are you thinking?'

'You just sit tight right there, buddy. I'll let you know how it goes.'

Iwanishi doesn't say anything. The sedan in front of Cicada starts to move, so he takes his foot off the brake.

'So, yeah, I'll call you later.'

'Wait.' There's something urgent in Iwanishi's voice. 'Where is it? Where exactly are you going?'

'I dunno, man, somewhere I can't explain to you.' *I gave you a preview, but you'll have to wait for the rest. The last thing I want is for your dumb ass to get in the way.* 'Anyway,' he says out loud, 'I'm free of you. That's the point. What, are you surprised?'

'I'm not surprised.' Iwanishi's voice doesn't have any edge to it, or sound like he's talking down to a subordinate. If anything he sounds affectionate.

'What'd you say?'

'You've always been free,' Iwanishi says plainly. 'I've got no control over that.'

Cicada spends a moment not knowing what to say. 'Whatever. You just stay right there at your stupid little condo.'

'Fuck you.' Iwanishi sounds casual but underneath it there's something heavier. 'All right then, Cicada. We'll meet again.'

'Yeah, well, if we did, you'll just be like, Hey, where's my gift from your trip?'

'You really need to shut the fuck up,' he says, putting on a show of exasperation. 'Hey, you know what Jack Crispin said when he retired?'

'You know I've been meaning to ask you for a while, does this guy even exist?'

'When Crispin was getting out of the game, a magazine reporter asked him what he wanted to do once he retired. Know what he said?'

'Of course I don't know.' Cicada feels like he's sat through literally dozens of these bullshit non-conversations. He considers hanging up but decides to humor Iwanishi. Once he kills the Pusher he's planning to cut ties and never see Iwanishi again. *Can't hurt to let him do his routine one last time.* 'What'd he say?'

'I wanna eat pizza.'

'Um, okay.'

'That's what he said. When I retire, I wanna eat pizza.' Iwanishi's laughing, but it also sounds like he's crying, which makes Cicada cringe.

'He could eat pizza whether or not he retired.'

'I know!' Iwanishi wheezes. 'Hilarious! He's so good!'

'It's stupid. Later.'

'Yeah, well, anyway, give it your best, Cicada. Don't lose.'

'What's with the cheerleading?'

He hangs up and puts his foot down on the gas. Opens the window. The wind flows in.

SUZUKI

'I'VE BEEN CALLED BACK TO the office for a matter regarding one of my students,' Suzuki lies. 'I have to excuse myself for a while.'

Sumire's teeth show white as she laughs. 'For a while? Does that mean you're coming back here? You don't have any other houses to get to?'

'No, I – well –' Suzuki stammers. 'Either way, I'd love to work with you.'

After all, I haven't yet found out if he's the Pusher.

As he's saying this, he can't help but think about Terahara's son. Hiyoko's words ring in his head. *Could he be alive? After that? Have there been bold advances in medical science? If so, they're a little too bold.*

In the end, Suzuki had agreed to meet Hiyoko. Of course he knew that it was probably a trap. She could very well be just trying to draw him out, dangling the lives of those two random kids, making up some nonsense about Terahara's son still being alive. He was fully aware of this. It seemed much more likely than not. Beyond likely. It was pretty much a certainty.

But he also guessed that nothing so very bad would happen. If he just exercises a little caution, he can keep them from being able to make any moves. So instead of meeting at an interchange near the station, he asked to meet somewhere there would be more people around.

'I just want to hear your story, so I'll make it as easy as possible,' she had said evenly. 'Cafe it is.'

The Asagao family all go to the door to see Suzuki off. Once he gets his shoes on, Kentaro says, 'Do you have to leave?'

'You're leaving?' The small voice at Suzuki's feet startles him and he looks down to find Kojiro hugging his left leg. He has his little sandals on, and he puts his hand in Suzuki's pocket as if to keep him there.

Suzuki gets an idea. 'Hey, I know. Why don't I mail those postcards you were writing? If you're still planning on sending them, that is.'

But Kojiro shakes his head. 'I'm still writing more.'

Suzuki wonders how many doubles of the same sticker the kid has.

Meanwhile Kojiro sings a little tune to himself. 'To-kyo-o, Bun-kyo waaard.'

'Then we'll see you later,' Sumire says.

'Thanks for your time and hospitality,' Suzuki answers.

Asagao says nothing. As Suzuki places his hand on the door-knob and is about to open it, Sumire speaks up. 'Hey, Mr Suzuki.'

He flinches, like the voice is a shot from behind. He turns toward her.

'I don't know how far you're going but maybe we can give you a ride?' She smiles, looking completely carefree. Then she turns to Asagao. 'What do you think?'

'Sure,' he assents. 'It's pretty far to the station from here. Faster to go by car.'

This puts Suzuki at a momentary loss. He mumbles something about it not being necessary.

'Where are you headed?' Asagao asks. There's still something about him that seems transparent. Suzuki swears he can see the stairs behind him.

'To Shinagawa.' He doesn't have time to weigh whether or not it's the best idea to tell the truth. It feels like he's being drawn in against his will. 'A cafe in the station.'

'I can take you to Shinagawa Station.'

'No, no, that's all right.'

'It's no problem.'

There's a blue sedan parked in front of the gate. Before he can process what's happening, Suzuki is in the passenger seat. He has no idea how it happened – suddenly the car was there, and he was opening the door, and fastening his seatbelt. Not even any sense of his feet touching the ground as he walked to the car. No one pulled him onward or pushed him from behind, he just somehow ended up in the passenger seat. *Just like being born*, he thinks. It just happened: he was born, and now here he is. With a start he recalls what his wife said: There's no proof that I was ever even here. *It's true, we're born and live our lives and there's nothing to prove that it ever happened. Like how we can't be sure Brian Jones was actually in the Rolling Stones.*

Asagao puts the car in gear with practiced movements and pulls away.

As the sedan glides along, Suzuki keeps expecting Asagao to turn to him and say *I see right through you*.

From the scenery out the window, he can tell that they are in fact headed toward Shinagawa, but this doesn't make him feel any better. His shoulders hunch as he tries to make himself as small as possible.

But after a bit it occurs to him that now is his best chance to ask questions. It's just the two of them together in the car, so it should be a good opportunity for him to find out if this man is really the Pusher. Suzuki begins to build himself up to it, feeling his courage stirring within him like an army of soldiers fomenting a revolution. *Now's the time*, they cry.

He turns to Asagao in the driver's seat. 'I've been thinking,' he begins, but then his words dry up. *I wanted to ask if you're the Pusher.* He can't say it. On a subconscious level he knows that if he takes another step forward he'll go tumbling off the cliff. His courage soldiers stop short, overawed by an obviously more powerful enemy.

'What?' asks Asagao.

'Kentaro is a really good kid.' He winces, annoyed at himself for going in such a drastically different direction, but at the same time he tells himself that if he's looking for a way in then the children aren't a bad place to start.

'You think so?' Asagao's reaction is hard to read. He might be uninterested, or he might just be keeping a poker face. 'He's no good at studying, but he's great at soccer.'

'He really is. In the right environment, I bet he could thrive as a soccer player.'

'The right environment?'

'Oh, I –' Suzuki falls silent. He can't exactly say that the boy won't succeed as a soccer player with the Pusher for a father.

'What about Kojiro?'

'He's adorable,' Suzuki answers honestly. 'He's like a cute little animal. But why does he always speak so quietly?'

'Oh that,' Asagao says slowly, his eyes on the road. 'I taught him that.'

'Taught him what, exactly?'

'When something's truly important, people will hear it even if you say it quietly.'

'Is that right?'

'When politicians scream and shout, does anyone actually listen?'

'No one listens to anything politicians say in any case.'

'Think about it. When someone is really in trouble, they can't raise their voice.'

Suzuki has no idea what Asagao is getting at, but somehow he can't press any further.

'Is there something you'd like to say to me?'

'No.' He feels a spasm in his gut. 'No, nothing at all.' His soldiers are in full retreat.

'We're here,' Asagao says. It's been twenty minutes since they left the house. The sudden announcement almost makes Suzuki jump out of his seat. He looks left and right.

'At Shinagawa?' He cranes his neck and looks around again, but he doesn't see the station building or any tracks anywhere.

'Just go straight ahead,' Asagao says, gesturing with his chin. He's pulled the car over on the shoulder of a one-way single-lane street. Sure enough, the station is fifty meters ahead. 'Where's your meeting?'

'At a cafe inside the station building.' Suzuki names the cafe. 'I can just walk from here. Thanks very much for the ride,' he says politely. He glances at the dashboard clock and sees that there are ten minutes before his four o'clock meeting.

'Thanks for playing with Kentaro.'

'Oh, it was my pleasure.' Suzuki unlocks and opens the passenger door.

He steps out of the car and bobs his head to Asagao, who is already putting the car in gear. The car turns right at the light and drives off.

'Are you the Pusher?' he's finally able to ask. The question is impressively late in coming.

*

The traffic circle in front of Shinagawa Station is hectic. Company workers in suits and travelers with oversize bags hurry this way and that. Taxis pull up one after the other, swallowing passengers and driving away. A large bus pulls in and barely comes to a stop before a wave of foreigners wearing clothing too light for the season pours out and flows into the station.

He slips by the bus and enters the station building. It's spacious and wide inside, with torrents of people. He goes up the stairs and heads down the long walkway.

The cafe he arranged to meet Hiyoko at is the one they went to on the day he first agreed to work for Fräulein. She apparently hadn't forgotten, as when he proposed it she said, 'A special meeting in our special spot.' She said it sweetly, like they were dating.

It's not a large cafe. The bearded owner is behind the counter, and there's one waitress, and besides Suzuki there are only two other customers, a pair of men. He takes a seat at a table where he can see the entrance. He checks his watch and sees that it's just four o'clock. Still no feeling of any danger. He reasons that if anything happens he can just call out for help and the other customers or the staff will call the police.

By the time he drinks half of the glass of water the waitress has brought him, Hiyoko appears. She's wearing a dark blue suit. The jacket is a conservative cut, but the skirt is extremely short, making for an imbalanced look.

'Well, well, I finally caught up with you.' She smiles almost wistfully and lowers herself into the seat across from him. Then she orders a coffee.

'Is Terahara . . . Mr Terahara's son really alive?' Suzuki's voice pitches upward.

'How respectful of you to call him mister. First tell me where you tailed our friend to.'

'All I want to know is if he's alive.'

'I'd say that first you have a responsibility to make your report.'

'On what?'

'On the Pusher. The man you were after is the Pusher, no? Tell me where he lives. Terahara's all worked up. It's not good.'

'I think,' begins Suzuki, giving the answer he had prepared, 'it's probably not him. I observed him closely until just a little while ago, and he's just a person.'

'What does that even mean, just a person? A murderer who stabs someone to death is a person. A woman who poisons her neighbor is a person.'

'I think he's got nothing to do with any of this. He's not the Pusher.'

Although in his heart Suzuki is certain that Asagao *is* the Pusher. The cool air about him, his sharp gaze, the way he seemed to see right through Suzuki – the power he projected didn't belong to any average man. Just talking with him felt like being cut open by a sharp blade. In their conversation about locusts, Suzuki detected a chilling contempt for humanity. Asagao is the Pusher. It's the most logical conclusion. There's nothing ordinary about the quiet threat that he gives off. If he isn't the Pusher, there's no way to explain the unease Suzuki feels around him. He's the one who pushed Terahara's son in front of a car. Suzuki is sure of it.

But he has no intention of telling Hiyoko any of that.

Just picturing Kentaro's and Kojiro's smiling faces makes Suzuki's chest catch. He can't let them get caught up in this.

'You should just forget about the man I followed. There's no way he's the Pusher.'

'It's my job to decide that, not yours,' Hiyoko says sternly.

Finally it starts to dawn on Suzuki that he's in much more danger than he anticipated.

'I don't think you're taking us seriously. If you were going to run, you should have actually run. Instead you came toddling

178

along when we called. People who can't pick a direction and go with it don't have the best time in life.'

'I don't know where the Pusher is. It's not the man I followed. Rough me up all you like, I still won't know.'

'Why, roughing you up is exactly what we're going to do, darling.'

Even as he hears the words, Suzuki feels his head getting heavier. He registers surprise, tries to look around, but feels more and more sluggish. His eyelids slide shut. Suddenly frantic, he tries to open his eyes, but the moment he does they fall shut again.

Drugs. His mind is moving too slowly. But when could she have drugged him? He knows that Hiyoko likes to use sleep meds on people. That's why from the moment she entered the cafe he made sure not to let her anywhere near his cup. She had no chance to spike his drink, he thinks, but then it occurs to him: *The Performers?*

'They'll play any role,' she had said. He realizes that the other customers, and the cafe staff too, are probably members of the Performers. And they probably dosed his water. *That's what happened*, he wails inside his mind, *How could I be so stupid?* But he barely has any time to feel regret before he passes out.

His body lurches and his eyes open. His head hurts. Right away he pieces together that he's been stuffed into the back of a car. Or a van. All the seats have been removed and he's lying on the floor of the vehicle. Two men are holding him down. His coat has been removed, and he can feel the cold metal of the car's body through his sweater.

His hands and feet are bound together. Not with rope or tape, but with some kind of strapped restraint.

'You really are pathetic, pal.' The short-haired man to the right brings his face close over Suzuki's, like he's about to spit on him. Suzuki thinks he recognizes him as one of the two men from the cafe.

'Are you with the Performers?'

He hears Hiyoko laugh from the front passenger seat. 'That's quite a memory you have. But these men aren't Performers. We're not getting along with them at the moment. These men are specialists in torture.'

'W-what?'

'We hire them to torture people.'

The only response Suzuki can muster is a low moan.

'And you really are dumb, you know that? I can't believe you fell for such a stupid lie.'

'Lie?'

'How could there be any way the idiot son was still alive after being squashed to death?'

That's what I thought. There's no way he was still alive. He feels simultaneously relieved and terrified. *It was a trap all along.* Just as he suspected, unfortunately. Disgust washes over him. *I'm an idiot.*

'What a moron,' says the man to the left with the flat nose. His hair hangs down, lank and dull. There's a bandage on his right cheek. Blood is visible beneath. 'You were so sure this guy would come,' he says to Hiyoko. 'Looks like you were right.'

'Well, you know. The thing about danger is that even if people understand it intellectually, it never quite feels real to them.'

'What do you mean?' The short-haired man turns toward her.

'They still think they'll be fine.' Hiyoko laughs again. 'No matter how dangerous the situation, they assume they'll be okay. When there's a box that says *Danger*, they figure it can't be that dangerous, right until the moment they open it. It's why a wanted criminal will go to a pachinko parlor. It'll be fine, they think. Nothing's going to go so badly so quickly. They're convinced that trouble comes gradually. That's why people keep smoking even though they know it could lead to lung cancer.'

She's right, thinks Suzuki. He had believed that danger would escalate slowly. He knew that Hiyoko could be lying to him, he knew that it could be a trap, he knew that his judgment could be wrong, but nonetheless, he never really believed any of those things would happen.

'You'd really better tell us whatever you know quick. We're specialists,' says the man with the short hair. Suzuki watches his mouth move, lips like squirming cakes of cod roe. 'When it comes to torture, we're the best of the best.'

Suzuki feels like his spine is being caressed by an icicle.

Pinned down face up, Suzuki stares at the ceiling of the van. *This is bad*, he thinks, but at the same time he keeps feeling like somehow he'll be okay. *I guess I'm still not taking this seriously enough.*

He remembers something his wife said, when she was staring at TV footage of wars unfolding in other countries. 'You know, I think that even if we were to see enemy soldiers lined up in front of us we wouldn't really feel like we were in the middle of a war. I'd guess that for most of the wars throughout history, people never thought it would get that bad.' She shrugged, but she sounded sad. *Looks like you were right.* He had forgotten that she said that, until now. He puts his focus into the nerves of his ring finger where her ring sits. 'So many of the troubles of the world happen because people don't take them seriously.' And she was absolutely right.

He has no idea where they're taking him. He peers left and right out the windows, but beyond darkening clouds and a tangle of powerlines there's nothing he can see that might give him a clue of where they are or where they're headed. His mouth is duct-taped shut. The tape smells so strong it makes him dizzy.

After some time, Hiyoko says, 'We're here.' She sounds excited, like a child who's been wanting to go to the zoo and is finally there.

'Oh.' The driver speaks up for the first time.

'What is it?' Hiyoko asks.

'There's someone here.' The driver's voice is devoid of life.

'Here, where? What did you see?'

'Someone in the road.'

'There's no one here.'

'There was. He ran off. Gone now.'

'You need to lay off the drugs.'

Suzuki gathers that the driver is one of Fräulein's customers. They get addicted to the illegal substances that Fräulein peddles, and to get more they end up pressed into service.

The flat-nosed long-haired man opens the door and gets out. There appears to be something wrong with his leg as he drags it behind him. Some kind of chain wrapped around his waist clinks as he moves.

'Hold still. We're gonna lift you.' The short-haired man wedges his hands under Suzuki's arms. All shackled up and unable to move his arms or legs, Suzuki just lies there flat like a plank of wood.

The two men hoist Suzuki up and carry him toward the building like they're moving furniture. He's facing upward, and all he can see is the dark sky.

He can't tell what floor the elevator takes them to. As soon as the door opens they tip him over sideways and lift him again. They go down a hallway, pass through a door, enter a room. It's a wide, empty space. Maybe once used for a business but now cleared out. Nothing left, just bare concrete walls. The floor is all cold tiles.

The whole space is suffused with a strong antiseptic smell, as if it had been scrupulously disinfected.

They lay him down on top of something like a mattress in the middle of the room. It's dusty. He coughs. For several moments he can't open his eyes.

'Let me just say that I don't want to have to hurt you.' Hiyoko sits down on a chair several meters away. It has wheels and she scoots toward him. If his mouth weren't taped shut he would tell her he believes her.

'But like I've told you in the past. Our operation doesn't exactly do things . . . legally.'

Suzuki's breath quickens. The odor of the duct tape stings his nose.

'And we're exceedingly persistent.'

That much I know.

He swivels his neck. An unsavory damp air wafts off the mattress. The two men stand on either side of him. The one with the bandage, to his left, slips on black leather gloves.

'I gave you plenty of chances. Even back there in the cafe, I gave you a final chance. I asked so many times for you to tell me the address of the man you were tailing. But you just won't spill. I'm not sure why not though. There's nothing in it for you. Is there?'

He notices the short-haired man to his left is now holding a grimy-looking hammer.

In that instant, for the first time, Suzuki is truly afraid. He can't move, and he doesn't know what they're going to do to him. His mind fills with terror.

He pictures Asagao, then Sumire, then Kentaro and Kojiro, one by one. He can see their home, remembers its location. *If I talk, will it save me?* He's shocked at how quickly his resolve wavered. He can almost feel his wife looking at him with contempt, asking how he could abandon those children so easily.

'I suppose there is something admirable about it. The aesthetics of silence. Or something like that.' Hiyoko's deep red lips curl upward. 'But it comes at a price. Have you made up your mind?'

Suzuki realizes with a jolt of dread that they haven't taken the tape off his mouth. She's apparently past the point of caring about what he has to say. They're no longer looking to get information out of him.

'We'll be sure to take our time.' The man with the bandage leers. 'We'll hurt you, but we won't let you die.'

A fist slams into Suzuki's stomach. He can't breathe in, he can only moan. It's less his voice than just sound escaping his body. Saliva wells up, but with the tape over his mouth it has nowhere to go and slides back down, catching in his windpipe. He chokes. Another punch. Something comes up from his gut. Probably undigested pasta.

'Fingers, toes, elbows, knees.' The short-haired man intones rhythmically, swinging his hammer. He swings hard, again, and again.

THE WHALE

HE LOOKS AT THE OPEN window. The curtain undulates in the wind like a tongue gently probing the inside of the room. He doesn't look out the window though. All there is to see is Iwanishi's broken body. And the residents now gathering around the corpse might spot him. For the past few minutes he's been hearing the sound of doors elsewhere in the condo building opening and closing urgently. Before long there was a clamor of shouts and shrieks.

The Whale surveys the room. Looking down at the phone on the desk, he pictures Iwanishi's praying mantis-like face bent over it, just before jumping out the window.

'Yeah, well, anyway, give it your best, Cicada. Don't lose.' Iwanishi was smiling broadly, which felt inappropriate, as he hung up the phone. He looked lighter, relieved, like he had set down a heavy burden. 'Well, that I did not expect.'

'What?' the Whale asked while sliding open the window. The curtain waved, an invitation to jump. 'Who was that on the phone?'

'Cicada.' Iwanishi flashed his plaque-stained teeth. His sour breath wafted out. 'Guy who works for me. The one who was supposed to kill you.'

The Whale's eyebrows twitch.

'You gonna go after him too?'

'Go after him?'

'You said you were settling all your accounts. Which I guess means you'd have to kill Cicada.'

Settle the score. Close out your accounts. The words echoed around the Whale. 'Where is this . . . Cicada?'

'A building. In Shinagawa.'

'There are lots of buildings in Shinagawa.' The Whale's immediate response is the same thing that Iwanishi had said on the phone.

'I was really surprised though. He's heading to a building owned by Mr Terahara.'

Terahara. The Whale has encountered the man several times. Terahara, boss of Fräulein. He pictured his face. A swarthy man with stubble. Straight spine, small frame, but hard, like a little chunk of mineral.

'If you're the famous suicide guy then I'm sure you know about Mr Terahara. But did you know his son just got run over?'

The Whale didn't answer. But in his mind he replayed the scene he saw the other night. The car accident at the Fujisawa Kongocho intersection. From among the crowd of people waiting for the light to change, one man pushed out into the street. Smashed into and sent flying by a minivan. *The Pusher.* The name flared in his head.

'The Pusher did it.' Iwanishi's face split in a lurid smile. 'Or at least that's what Mr Terahara's decided.'

'So what?'

'Apparently there's a guy who knows where the Pusher is.' Iwanishi gave all the details he knew, despite the fact that the Whale didn't ask. He had heard that this employee of Terahara's had followed the Pusher home. But since he wasn't telling his bosses where that was, they called him back to home base. They were planning to rough him up to get it out of him.

'Sounds like you don't know anything for sure.'

'That litte fucker Cicada says he's going to go intercept this employee. He told me just now.'

'Where?' The Whale noticed that the inside of his mouth was dry. 'Tell me.' His demand was like a shot fired at Iwanishi. 'Where did your guy go? This Cicada.'

It's all connected. The Whale looked down at his chest and saw that it was heaving, even if only slowly. *Just like Tanaka said. One thing will lead to a series of connections. The future is written according to God's recipe. He may well have been right.*

'So you're gonna go after Cicada, huh?' Iwanishi's smile spread wider.

'You going to stop me?'

'No way.'

'Then you're happy about it?'

'It just feels good when someone who works for you takes on a job bigger than what you thought they could handle.' Iwanishi snorted and laughed through his nose. 'Although he hates me.'

'And you don't hate him?'

'I don't like him or hate him. But when my only guy goes out on his own, I guess I can feel free to fly, no regrets.' Iwanishi seemed to have regained his senses, but he was still planning to throw himself out the window.

'You won't fly. You'll die.'

'I gotta say,' Iwanishi huffs proudly, 'I can't stand people who kill themselves. Humans are the only animals who kill themselves as an escape. Real tough, right? Whereas other animals would never kill themselves, no matter how bad their situation. They know what sacrifices had been made so that they could live. Humans are arrogant, you know? That's why I'm gonna fly.

Dying is just incidental.' He yanked open the desk drawer. For a second, the Whale thought he was going for a weapon, and he aimed the gun. 'Don't shoot, I'm not trying anything,' Iwanishi said, raising his hands. 'I don't wanna get killed before I die.'

He lowered his hands calmly and reached into the drawer. Then he turned toward the Whale and held up a small photograph. It was a black-and-white headshot for an ID.

'What's this?' The Whale takes the photo between his fingers.

'Cicada.'

The young man in the picture has soft-looking hair down to his ears and a sharp nose. His brow is furrowed with annoyance. But he looks boyish.

'I was gonna get him a passport but I forgot.' It seemed like Iwanishi was proud of having forgotten. 'This is what Cicada looks like. Don't mess it up.'

'Why are you giving me this?'

'I wanna see you and him duke it out.'

'You won't be able to see anything.'

'He said it's in Shinagawa. Terahara's headquarters is somewhere around there. But I think he's somewhere else. If they're gonna mess up one of their employees, they'll probably do it at the other location. I bet you even know it.'

'Know what?' The Whale peers searchingly at Iwanishi.

'Terahara's other spot. It's off the main drag, on a dirty little backstreet. By a bunch of cedars. It's famous in our industry.'

'We murder people. You call that an industry?'

'Funny. Cicada said the same thing.' Iwanishi grinned impishly, then grabbed a detailed map off the table and handed it to the Whale. 'Here. This building. This must be where they are.'

'Are you on my side, or against me?'

'Neither. I'm just a spectator. I'm the audience.' Iwanishi got up from the desk chair and stepped over to the window. 'Well. So long. I don't wanna live like I'm dead. What a great line.'

And then he jumped out the window. He didn't scream. It was only a moment before there was the sound of his body bursting on the pavement.

The Whale doesn't want to run into any of the other residents, so he briskly makes his way down the back stairs to the ground floor. There's a police cruiser in front of the entrance to the condo. The siren isn't on but the lights are flashing. He leaves the building and heads back on the road he came by. He follows the river, toward the station, intending to go from there on to Shinagawa. He checks the time on his phone. Four fifty in the afternoon.

He walks with long strides, and when a taxi happens to turn onto the road beside him he hails it. Faster to go by car. He shows the driver the section he tore from the map.

'This is where you want to go?' The driver sounds a bit annoyed.

'That's where I want to go.'

As soon as the taxi starts moving the Whale feels a pain in his stomach. Like screws turning in his guts, drilling deeper. He presses his hand against his belly and leans his forehead on the windowpane to his left, trying to steady his breathing. He can't take in any air, and his mouth moves helplessly. It feels like his blood has stopped flowing.

'Hey, you okay, buddy?' The driver peers at him through the rearview mirror.

The Whale can't get any words out to answer.

'If you need to vomit, let me know. I'll pull over.'

Eyes shut tight, the Whale concentrates on his breath. His teeth chatter. *Cold*, he thinks, and his body begins to shake. He thrusts his hand into his coat pocket, finding the coverless, dog-eared book. He grips it tightly. *There is nothing in it at all to worry about! It's simply physical derangement.*

No doubt any moment now a ghost will appear and mockingly pronounce that it's all from his sense of guilt.

Fifteen minutes later, the taxi pulls to a stop. 'This work?' the driver asks. 'Head left in there, make the next right, and you'll be there.'

The Whale looks around, checks his map. He's feeling a bit more like himself. 'Don't want to take me all the way there?'

'There's a lot of cedar trees by the entrance. You can see them up there.' The driver turns his five-o'clock-shadowed face and points off to the left. 'I get hay fever really badly. If I get any closer I'll be in trouble.'

'Trouble.'

'My eyes get all watery, I could get into an accident.'

'It's November. Is there even any pollen right now?'

'Shh. Don't let the pollen hear you say that.'

This driver with his stubble could easily be one of my ghosts, he thinks, even though he knows that isn't the case.

He takes the fare from his wallet and hands it over, then gets out of the car. The taxi speeds off and is gone in an instant. *Must be really afraid of that pollen.*

A left turn takes him to a narrow street. There would barely be enough room for a car to squeeze by him. Dingy buildings line the street on either side.

Soon the space opens up onto a larger thoroughfare. There's a parked SUV twenty meters ahead. It's facing toward him and half up on the curb, tipped on a diagonal.

A young guy is getting out. The Whale immediately ducks into a recess in a wall of the nearest building. The young guy is skinny, but he carries himself with a fluid ease. His graceful movements and his soft-looking hair call to mind a cat.

The Whale catches his face in profile. It's the face in the photo from Iwanishi. *Cicada.*

CICADA

THE STOLEN SUV ZIPS ALONG at a decent clip, and before long he arrives at the building. It's right where Momo said it would be.

Five stories high, dark gray. All the windows are opaque, maybe from a buildup of grime. Water drips from cracks in the walls like seeping blood.

He drives past it and takes the first left turn. The tires squeak lightly but now's not the time to worry about that. A few meters in he pulls up onto the curb and stops the car, leaving it on an angle.

As he's about to get out he notices a blanket in the back seat. He flips it up. *Better not be someone hiding in there*, he thinks, but it's just two empty cardboard boxes. He puts the blanket back over them, opens the door and steps outside.

He heads for the building's entrance.

On the other side of the street he sees a grove of cedar trees. Gloomy and menacing. Rearing four or five meters tall. It's hard to tell how far in the grove goes, but it looks deep. The dark red trunks stretch straight up into a crown of needles. *They're like spears*, he thinks, impressed. *Piercing the sky.* They're swaying in the wind, the needles rustling. Now it reminds him of a giant animal stamping and bristling its fur.

Just then he sees a van approaching. He darts around a corner, out of sight.

Cicada focuses his hearing. The van stopping. A woman's voice. He peeks out from behind the wall.

The woman is opening the back door. Two men emerge from the van. They don't waste any time getting into the building so he doesn't get a clear look at their faces, but they're carrying some kind of cargo. Then he sees that it's not just any cargo: it's a person, all tied up.

So that's the famous employee. Cicada licks his lips. *The tight-lipped, uncooperative, unfortunate, soon-to-be-tortured employee.*

After watching the van pull away, he starts toward the building.

Yeah, well, anyway, give it your best, Cicada. Don't lose. Iwanishi's words replay in his mind. *I'd give it my best without you telling me to.*

The area in front of the entrance is covered with white tiles. Cigarette butts and wads of gum litter the ground.

He enters, walks up to the elevator, sees that it's stopped on the fifth floor, then turns around and goes back outside. He heads toward the fire escape. It would be easier to ride the elevator up, but if he called it down the people on the fifth floor might notice. Then they might be ready and waiting for him, which wouldn't be good.

He carefully climbs the fire escape. When he reaches the fifth floor he pulls open the emergency door and slips inside. A hallway. Elevator at the far end. Walking down the hall he comes to a sturdy door on the left. He brings his ear close to the panel of frosted glass beside the door, trying to get a sense of what's going on inside. It doesn't feel like there's any kind of a crowd in there. And when he watched the van pull up, it was only the one woman and two men who got out.

He rams open the door and dashes in, knife in hand. When you're launching a surprise attack, the most important thing is speed.

The room is lit by fluorescent bulbs, but they must be old or run down because they don't give off much light. Still, he can see what's what. In the center of the room, a woman turns toward him. At first she just looks alert, then she spots Cicada and her eyes widen.

He bounds toward her. Notices a man lying flat on a mattress. *I've come to rescue you, my dude.*

As he advances he sizes up all the people not on the mattress. Sharpens his nerves in their direction one by one. As he suspected, it was just one woman and two men. That's all. The woman had been sitting on an office chair with wheels but now she's on her feet, rigid.

The woman first. Easy enough decision. Neither of the men is holding a gun. The one on the left side of the mattress has leather gloves on, and the one on the right side is holding a tool. A hammer. If anyone has a gun, it'll be the woman. The more delicate a woman looks, the more likely she is to be calmly concealing a pistol.

He darts in and slams his fist into her jaw. She tumbles to the ground looking flabbergasted, like this is the first time she's ever been punched. Her high heels go flying. Just as he guessed, she was hiding a gun, because now it clatters to the floor and slides off to one side.

One of the men comes in punching. Cicada's knife flashes.

The position of the man's neck, the reach of his own arm, the length of the blade, the distance to his opponent – he had accounted for all of it. He swings the blade, picturing himself slashing through a sheet hanging down in front of him. It's a well-practiced movement with his full bodyweight behind it. The result of the years of practice slicing at sheets hung from the ceiling, something he's been doing since he started working for Iwanishi. 'Look at you, with your training routine, taking practice swings just like a baseball player. Aren't you the wholesome little sportsman?' Iwanishi would chortle.

The blade catches the man's neck. Cicada can feel it dig into the flesh, sever the carotid artery, and snap the bone.

The man glares at Cicada, mouth open, his movements coming to a stop. His tongue twitches but no sound comes out. His eyes cloud over. Blood bubbles out of the wound, then bursts forth in a geyser, like a stopped-up hose suddenly released. Cicada tips the man over. The body falls to the floor, bleeding out in an expanding puddle.

Cicada resets his stance and turns to meet the short-haired man.

The man swings the hammer in his right hand. Cicada catches a glimpse of his face. 'Hey!' He pivots and the hammer swings by him. The man lurches forward with the momentum of his swing. Cicada grins. 'If it isn't my old friend Shiba.'

The same man he encountered just a few hours ago in a back alley near Tokyo Station. Whose buzz cut makes him look like a Shiba inu. Cicada glances at the other man on the ground, whose neck he just slashed open. Chain wrapped around his waist. *And that was Tosa. Huh. Well, this is a happy reunion. Shiba and Tosa. Or maybe Taro and Jiro, the wonder dogs.*

Shiba comes in with another hammer swing. Cicada narrows his eyes. He can read the trajectory of the arm, see its arc. It's coming from the left toward his face. He dips his upper body backward, letting the hammer brush past his nose just to test how fast it's actually going.

He snaps back upright. 'I let you guys off last time, but this time, no way. Sorry. "I can only forgive you once," like the song says.'

The force of Shiba's attack throws him off balance, but he somehow catches himself and cocks the hammer back. *He's gonna throw it*, Cicada realizes. *Who throws their weapon from this close?* As the thought forms he whips forward his own hand and throws his knife.

It pinwheels through the air and buries itself in Shiba's right eye.

Shiba reels backward, not making a sound. Unable to understand why his right eye has stopped working, seemingly overcome with heaviness more than pain, he sinks down. 'Why?' he croaks in confusion.

Thinking he's being asked why he stabbed the man, Cicada answers, 'Cos you aren't as tough as Taro and Jiro.'

He takes out the second knife he has in his pocket, steps up to Shiba, and stabs him in the solar plexus. He pushes the blade upward into the chest. Same as he always does. Another familiar movement. The same vibration in his hand as when he cuts through heavy cloth. When he yanks the knife out he can hear the sound of blood pumping.

Shiba's down. Cicada turns back to face the woman once more. He checks to make sure that the gun is still on the ground, out of her reach. She must have just gotten to her feet because she hasn't retrieved the gun yet.

'I'll let you know up front, I'm not gonna give you any special treatment just cos you're a woman.'

'Who are you anyway?'

Cicada can tell that she's not nearly as relaxed as she's trying to sound. He scans her from head to toe. Short hair, suit, black stockings. High heels toppled over next to her. Pale skin. White like a mannequin.

'Sorry to tell you, but I'm taking this guy with me.' Cicada squats down, putting his knife down beside his shoe, and takes a good look at the man on the mattress. He's bound with leather straps. They're on tight, so tight that Cicada can barely move them. He works at them with both hands, trying to make openings between the straps, aiming to gradually pull them apart, but he doesn't make much headway. 'Damn, these are on good.'

What's the deal with these straps? Killing those two was easier than getting these off.

Then he senses the woman's feet moving. Before he even stops to think, he wheels around, grabbing his knife and standing back up.

She's running full tilt for the door, leaving her heels behind. Cicada clicks his tongue and winds up to throw his knife again. But then he stops himself. *So what if she escapes*, he thinks.

He squats down beside the mattress once more and starts on the straps again. Patiently working, little by little, he manages to get them loose. Then something falls from the man's hand. It makes a small metallic noise when it hits the floor. Cicada snatches it up and holds it at the level of his eye. A ring. The inset jewel doesn't look too fancy, but he can probably turn it into some cash, so he puts it in his jeans pocket.

'I'm here to rescue you,' Cicada says in the man's ear. The man blinks rapidly. 'Aren't you impressed?'

SUZUKI

HE HAS NO IDEA WHO this person is who came to his rescue. He's almost certain they've never met before. What he does know for sure is that this man has released him from the straps that were holding him in place.

The man appeared just as they were about to smash Suzuki's fingers with the hammer. They had punched him in the stomach, kicked him in the ribs, and then the long-haired man had yanked Suzuki's hand and pressed it down on the mattress, holding him hard by the fingers. 'All right, crush 'em,' he had signaled to the short-haired man, who was taking vigorous practice swings with his hammer. 'We're gonna destroy one or two of your fingers, and then you'll talk.'

Suzuki imagined his fingers being pulverized by the hammer, pictured the shattered bones and mangled veins and splintered fingernails. His skin felt icy. He had a sickening moment where his stomach twisted with the certainty that there would be no coming back from this.

That was when he heard someone burst into the room.

His two tormentors stopped to look up. They had no idea what was happening.

From his position, Suzuki was unable to make out what was going on, what kind of fight had broken out. He just shut his eyes.

When the noise and reverberations died down, he gingerly opened his eyes. In front of him was the body of the man who had been on his right. The short-haired man with the hammer. He was lying face down, looking in the other direction. Suzuki could see skinny ankles protruding from the man's trousers. His body was twitching.

Suzuki looked to his left and saw the long-haired man, also on the ground. Lying in a dark puddle. After a moment Suzuki realized it was the man's own blood.

The only other person in the room was the one who had come to save him, a rather young-looking man. Couldn't have been any older than his early twenties. He looked to Suzuki like a kid with a short attention span, fidgety, the kind of guy who delighted in shoplifting and shaking people down for money. 'I'm here to rescue you,' the young man said, but he didn't strike Suzuki as a very likely savior.

Now the man gets him up and tells him to walk. Suzuki wipes the saliva caked around his lips with his sleeve. There's a sour taste in his mouth. He feels the urge to vomit.

'Whiskey,' Suzuki says, surprising himself. 'I need whiskey from your barrel.'

'What?'

'Ah, um, nothing.' The fog in his head had given him the sense that he was being rescued from high in the mountains.

The young man introduces himself as Cicada. There's no reason for him to give his name but he does it proudly. Must be an alias. He must also be impatient with Suzuki's pace because he urges him to go faster. 'Come on, hurry it up.' Then he comes closer and offers his shoulder.

'Wasn't there a woman here?' Suzuki wonders what happened to Hiyoko.

'She got away. She's pretty fast. Probably went to call reinforcements. Criminal types are always quick to call for backup. Dummies. Like you can just solve everything with a crowd of goons. Am I right?'

'Who are you, exactly?' Suzuki can't help himself from asking.

'I'm Cicada. Like I told you.'

You don't look like any kind of singing insect to me. 'Do you work for Terahara?'

'Don't lump me in with those assholes. You're the one who works for Terahara. I've got my own thing going on. A tiny little personal business. But hey, you're apparently pretty famous.'

'I'm famous?'

'You know where the Pusher is, right?'

Suzuki doesn't know how to answer. A quick 'What are you talking about?' or 'Everyone says that about me but I have no idea what they're talking about' would have probably worked to deflect, but he misses the moment. Instead he stammers, his face tenses, he swallows hard. All of this says far more than any words might have.

'Yeah, you know about the Pusher,' the young man presses. 'Right?'

They walk down the hallway and come to the elevator. It's stopped on the ground floor. 'I don't think anyone's coming up,' says Cicada. He pushes the down button and the elevator whirrs to life.

'What if we take the elevator down,' Suzuki starts, suddenly worried, 'and Terahara's men are there waiting for us?' He can picture the scene. The elevator reaches the ground floor, the door opens. There's Hiyoko and her crew, guns drawn. They all open fire at once. It's a scene he's watched in movies countless times, but he only needs to live it once and it'll all be over for him. 'It'll be like walking into a hornet's nest.'

'A cicada in a hornet's nest, not something you see every day.' Cicada smiles, unconcerned. The elevator door trundles open. Cicada takes his arm from around Suzuki and pushes him from behind, into the elevator. 'Guess we're taking our chances. But I think we're still okay. I didn't hear a bunch of cars pull up to the building. Even if she called all her goons, that type usually isn't the brightest, and they'd show up making a ton of noise. We'd hear all kinds of brakes squealing and everything. Unless we hear that, I'd say we're good.'

'You have a point. But it's not a sure thing.' Then Suzuki realizes that Cicada has him from behind, holding his hands in place.

'Well,' he hears Cicada's voice say, 'if the door does open and there's a bunch of guns aimed at us, I'm using you as a shield. Sorry.'

The elevator is maddeningly slow. It seems to be purposely trying to aggravate them as it crawls down the shaft, swaying back and forth as if at any moment it might suddenly drop.

'I want you to take me to the Pusher.'

'The Pusher.' Suzuki rolls the name around his mouth. Everyone seems to be looking for the Pusher. 'What do you want with the Pusher?'

'To meet him. Talk to him.'

'Is that it?'

'What do you think?'

'Do you have a score to settle with him?'

'Do I need to have a score to settle if I wanna meet him?'

They reach the ground floor. Suzuki holds his breath. The door begins to slide open. All he can do is pray. His head fills up with images: countless gun barrels, countless fingers on triggers, a hail of bullets ripping into his flesh, a wave of blood, a crush of pain, his own shriek of anguish, his organs perforated. He makes a useless promise to himself that if he's shot then he'll shout his wife's name. His legs feel like they're about to give out.

Why is this happening to me? Doubt and fear flood his body. But he tries to banish the feeling with his wife's favorite saying. *I just have to do it. Right. For her.* He steadies his legs and clenches his jaw. *I'm doing my best. I'm doing it for you.*

The door opens all the way. He nearly closes his eyes, but he fights down the urge by tensing up the muscles in his cheeks and forehead. Whatever happens, he wants to see it.

The ground floor spreads out before them, silent and empty. The air is completely still. No ambush.

'Safe,' Cicada says lightly. Suzuki presses his lips together, then exhales with relief.

They head toward the exit.

'So what's the Pusher like?' Cicada's voice needles him from behind.

'He's got a family.' Suzuki decides to try and change Cicada's mind, appealing to his sympathies. He imagines that if Cicada doesn't bear any particular grudge then he won't be dead set on killing a man with a family. 'Two young kids. So maybe you'd want to go easy on him?'

Cicada whoops, apparently with delight. The noise is bright like a flute. 'Well, that's my specialty!'

'Wha—?'

'I'm the guy you send in when you need the whole family killed. Oh, this just keeps getting better.'

Not sure what kind of a joke this is supposed to be, Suzuki looks at Cicada. The young man's face doesn't look like he's joking. He looks genuinely excited. *Another locust. They're all locusts.*

Suzuki walks, pulled along by Cicada. They soon make a left turn onto a narrower street. Up ahead is an SUV parked half on the curb.

'Get in.' Cicada pushes Suzuki by the shoulder. The door to the passenger seat is unlocked and Suzuki opens it. 'Not thinking of escaping, right?'

Suzuki turns to look at Cicada, straight into a punch to the face. He crumples into the passenger seat. It takes him back to his experience on the mattress and his gorge rises again. He loses his sense of up and down, left and right.

Next thing he knows he finds his arms are pulled behind him, contorting his body and further disrupting his sense of direction. His hands are bound together. Cicada has apparently brought the leather straps and he wraps Suzuki back up. The car door closes.

Cicada circles around to the driver's side and hops in. 'Let's go for a little drive.'

THE WHALE

'LET'S GO FOR A LITTLE drive,' says Cicada from behind the wheel. The Whale is hiding under the blanket in the back seat. He had broken down the cardboard boxes and spread them on the seat so he could get under the blanket.

He has a gun jammed into the back of his belt. The one he took from Iwanishi's condo. He had taken his own gun, the one he never kept loaded, and wiped off the prints before tossing it in the river.

'Why do you want to know where the Pusher is?' asks the man in the passenger seat. 'Why are you looking for him? As far as I can tell you're not with Terahara. Why are you so set on this?'

This man in the passenger seat must be the one that knows the Pusher's whereabouts.

'I'm not set on anything. Look, you've got two choices. You can either tell me what I want to know or I can get it out of you. Option two will probably be a lot rougher. It'll hurt, and the result will be the same as option one.'

'That's what I just went through,' the man in the passenger

seat wails. 'The exact same situation that Terahara's crew had me in. They were hurting me to try to get me to talk. What you're saying is no different from what they were doing!'

'Yeah, so?'

The man in the passenger seat falls silent. From under the blanket, the Whale can't tell if the man is still deciding how to answer or if he's made up his mind not to talk.

'Well, let's just get a change of scenery and we can have a little chat,' Cicada says, at the same time fidgeting around noisily. 'Where's the key? Have you seen it anywhere?'

The Whale feels like the question was directed at him, although he knows that isn't the case. It's also the case that if the car stays put it works to his advantage. He slowly starts to prop himself up, getting ready to emerge.

The car trembles, and the Whale falls back onto the seat. He thinks for a moment that the engine started, but that's not it. *No*, he thinks. But of course it's yes. The vertigo sets in. His head throbs. The pain almost splits him in two.

'Looks like it's my turn to say hello,' says a voice close to his ear. He opens his eyes and looks left.

Beside him is a man in a suit with black hair parted in the middle. He's under the blanket as well, and his face is right next to the Whale's. Two grown men stuffed under the same blanket isn't exactly comfortable, but the Whale can't chase him away. After all, he's a ghost.

'You got Kaji for me,' the man says gratefully.

It's the man who hanged himself in the hotel room the night before. The loyal secretary who played the part of sacrificial lamb. Victim number thirty-three.

'I was very happy when I found out that you forced Kaji to kill himself.' His words flow smoothly. 'Now that he's dead, I'm sure it won't be long before he'll hire me as secretary again, here on the other side.'

The Whale says nothing. Just waits patiently for the man to disappear. Hoping desperately that Cicada doesn't discover him in the meantime.

'But doesn't doing this kind of work make you sad?'

The Whale doesn't answer. He pinches the bridge of his nose between his fingers and shuts his eyes tight.

'It seems like you have all sorts of problems.'

The Whale still keeps silent, but he has the strong sense that he can only stand two or three more utterances from the secretary before he explodes with rage. *Since when have I had any trouble controlling myself? . . . It's all written in the recipe.* He remembers Tanaka's words. *Is this part of the recipe too? Because if it is,* he tells himself, *I have to make a move. Ghost or no ghost.* He doesn't sense anyone in the driver's seat or the passenger seat. But he knows they're there. Even if he can't see them, he can still make his move. *I need to settle my accounts.* His mind is made up.

He slowly bends his knees. The secretary's face is unnervingly close to his. He can feel the breath from the man's nostrils. The Whale is ready to emerge from under the blanket like he's bursting out of his illusion. His head swims. He hears the secretary's voice right beside him.

'Now's the time.'

The Whale bolts up and flings his arms toward the driver's seat. His left hand latches onto Cicada's forehead from behind.

The ghost is gone. He can see Cicada in the front seat. He can feel what his hands are touching. Cicada is reflected in the rearview mirror, rigid, like he's frozen.

The Whale jerks Cicada's head back, slamming it into the headrest. The impact rings out.

CICADA

HE HAS NO IDEA WHAT'S going on. By the time he can process anything he's being dragged backward. His ass floats in space and his heels scrabble at the ground.

He's being held by the back collar of his jacket. Someone's pulling him, he realizes. Someone extremely strong. So strong it feels like he's being dragged behind a car or a motorcycle.

He can see the asphalt below him, and there in front of him is the SUV that he was just sitting in. His body is suddenly weightless. Lifted like luggage. Hoisted up over the curb, apparently. The ground below his feet has shifted to dirt.

Just a minute ago he was in the driver's seat of the SUV. Of that much he's certain. After threatening the man he'd rescued, he was fishing around in his jeans pocket for the car key. Suddenly a hand appeared from behind him. He didn't quite believe what he was seeing. There was no time to react. By the time he blinked once the hand had him by the forehead. Then his field of vision was blocked off. All he could see was palm lines right in front of his eyes, with stray glimpses in the gaps between fingers. An instant later his head was yanked backward, bashed into the headrest. Light burst inside his head and his awareness floated. His brain must have been rattled, because all he could register was a tremor at the very core of his being, and after that everything was hazy.

He had the vaguest sense that the door was being opened. By the time he regained any awareness, he was out of the car, being dragged.

Something pricks his left cheek. The smell of grass. Green tufts scratching at his body.

The cedar grove.

The same cedar grove he had seen in front of the building, gloomy and oppressive, giving off an air of menace. Now he's in among the trees. It's not far from the road at all, but no outside sound penetrates the wood. He's being pulled further into the thicket, but it feels more like the depths of a cave.

Who is this guy? For the first time the question swims up into his mind. *Hiding in the fuckin back seat.* It's almost impossible to believe. He tries to twist his neck around, but he can't get a clear look.

From the pulling power and savagery, the sheer wildness of it, he almost wants to believe he's being dragged by a crazed horse, and not any human.

Even while he's being towed backward and tossed around like a sack, he manages to get his hand in his back pocket. His grip closes around the handle of his knife. Then he swipes it in the direction of his assailant's back.

His first attack misses. Maybe he misjudged where the man is, or the angle of his cut, but the blade only slashes air. 'How could I miss?' Cicada rages, like a man who had bet his life savings on the lottery only to find out he didn't win. 'There's no way I missed!'

Then he drops. The hand lets go of his collar and he falls on his tailbone, then tips backward. After a flash of pain, he feels the cool damp of the earth on his back. Immediately he bends his body and rolls to the side. Dirt and grass stick to him. He scrambles to his feet.

Still staggering. 'Who the fuck are you?' Knife in hand, he faces his attacker. *Whoa, this guy's huge.*

The man is standing at a slight distance. His body looks solid and strong. Cicada can see him clearly enough, even in the gloom among the trees. A full head taller than himself. Broad shoulders. Short hair. Eyes sunk deep beneath the brows. The nose is well shaped, handsome even, but the sunken eyes are shadowed. Wearing a coat. Arms hanging at his sides – no sign of a gun or a knife. Cicada can see him breathing. Read the rhythm. In, out. He matches his own breath to the big man's.

'You're Cicada,' says the big man. His voice is soft but somehow daunting. It seems to ripple through the air between them. Almost feels like it was the cedar trees that said it.

Cicada looks upward. The giant trees block out the sky. The trunks are spaced a few meters apart. There are vertical lines running down the dull red bark, making it look like it would be easy to peel off a strip. The branches curve upward, covered in spirals of needles, rustling in the wind. Narrow bands of late-afternoon light find their way between the boughs.

'How do you know my name?' Between the easy power that the big man dragged him with and the impassive composure on the man's face, Cicada can tell this is no ordinary criminal. Nothing like Shiba and Tosa, that much is obvious.

'You were supposed to kill me.' The man's lips barely move. His voice crawls across the ground to Cicada.

Now I get it. 'So you're him, huh? The big guy Kaji wanted taken out.'

'Why didn't you come to do the job?'

Cicada checks his own breathing. The man doesn't seem like

he's about to attack. Cicada takes a step closer, still relaxed. But always gauging distances. Controlling distance is the key. Striking distance with the knife, the reach of his arm, the right range to slash the carotid, or else close enough to fling his knife and hit the target.

He knows that a single miss will be the end of him. That's how serious a threat this big man is. Cicada takes another step, measuring. The big man holds perfectly still. Just stands there glaring.

Like a stone statue, Cicada marvels.

Two more steps. One more. Another. Then he launches. There are two meters between them. He speeds in, knife ready.

Cicada is confident the man won't be able to dodge. His attack is coming in from too close. Fallen twigs crack beneath his feet.

The big man's face goes taut and he hastily shifts his center of gravity to the left.

'Too slow!' Cicada slashes with his right hand. At the same time he thrusts with his left – he had been concealing a second knife.

The big man moves much more nimbly than a big man should. But he must have been too focused on the right hand, because he's a split second too slow. Cicada had aimed at his gut. The big man turns, and Cicada connects with his side, like a boxer landing a hook. The blade pierces the coat and the knit sweater beneath. Cicada focuses all his attention on it. He envisions it: the feel of the blade sinking into flesh, the pressure of his fingers on the handle, the impact in his palm, traveling up his arm, reaching his brain. Blood starts to flow from the wound. Cicada pushes it deeper.

The big man lurches backward. He falls on his ass, the impact reverberating through the trees. The swinging knife slashes air. The man is still facing up, hands behind him, propping himself on the ground. In the next second he's back on his feet.

Cicada retracts his hands from the attack, regaining his balance. 'You're big, but you're fast too, huh?' As he says it, he thinks, *This is not good.*

The big man is standing tall, wiping the dirt off his hands. He looks down at the hole in the right side of his coat. He presses his hand to it, then looks at the blood on his palm. He regards the dark fluid that came from inside his body with curiosity, like it's something new for him.

'Didn't get you that bad, I guess?' Cicada feels his own palms sweating. 'This time I'll get you good.'

Can I really do it, though?

'You seem to be enjoying yourself,' the big man says quietly. His voice carries no mockery or contempt.

'Yeah, well, cicadas like to make a lot of noise.'

'And whales are big.'

Cicada pulls his chin in. 'Ohh. I just heard about you from Iwanishi. So you're the Whale. What's your thing again, you make people kill themselves, right?'

'People who meet me just wind up dying.'

'I bet.' Cicada plasters on a forced smile.

'All people want to die.'

'If that's the case, then I got a favor to ask.' As he speaks, Cicada slowly shifts his weight on his feet. He's looking for a way to get closer. He needs to get in range. Needs to find a way to take this guy out.

'What is it?'

'The guy I work for, his name's Iwanishi – well, I don't really work for him, he just answers the phone. I want you to have a meeting with him. You're saying anyone you meet ends up wanting to die, right? Iwanishi's a stubborn fucker so it might be tougher than usual, but I'd love for you to get rid of him.'

'It wasn't tough at all.'

'Huh?' Cicada's voice pitches up crazily.

'Iwanishi was the same as everyone. We met. He died.'

Cicada swallows. Almost drops his knife. 'So you already met him.'

'Before coming here.'

'How did he die?'

'You want to know?'

'Yeah, I wanna know.' Cicada shrugs.

'He flew,' the Whale says simply. Cicada can't tell if the Whale is trying to put it gently or if the man just doesn't care. 'He flew out the window.'

'Oh.' Cicada doesn't know what else to say.

'This man Iwanishi,' the Whale goes on, apparently stepping closer, though Cicada doesn't see him approach, he just sees him looming larger. 'He wanted the best for you.'

'For me? Him? . . . He didn't want anything for me one way or the other.'

The Whale seems even bigger than before. Cicada has no idea how; he definitely didn't see the man come any closer. The giant body seems to block out everything else. Like a mountain range. Impassable.

'But I guess I should thank you. There's nothing I wanted more than to get rid of him.'

'Do you really mean that?'

'Of course I mean it. I couldn't stand the guy. What, you think I'm just trying to act tough to cover up how sad I am?'

Iwanishi's dead. That means I'm free. It's a totally different ending from the Gabriel Casseau film. *Iwanishi's dead, and I'm still alive. Which means I was never his puppet.* He pictures the pitiful last scene of the movie, with the young man moaning, 'I'll be a good puppet, just let me be free.' *Not like me.*

Then Cicada cranes his neck to look directly into the Whale's eyes. The moment he does he feels a chill wind on his back. The hair on his body stands on end and his chest trembles. He knows instinctively that he absolutely should not be looking into these eyes, but he can't pull his gaze away. He's rooted to the spot.

The Whale seems to have black holes for eyes. Maybe it's just the shadows under the trees, but where there should be eyelids and eyeballs there's only void, like the blackness in the eye sockets of a skull. Cicada squints hard and can just make out the whites of the eyes, but the pupils and irises are holes in space.

The holes are pulling him in. *What is this?* Cicada thinks, but by the time the thought forms he's already been sucked into the abyss. His whole body has been swallowed, sinking deeper, to the darkest depths of the ocean. Water everywhere, blacker than night, flooding him, filling his mouth. There's no pain. The water fills him up. Eating away at him. A foreign substance entering his body, penetrating, devouring. He's entirely saturated with black fluid. And the whole time, he can't tear his eyes away from the Whale's.

A gelatinous sorrow spreads through his chest, then his head. He can feel it.

Dark thoughts and feelings take over. He feels damp, sticky, but at the same time completely parched. *What*, he wonders vaguely, *is going on?*

He tries to make his mind work, which feels like struggling through the clinging sludge of a swamp. The unfamiliar sadness and confusion frighten him. He's under assault by some kind of disillusionment, a feeling of disappointment with himself. It's not quite sadness, and it's not purposelessness.

Then he hits on something. *Could it be . . . ?* It occurs to him: *Do I feel guilty?*

He hears a chorus of voices, too many to count. Whispers, screams, shouts of rage, pleas for mercy. Faces appear, crowding around him. Faces upon faces, and all of their voices. The throng of faces and voices threatens to overwhelm him. Pressing in on him, flooding his ears and crushing his eyes.

That's when he realizes that all these faces, all these voices, belong to the people whose lives he's taken. Their curses and lamentations speed the encroaching blackness. *I don't feel guilty, this is bullshit,* he rages inside. But it doesn't make a difference.

'This is Iwanishi's fault,' says one voice. It seems to have come from the Whale's mouth, but Cicada knows that isn't the case. 'Now that Iwanishi's gone, the lid's off,' the voice continues. 'The only reason you could kill all those people without feeling any guilt is because Iwanishi was there. Now that he's dead, it's all coming out. And you're drowning in it.'

The Whale's eyes are still locked on Cicada's.

Iwanishi's got no power over me. So what if he's gone, doesn't make a difference to me, Cicada insists to himself. *I had a life before I met him.* But as soon as he tells himself this, he realizes something with a shock. His vision goes dark. Like a clump of mud had hit him right in the eyes. In the next moment he's down on his knees. 'I can't remember anything before I met Iwanishi.'

Facing this fact crushes him. *It can't be,* he tries to say, but all that comes out is ragged breathing.

'Do I even exist?'

All people want to die.

The words bear down on him. *No fuckin way.* But there's his right hand, stretched out in front of him. It's the only part of him that has any feeling. The rest of his body is numb. In his hand is his knife. The blade is aimed back at himself.

Wait –

Cicada realizes he's about to stab himself, and panics. But his body won't listen to him. *All people want to die.* This time when he hears it he answers, 'Yeah, you know what, I do wanna die. This is exactly what I want.'

Still staring into the Whale's eyes, he raises his hand. He's sitting up on his knees, sticking his belly out. *I never even existed in the first place.*

He can see faint illumination coming in from between the

cedar branches. Not sure if it's the sun or streetlamps. Thin bands of light, barely a glimmer.

The trees begin to sway. The wind must have picked up. Heavy rustling from the branches and needles urge Cicada onward. *It's time now, time to die,* as if something were pushing him onward from behind. *Shut up, shut up, if I die will you please just shut up?* He's reached his decision; he feels calm now. He raises the hand with the knife, ready to strike – then everything seems to brighten. The fog that had been surrounding him disperses, just like that.

For a moment he's confused, unsure of what's happening. Then he sees.

The Whale looks different. Standing just where he was, but his eyes are half closed. Almost as if he's dreaming.

SUZUKI

SUZUKI HAS NO IDEA WHAT'S going on. All of a sudden the driver's side door was flung open and Cicada was being dragged out of the vehicle.

Left on his own, for a moment he just sits there, utterly bewildered. With his hands and legs tied up he's like some giant caterpillar, but by rocking his body back and forth he manages to hoist himself upward a bit, squirming up the seat, so that he can get a better view out the driver's side.

Off in the distance he can see Cicada. A solid-looking man is pulling him along by the collar, headed into the cedar trees.

Got to get away, he thinks, wriggling his upper body and legs, trying to shift his position. He attempts to open the passenger door but it doesn't go well. Turning his back to the door so that his tied-up hands can get to the handle, he stretches his fingers as far as they'll go, clutching and reaching, but fails to open it. His heart is hammering. He moves his arms and twists his upper body. Every muscle from his index finger to his bicep feels like it's about to cramp, but he can't afford to worry about that.

He thinks about his wife. He can see her, crushed against the telephone pole, beyond any hope of resuscitation. *Don't think about her now.*

Just then he hears the door open behind him. Startled, he turns his head to look. *Now what?* he thinks, both frustrated and frightened.

'Looks like you could use a hand.' Standing there is Asagao.

THE WHALE

TRYING TO GET HIS BEARINGS, he scans the area. Cicada should be right there, on his knees, but he's gone.

Until now, every time he had one of his visions it would come with vertigo and head pain. This time there was none of that, so he had no warning that it was about to happen. The rustling of the cedar branches and the sighing of the wind in his ears were both suddenly louder. Then he realized that there was no one in front of him anymore and thought, *This is not good.*

Cicada had been aiming his knife at his own belly, his eyes giving off the dark light of someone ready to die. It was only moments away. But now thanks to this physical derangement, it's all ruined. The Whale feels a spike of danger.

He thinks back to what happened in Iwanishi's condo. Vertigo had overtaken him, and while he was in the grips of his vision Iwanishi had crawled over to his gun. He came to in the nick of time. If he had been one second later in coming back to reality he would have been shot. He knows that this time is even more dangerous. Cicada is nowhere to be seen.

He steps forward and swings his leg wildly, almost convulsively, kicking at the spot where Cicada had just been. He's afraid that at any moment Cicada will pounce. He tries to kick away the dark clouds of doubt, but as he expected, he doesn't connect with anything.

'Looks like the Whale's not such a big a deal after all.' He hears a voice and turns. It's Iwanishi. Standing right in front of him. Iwanishi who had jumped out of his window no more than an hour ago. Wearing the same purple cardigan the Whale had just seen him in, flashing his crooked teeth. 'And you were so close to taking out Cicada.'

'I would have if you hadn't shown up,' the Whale shoots back.

'So you're saying I saved Cicada?'

'Looks like it.' The Whale's neck swivels back and forth as he urgently tries to take in all 360 degrees around him. 'And now I'm the one who needs saving.'

'Nah, Cicada's still out of it.' Somehow Iwanishi sounds happy and sad at the same time. The ghost starts walking, stepping on fallen twigs and branches, but there's no cracking sound. No footfalls in the dirt. 'Cicada's a lot tougher than me,' Iwanishi says with a smile. Then he looks down at the ground, working his jaw. 'Hey, you dropped that book of yours.'

The Whale looks down too, alarmed. The book should have been in his pocket, but somehow it slipped out and landed on the ground. It's lying face up. The wind blows it open, fluttering the pages audibly. The pages turn, then stop.

He's just about to lean down and pick it up when Iwanishi speaks.

'Take a look at what's on that page. See that? "He has the happiest life who manages to hoodwink himself best of all." How about it? You doing a good job of fooling yourself?'

'I'm not fooling myself.'

'Then you must not be living a happy life.'

The Whale ignores the taunt and reaches for the book. The wind blows again, somehow from the other direction, flipping back through the pages. When it stops another line catches his eye: *But what does God do for you?*

The words give him momentary pause. He tries to recall who speaks them. Raskolnikov, or Sonia? Or someone else? The line on the page seems to bypass his lenses and retinas and go directly into his mind.

'God? What, you mean Jack Crispin?' Iwanishi's saying something nonsensical. The Whale shuts his eyes.

Rather than asking what God does for you, he thinks the real question is whether God has ever done anything for anyone. Forget about God, forget about other people – has anyone actually ever done anything for themselves? Can they even? As soon as they understand the impossibility of it, they want to die. People simply live, with no goal, no destination. They live like they're dead. Once they realize this, they make up their mind to die.

Where is Cicada? The Whale has no idea what his opponent is doing, whether he's down on all fours or sitting up on his knees or if he's even still in the grove of cedars.

He holds still and listens, straining to hear any breathing, any footsteps, the rustle of clothing or the sniff of a nose. He *feels* for breathing. He even feels for the moisture seeping out of the bark of the cedars. His skin is alert, his ears are sharp. He opens his eyes to see a flash of light.

A car is passing along the road, dozens of meters distant, its headlights traveling horizontally across his field of vision. He follows the white light. At that moment his head lurches, like he was hit with a blast of air. *Back in reality?* He narrows his eyes.

He was reaching for the book at his feet, crouched down, arm extended.

Now he sees two things at the same time.

One is a gun. The gun he took from Iwanishi's, on the ground, his hand stretching toward it. Not a book at all, but a gun.

The other is Cicada. Legs planted, back to the Whale but looking over his shoulder at him, knife in hand.

He had just taken a swing, but cut only air, as the Whale had crouched down. He looks momentarily off balance from the missed attack. The Whale takes the gun and straightens up. Extends his arm, finger on the trigger.

CICADA

HE RESETS HIS STANCE AFTER his missed attack, turning back to face the Whale. As soon as he raises the knife again he feels warmth spreading in his chest.

'Wha—?' His movement stops limply, then he presses a hand to his chest. *Hot*, he thinks, but he doesn't know where the heat is coming from. He tries to inhale, but only manages one choked breath, and he can't exhale. He can't breathe at all. He reaches up to feel his throat. By the time he realizes he's been shot, his knees are starting to buckle. He topples over sideways, falling onto a branch. Pain shoots up his side. His ear is flat on the cold, damp earth.

He looks upward. Far overhead, the swaying cedar trees are blacker than night, gazing back down at him. The branches are rustling as loudly as they can, needles falling down through space. Off to the side of his vision, much closer than the tree-tops, floats the Whale's face. He too looks down at Cicada, silent.

'Hey now, you're not gonna lose, are you?' The voice clearly didn't come from the Whale. Cicada looks to the right. There's

Iwanishi, grinning from his praying-mantis face, his crooked teeth like so many staring eyes.

'What about you? I heard you jumped out a window.' Cicada grits his teeth against the pain.

'Fuck you.'

'So what's the deal with this big guy? He makes people kill themselves, huh?' He extends a finger to point at the Whale, but his finger is shaking badly. Seeing this makes him shake even more.

'Well, he is the suicide guy.'

'He didn't make me kill myself.' Cicada manages a twisted smile, then points at his own chest. 'He fuckin shot me. Totally different story.'

'That's cos you're strong.' Iwanishi suddenly appears less distinct, like he's blending in with the scenery.

'Hmph. Not much a cicada can do against a whale. An insect versus the world's largest mammal.'

'You know what's happening though, right?' Iwanishi's chin thrusts forward.

'What?'

'You're dying.'

'I damn well know that.' Cicada turns his head and spits. There's blood in his saliva. A thread of it sticks to the corner of his mouth.

'Any last words?'

'Nope,' Cicada replies, but then he groans with frustration. 'The clams!'

'The clams?'

'I left my clams in the bowl, to get the sand out.' Cicada's voice sounds distant. He thinks about the little shellfish, breathing in a bowl on his kitchen counter. The tiny bubbles that float up when they expel a grain of sand. 'Wonder if they can just stay there forever.'

'You're talking about clams?'

'Yeah, clams. Which do you think is more advanced, people or clams?'

'People, obviously.'

'Dummy. All the knowledge and science that human beings have, it only helps humans. Get it? No living thing in the world besides humans is happy that humans exist.'

'Maybe you'll be reborn as a clam.'

'I'd love that.' Cicada presses his hand against his chest again, then looks at the blood on his hand.

'Hey. You dropped something.' Iwanishi points at the ground beside Cicada. There's a small ring, smudged with dirt.

'Oh that. I took it off that guy before.'

'Is it valuable?'

'You want it, you can have it.'

'I don't need it.' Iwanishi smiles cynically. 'But hey.'

'But hey what?'

'You really were strong. I was proud of you.'

'I don't need you to be proud of me.'

SUZUKI

ASAGAO'S SEDAN FLOWS ALONG SMOOTHLY, like it's riding the current of a river. The headlights brighten the darkness of the evening road. Suzuki rubs his bound hands together in his lap, looking down at the restraints. They're made of black leather and fastened with buckles. *These are no joke.* He tries to pull and twist but they won't come off.

He looks over to the driver's seat, at Asagao's face. It seems amazing to him that this man is at the center of a conflagration threatening to burn the whole city down but doesn't appear to show the slightest concern.

'Mr Asagao,' he says finally, as they pull to a stop at an intersection.

'What is it?'

'How did you know?'

'What do you mean?'

'How did you know where I was, sitting tied up in that car?'

'I followed you.'

'You did?'

'When I dropped you off at Shinagawa I just had a feeling so I followed you.'

'To the cafe?'

'Yeah. I found a place to park and kept an eye on the cafe from outside.'

'Is it because you . . . suspected me of something?' If Asagao really thought he was a home tutor, he probably wouldn't have followed.

'Did you think you weren't acting suspicious?' Asagao's tone is mild. 'A salesman for a tutoring company wouldn't have been so persistent.'

'Salespeople can't do their jobs if they aren't persistent,' Suzuki answers stubbornly, even though it's barely an excuse and not exactly a refutation. Then he exhales. 'When did you know?'

'From the moment you showed up.'

Suzuki's shoulders slump. He'd suspected that Asagao had seen through him from the beginning, but hearing him say it so plainly is still deflating. It feels like being a magician who has barely started his stage act when someone in the audience shouts *I know how you're doing it*.

'From when I first met Kentaro?'

'From the beginning.'

Suzuki almost feels like he means since the moment he was born.

'Did Kentaro and the others figure it out too?'

'They also got it from the beginning.'

'It was that obvious? Right from the start?'

'That's why I followed you. I saw two men carry you out of the cafe. You were completely passed out, like you were dead drunk. Did they drug you? Then they put you in a van that was parked at the traffic circle. These men didn't look like the nicest guys. They looked, how can I put it . . . ?'

'Illegal?'

225

'Yeah.' Asagao nods, taking his foot off the brake and easing the car forward. 'That's right. What they were doing did not seem to be legal.'

But aren't you illegal too?

'I was concerned, so I tailed them. They led me to an area that seemed fairly shady. I parked some distance away and came back on foot. I saw the SUV, and when I looked inside, there you were.'

'The whole thing was awful.'

Asagao glances down at the straps around Suzuki's hands. 'What did they do to you?'

'Have you ever heard of a company called Fräulein? . . . It's German for maiden.'

'Should I have heard of them?'

'I would think so.' Suzuki is building himself up. There's no more need for charades or ruses. The soldiers of his courage are gathered once again. *Here it comes.* 'Since you killed Terahara's son, Mr Asagao.'

'I did?'

'Yes. You.'

'Well, that's funny.' His expression is the same as always. It doesn't look like he thinks it's funny. 'How did I kill him?'

'You pushed him.' Still no reaction from Asagao. 'You pushed him, didn't you? He was standing at the corner of the intersection and you pushed him from behind.'

'I don't know what you're talking about.'

'You're the Pusher. You push people. And then they die. I mean, I saw it happen.'

'You saw?'

'I saw you push him.'

Suzuki is expecting a denial, but it doesn't come. Asagao is silent for a moment. The moment stretches, past the point where he might still be thinking of how to answer, until finally: 'You didn't see anything.'

'What?'

'I'm sure that nobody saw me do anything.'

This throws Suzuki. He searches his memory of that moment. 'Well, now that you mention it, I guess I didn't see you actually push him. But I did see you leaving the scene. That I'm sure of.'

'So just leaving the scene makes me the culprit?'

It's obvious enough that this is just a dodge. The way Asagao refuses to confirm or deny, the way he's deflecting and answering with more questions. He seems to be enjoying himself.

'Where are we headed now?' Suzuki looks out through the windshield. They had long since passed Shinagawa, and must have avoided the inter-prefectural route because they're on a narrow one-way street. There are regularly spaced streetlamps, but it still feels dark.

'Netozawa,' Asagao responds. 'I'm going home. Do you want to come with?'

'Yes. But I'm not sure your house is safe.'

Suzuki's vision replays in his mind. The horrifying scene he had pictured when they were eating pasta, just a few hours earlier.

Jet-black imported cars speeding into Netozawa Parktown, Fräulein staff spilling out and bursting into the house, Kentaro and Kojiro hiding under the table, Sumire white with shock. And then another scene, the boys on the ground in a dimly lit warehouse, and Sumire screaming. They cling on to her. In the next moment her face becomes his wife's face. He doesn't know why his wife would appear there, but it's like a stake to his chest.

Trying to push down the anxiety that's welling up in his throat, he explains, 'They're after you, Mr Asagao.'

'What's this, all of a sudden?' Asagao looks completely calm. Turning the wheel to the right, he accelerates into a curve. The centripetal force presses Suzuki's body against the window. Meanwhile, Asagao leans a bit and puts his hand in his rear pocket. He produces his wallet, which he hands to Suzuki.

'What's this for?'

'Look inside. There's an employee ID card. From the place I work as a systems engineer. Does that work for proof?'

'That hasn't got anything to do with anything!'

'I'm not this Pusher person you're talking about.'

'You still won't admit it? Well, either way, you're in danger.'

The sedan pulls to a stop. Suzuki looks ahead and sees a red light.

'You lied about being a tutor, you got carried out of a cafe by some unsavory-looking characters, and now you're telling me I'm the one in danger? If I wasn't a patient guy I'd toss you out of my car.'

'You don't toss people out of cars, you push them in front of them.'

Asagao sighs.

'Terahara's outfit, Fräulein, that I mentioned before, they're out to get you.'

Now Asagao exhales through his nose, apparently pleased. He even looks a little coquettish. 'Say for a minute that's true. How would they know where I live?'

Suzuki says nothing.

'Doesn't look like anyone's tailing us now. Did you tell them my address?'

'I hadn't told them anything yet.' As soon as the words leave his mouth he feels overcome with shame. Asagao sees this and exhales again placidly.

'It's nice that you're being honest. So does that mean you would have told them?'

'If they tortured me enough, I might have.'

'Yeah, I get it. Torture is one of humankind's most effective inventions.'

'Anyway, I didn't talk. I didn't tell them where you live.' Because

228

Cicada had saved him. If that hadn't happened, he very likely would have given in.

'Then we shouldn't be in any danger at my house.'

'Well, I suppose that's true.' But as he says it Suzuki feels uncertainty welling up from an unknown source. 'What if they put something on me though?' The thought sends a jolt through him and he immediately begins patting himself down, looking for some device that might give away his position via satellite location. It seems entirely possible that they might have stuck him with something like that when he was tied up and incapacitated.

'I checked you when I pulled you out of that SUV before. Nothing was on your clothes.'

'You did?' *He did?*

'Unless it's up your ass, you're fine.'

Suzuki focuses on his rectum, but nothing seems to be amiss. *What kind of systems engineer thinks to check for tracking devices?*

Then Suzuki starts to worry about his phone. It occurs to him that the phone he got from Fräulein might have a tiny tracker on it as well. He reaches into his back pocket. 'What?'

'What's wrong?'

'My phone is gone.'

'You lost it?'

'It must have fallen.' As soon as he says it he realizes that his coat is missing too. 'I think my coat must still be in that SUV. The phone's probably in the coat pocket.'

'That's too bad.'

'But it's my company phone, so it's not such a loss.' The only person who ever called him on it was Hiyoko.

Just then a phone rings. A low, curt ringtone. It belongs to Asagao. He pulls it out of his pocket and brings it up to his ear. 'Sorry, I was late because I was waiting for him. I'm bringing him back now,' he explains. 'That's right. He's coming back to the house again.' Then he hands the phone to Suzuki. 'Sumire wants to tell you something.'

Wondering what it could be, Suzuki takes the phone.

'Hi, Mr Suzuki!' She sounds extremely upbeat. 'Glad you're coming back here. It's funny, what happened –'

He must be imagining things but it seems like the view out the windshield grows darker. An unsettling premonition flashes in his mind. Thick mist seems to wrap around him, ominous and unwelcome.

'Our Kojiro actually has your phone.'

'What?'

'He came to the door to say goodbye when you were leaving, remember? Apparently he took it out of your pocket!'

He struggles to recall that happening but can't. There's the clear memory of Kojiro clinging on to his legs, but no notion that the boy had pinched his phone. Immediately he asks her, 'No one happened to call on that phone, did they?'

THE WHALE

IT'S BEEN A LONG TIME since he's actually fired a gun. Probably not since he was working as a newspaper delivery boy in his teens and got angry enough at his boss to shoot the fat bastard.

He gazes at Cicada's body until it stops twitching, then heads toward the edge of the cedar grove.

Back on the road. The opposite side is lined with buildings. There are barely any cars. In the darkness it looks less like a road and more like a ditch. He cuts across, going back to the place where Cicada's SUV is parked.

There had been a man in the passenger seat. A man who knew about the Pusher. All he has to do is get rid of the Pusher and his accounts will be cleared.

Settle your scores. Then you'll have no more regrets, and you can retire.

He turns the corner around a building and approaches the SUV. The passenger-side door looks to be ajar. *Did he run?* There's no sign anywhere of the man who was all tied up. The

Whale stares at the interior of the car. Then he takes a few steps backward.

His lead on tracking down the Pusher is gone. With Cicada and Iwanishi dead, there's nothing more he can do. He looks left and right, hoping to spot some trace of the man. On the dark sidewalk he's unlikely to find any footprints or clues. If only the man left behind a gleaming, sticky trail like a slug.

That's when he hears a woman's voice.

'I'm on my way right now,' it says, high-pitched and urgent, coming from somewhere behind him.

He wheels around to find the speaker.

She's leaning up against the wall of one of the buildings. He walks briskly over to her with long strides and seizes her wrist in his hand. She shrieks and drops her phone. With his other hand he grips her by the forehead, lifting her up and pressing her against the wall. A scent wafts off her, perfume probably, an artificial citrus smell that's almost medicinal.

'Who the hell are you?' Her voice is sharp, more angry than afraid.

He's met her before. The memory swims up to the surface. 'You work for Terahara's outfit. You were at the site of the accident.'

She had given him her card last night at the Fujisawa Kongo-cho intersection.

Her feet dangling in the air, she struggles against him, aiming a knee at his crotch, but the Whale ignores her attempts and keeps her pinned to the wall. He glances down and sees she has no shoes on. There's something creepy about the fact that she was walking around this grimy area in her stockings.

'What are you doing here?'

'What am I doing?' She grimaces. 'Some crazy guy kidnapped one of our employees.'

'One of your employees?'

'I called for backup, but he got away.'

232

'And you survived.'

'I ran, but if I just waltz back into headquarters empty-handed who knows what'll happen to me,' she moans. 'So I was hanging around here. Trying to figure out what to do next.'

Then he asks the key question: 'Where is the Pusher?'

'Wha—' She's enraged. 'What are you talking about?'

He tightens his grip on her forehead. It fits neatly in his hand. If he were to squeeze full force it wouldn't be hard to crush her skull. 'Where's the Pusher? I know one of your employees knows where he is.'

She goes a shade more pale.

'All I have to do is bash your head against this wall. I wouldn't mind seeing it split open like a fruit. I might just do it. Well?'

'Okay, okay.'

'Okay what?'

'I'll tell you where the Pusher is.'

He lets his grip loosen, then removes his hand from her forehead. She falls from where she had been hanging in space. Her balance is unsteady and she drops into an awkward crouch. The Whale lowers himself down to her level and brings his face close. His hands are ready in case she shows any signs of resistance. She retrieves her phone and wipes the dirt off of it.

'Do you actually know where the Pusher is?'

'It just so happens,' she begins, steadying her breath but already sounding proud of herself, the scent of her perfume seeming to spread and make it harder for him to breathe, 'that I called Suzuki.'

'Suzuki?'

'My employee. The dumb one who tailed the Pusher but won't talk.'

'So his name's Suzuki.'

'And some kid answered.'

'A kid.'

'The Pusher's kid, I think. Just a hunch. Anyway I asked for Suzuki and the kid tells me, oh, big bro Suzuki forgot his phone.' She mockingly imitates a child's voice speaking in a whisper. 'Kids are so dumb. I can't stand them.'

'The Pusher has kids?'

'I just asked nicely and he gave me the address.' A satisfied smile spreads across her face, like a hunter who has their prey cornered. 'What a dummy.'

'Tell me the address.' The Whale grabs her by the shoulders and hauls her up, already pulling her toward the SUV. 'Get in.'

SUZUKI

'THIS IS BAD,' SUZUKI KEEPS saying. But Asagao doesn't show any signs of being in any hurry at all. It's agitating Suzuki no end.

'Rushing won't get us home any quicker,' Asagao says evenly.

'Hit the gas!' Suzuki sputters. 'You have a gas pedal – if you push it all the way down the car goes faster. That's how a car works. Then we'll get there faster.'

Streetlights and vending machines glow through the window as they pass. Otherwise it's totally dark out. The details of objects fade into the night, buildings becoming nothing more than deep shadows that flow by.

'They know where you live,' Suzuki wails. 'Terahara's people are on their way!'

Hearing the story from Sumire on the phone was enough to make Suzuki's blood run cold.

'Kojiro snuck your phone, and then a call came in and he took it,' she said. 'I was in the kitchen so I didn't realize what was happening, but then I heard him talking on the phone.'

It could only have been Hiyoko calling. At first maybe she was surprised, but likely she remembered Suzuki telling her that the Pusher has children. Then she asked all kinds of questions – Is a man named Suzuki there? Where are you now? Where's your house? Do you know your address?

How is this happening? Suzuki felt lost when Sumire told him, plunged into blackness. His ears were ringing.

'And did Kojiro answer?'

'Sounds like he did,' she replied brightly. Her cheeriness only made Suzuki feel more hopeless. 'Sorry about that. You might want to apologize to whoever it was.'

'This is very bad,' he half shouted.

'What's so bad about telling them our address?'

'It's about as bad as it could be.'

'You think they're coming because they think you're here? Is it your girlfriend? Someone your wife doesn't know about?'

'No, nothing like that.' He was almost jumping out of his seat. 'You're in danger. Please get out of there.' By that point he was fully shouting, but Sumire sounded as carefree as always.

'What are you up to, Mr Suzuki?' she said with a laugh.

This did nothing to settle his nerves. 'Talk to your husband. Here, please explain it to her.' Suzuki thrust the phone back toward Asagao.

Asagao took the phone and listened, interjecting a few yeses and that's rights, then gently said, 'He's a little worked up right now,' giving Suzuki a sidelong glance.

'Tell her they need to get out of there!'

But Asagao's attitude didn't shift at all. It sounded like he was just having an ordinary, everyday conversation with his wife. After a few more words he said, 'Talk soon,' and ended the call. Then, to Suzuki, 'Guess that's that.'

'What's that supposed to mean?' Suzuki was genuinely angry.

'This is no time to be so casual. Do you understand what's happening here?'

'You're the only one who's upset about it.'

'I'm telling you, your boys are in danger!'

'That's assuming everything you're saying is actually true. Right?'

'It's all true!'

Suzuki had no more reason to conceal anything, and no time to try to formulate a story in any coherent way. He just let it all come pouring out, speaking loudly and urgently.

The car hitting Terahara's son, being tasked with following Asagao, Terahara's operation mobilizing to find the culprit, and now that they know Asagao's address likely sending a crew there at that very moment. He explained it as quickly as he could, the veins in his neck bulging.

'That's why I keep telling you you're in danger!'

'And you expect me to believe all this?' It's like Suzuki's words were a spear thrust that Asagao had neatly sidestepped.

'Please believe me.' Suzuki looked at the compact car in front of them with frustration. 'We need to hurry.'

Asagao eyed the side mirror and turned the wheel, changing lanes, saying nothing. He passed the compact car. Suzuki put his hand to his forehead, squirming at his own powerlessness, furious at his inability to find a solution.

'Tell me something,' Asagao began.

'What?'

'Do you have any proof?'

Suzuki was all too conscious of the fact that this was the weak point of his argument. He felt a stab of physical pain. 'You want proof?'

'Yeah. Something to convince me.'

'No, I don't.' Suzuki was not quite defiant, but his voice was hard. 'You'll just have to believe me. You saw them stuff me in that van, right? Those illegal people? That's who I'm talking about. These people tied me up,' he said, showing the leather straps.

'Could be that it's all an act. That you're in on it.' Asagao smiled.

Now they're driving along in silence. There's the sound of the engine, the noise of the other cars they pass, and that's it. No radio. The tires are humming, but everything feels quiet.

'We're here,' Asagao says before too long. The sedan comes to a stop. Outside the car it's quite dark. Suzuki can't see any identifying landmarks, but the grid of streets does feel like what he recalled of Netozawa Parktown. Asagao starts to put his car into the carport, spinning the wheel to back in, but Suzuki protests, eyes wide.

'We need to get out of here. You need to leave the car out on the street so we can get away easily.'

'Still going on about that?' Asagao sounds like he's watching a boring movie and would like to fast-forward.

'You have to believe me. I'm telling the truth. Terahara's people are on their way right now.'

Asagao unlocks the doors and turns to look at Suzuki. 'And the proof? Where's the proof that any of what you're saying is true? Proof that I'm the Pusher, that my house is being targeted, that I need to worry about any of this?'

Suzuki looks into the other man's eyes. They remind him of the depths of a lake. He wants to run away as fast as he can. Instead he screws up his courage. He tugs at his hair and takes a deep breath. But when he speaks, his voice is forceful. 'Proof doesn't matter.' It's a tone he never even used when scolding his students. 'Proof has nothing to do with it. Just *believe* me. You're so concerned with proof, but proof doesn't change the fact that no one even remembers Brian Jones was in the Rolling Stones!'

The car interior falls silent once more. Suzuki starts to doubt himself, wondering what he's even saying, until Asagao lets out a small laugh. 'That's interesting.'

'Sorry?'

'It's not bad.'

'Sorry?'

'I'll believe you.'

For a moment all Suzuki can do is blink rapidly. 'You will?' It almost shocks him, as if rain that had always been falling suddenly stopped.

'I wanted to see how you would answer. Never thought it would be with Brian Jones.'

Suzuki thinks about his departed wife. *I'm not sure what just happened, but it looks like you were absolutely right.*

THE WHALE

WHILE DRIVING THE SUV, HE keeps looking over at the woman in the passenger seat. The curves of her body are appealing, but she also gives off a spiky air that suggests she would be hard to approach. The same feeling he got off of her that first time he met her in the street.

She seems to have settled in since first getting into the car. She doesn't look as wary.

'I'll tell you how to get to the Pusher's house,' she says, speaking to him like they know each other. 'It's in a residential neighborhood. I've been to the area before, it was a while ago, but I think I can get us back there now. Take a right at the next light.'

The Whale merges into the next lane. 'So your outfit has a grudge against the Pusher? What are you planning on doing to him?'

The sky and the ground are the same shade of deep indigo. Lamps line the street on both sides. There's barely any traffic on the road, though he does see a group of headlights up ahead at the intersection. They look like beetles, or ants.

'Oh, well, about that.' She sounds relaxed now. She pouts her lips a bit. It's an act. The Whale can see right through it. She's clearly covering up her fear and anxiety. Probably watching for a chance to escape. 'Just before I ran into you I called into base. So I imagine they're on their way now.'

'To the Pusher's house.'

'We'll pay a little visit to his happy family home.'

'That seems cruel.'

'What in this life isn't cruel? From the moment we're born, we're destined to die. Everything's always already cruel.'

Her phone rings, the tone jarring. She answers right away. 'Yep. I'm headed there now.' She glances sideways at the Whale. 'Getting a ride from a very nice big man. It shouldn't take too long to get there. We're about to get onto the inter-prefectural road. Where are you guys? . . . Sounds like you'll get there first. Call when you do.'

When she hangs up, the Whale asks, 'Who?'

'Fräulein employees. I'm pretty high up at Fräulein. I guess you'd call those guys my staff.'

'How many are headed there now?'

'What's that got to do with you?'

'What indeed.' It has plenty to do with him. To settle the score with the Pusher, he'll need to get rid of any third-party interference. Which means when they get to the Pusher's house he'll have to get rid of Terahara's underlings. 'How many?'

'Four or five cars, so, almost twenty guys I'd say.'

'That's a lot.' Sending that many to deal with one family seems almost childish.

'When you show up with a crowd it makes it easier for the other side to give up. They know that even if they fight back, even if they try real hard, they're just outnumbered. And these are tough guys who are on their way. Violent and cold-blooded. I'd say our friend the Pusher is in big trouble.' She says it breezily, as

241

if she's not the one making it happen. 'Against that many guys, the Pusher will just have to do what's best for his family.'

'What do you plan to do to him?'

He sees her inspecting her nails – probably another gesture intended to show just how calm and collected she is – then her full lips part. 'Probably put the whole family in a car and take them all back to headquarters.'

'So you're not planning on doing anything there at the house.' If that's the case, he can likely get to the Pusher in the time it takes them to return to their headquarters. *Settle your accounts.* Tanaka's voice reverberates.

'If they don't give us any trouble, we won't shoot them or anything like that. After all . . .'

'After all what?'

'Terahara's the one who's apoplectic about all this. He won't be satisfied unless he watches them die.'

'So Terahara's waiting back at headquarters for you to bring his son's killer to him.'

'He should be. I'm sure right about now he's there all alone, nostrils flaring, spreading plastic sheets everywhere.'

'Plastic sheets.'

'For all the blood and piss and shit. When you torture people that stuff gets everywhere. I imagine he's getting the place ready. Torture prep. The boss is into that kind of stuff. Make a left up ahead.' He follows her instructions, easing the SUV onto the narrow street.

'Sounds like quite a boss.'

'Oh, he's in high spirits today. He'll get to avenge his son. I don't think I've ever seen him this excited.'

'What about the wife and kids?'

'I'm betting we'll kill the kids first. Then the wife. By that time the Pusher will be feeling terrible about the choices he's made. And then we'll start on him. Once we get the name of who hired him, then we can get into the really bad stuff. We have lots of different methods. And we have plenty of time.'

'I see,' the Whale says, all the while thinking of how he can have his own time with the Pusher, uninterrupted.

They reach the end of the narrow street just as the light is turning green, then merge onto the inter-prefectural road. Something occurs to him. 'Are you sure this guy is really the Pusher?'

'What's that supposed to mean?'

'The man you're about to take prisoner. Are you sure he's the Pusher?'

'We had him followed.'

'And you're sure about that.'

'Well.' She cocks her head gracefully. 'We don't have proof. But even if we're wrong, and this man and his family have nothing to with the Pusher . . .'

'Which could be the case.'

'. . . what does it really matter?' She smiles, serene.

SUZUKI

THEY ENTER ASAGAO'S HOUSE, BUT the man still doesn't show any signs of getting ready to run. Despite having said that he would believe Suzuki.

'Welcome back,' Sumire greets them.

'Hi,' Asagao says, then gestures to Suzuki. 'He finally confessed.'

'Confessed?' She looks at Suzuki, making no attempt to hide her curiosity. 'What did you confess, Mr Suzuki?'

Unsure exactly how to answer, Suzuki begins, 'I'm not actually a home tutor.'

'Aww, you're giving up already?' She smiles ruefully. It's like she's watching some silly quiz show and she's disappointed that they gave away the answers too early.

Suzuki follows Asagao through to the dining room. 'You knew?'

'We knew from the start,' she says. 'I was having fun with it.'

'Either way, more important – the situation has gotten dangerous, fast.'

'That's what you were saying on the phone before,' she replies, beaming. Suzuki is almost offended by how cheerful she's being.

'Hey, big bro came back!' Kentaro shouts from the living room. The sound of his voice makes Suzuki's worry spike. He knits his brows. *We don't have time for this!* Kentaro marches right up to Suzuki and cranes his neck to look at him. 'I knew all along you weren't a tutor,' he announces.

Suzuki's face flushes. At the same time, the relaxed mood in the house has him more and more anxious. 'Mr Asagao,' he cries, angry that he's the only one who seems to care about the situation. Asagao has taken a seat at the table, pointing at the facing seat, evidently inviting Suzuki to sit as well. Realizing that Asagao won't speak to him unless he complies, Suzuki grudgingly lowers himself into the seat. 'We have to get out of here. Now. You said before that you believed me.'

'Yes,' Asagao nods, 'you are telling the truth.'

'Then in that case –'

He notices Kentaro and Kojiro, who have suddenly appeared at the table.

'Here,' Kojiro whispers, even quieter than usual. He leans forward off his chair and holds a mobile phone out toward Suzuki. 'I'm sorry.'

Suzuki grabs it.

'I'm very sorry I took it from you.' Kojiro bows his head.

'Don't worry, it's all right.' It's not all right, but it won't do any good to give the boy a hard time.

'It's not Kojiro's fault,' Asagao says. Suzuki looks back up at him. 'I asked him to do it. I wanted to get a look at your phone.'

'Wh-why would –' The confusion trips up Suzuki's tongue. 'Why?'

'I knew from the start that you weren't a tutor. I wanted to find out more about you. So I told Kojiro to take your phone.' His voice is completely calm.

Now Sumire is seated as well. Her expression is mild, but with the whole family there Suzuki has the uncomfortable feeling he's being called to account for his crimes. His heart starts pounding.

'Mr Asagao, either way, we need to leave as fast as we can. They're coming.'

'You're right.' But Asagao makes no move to get up.

'We should call the police!' Suzuki shouts out his sudden thought. 'I'm calling. You may prefer that I don't, but it's better to deal with the police than have something terrible happen.' He goes to call, but sees that his phone is dead. *Of course.* He wants to smash it onto the ground.

Suzuki can feel the Fräulein crew closing in on them. Cars pulling up to the house, violent men bursting in. He swears he can hear footsteps, though there aren't any. An unsettling heat envelops him. He knows exactly the kind of unsavory place that the whole family will be taken to.

I'll just have to make as much noise as possible, he thinks. *Get the neighbors involved. Scream, shout, start a fire if I have to.* If he creates a big enough disturbance, the men from Fräulein might call it off.

Or maybe we could go up onto the roof and escape to the next house over.

'We'll call the police. Then we'll go upstairs and escape via the roof. Can I use your phone?' Without waiting for a response, he stands and walks back toward the living room.

He paces around. His legs are shaking. It feels like they may give out at any moment. Maybe he can take the boys and escape. Frantic, he rubs his hands together. That's when he notices his ring is missing. 'What?' *Where did it go?*

You lost it, didn't you? He hears his wife's accusation in his ear.

'We don't have a phone.' Suzuki looks back to see Asagao standing at the threshold between the dining room and the living room, shrugging. 'Sorry to tell you. No phone in the house.'

'No phone?' The words sound to Suzuki like the death of hope.

246

THE WHALE

AS THEY REACH THE RESIDENTIAL neighborhood, the woman gets another phone call.

'We should be there soon. But don't wait for us, you can go ahead and get started.' She gives orders with confidence. 'Get the kids in a car too. Yep. If the neighbors show up just say that they weren't feeling well and you're taking them to the hospital. Make something up. That's right. All right. Get it done.' Then she adds, 'Oh, one more thing. The houses are close together. They might try to escape from a balcony or from the roof. Keep an eye out for that. Watch the back too. Surround the place. No slipups. The Pusher is not your ordinary guy. If you let your guard down he might get the jump on you.' She rattles off instructions with authority. Finally she confirms the route from the entrance of the neighborhood to the house, then ends the call. She turns to the Whale, a satisfied look on her face. 'Looks like it's all happening.'

'They're going in?'

'So it seems. It'll probably be over quick. They just need to bring the family out. Surround them, threaten the kids, the parents will fall right in line.'

'Do you think that one employee of yours is also at the house?'

'Who, Suzuki? You think he went back? I don't think he's that stupid, but either way it doesn't make a difference. There's not much he can do. He didn't really help us, but he also can't stop us.'

'Mmm.'

She tells him to make the next left. 'Then we just go straight to the end.'

It's an unremarkable residential neighborhood. Similar-looking houses lining a grid of streets. *Almost like a prison*, he thinks.

'Up ahead,' he says. Through the windshield, a hundred meters down the street, there's a line of several parked cars. They're tight up against the left side of the street, like they're crowding toward the house. All the headlights are off, but he can see their shapes in the darkness.

She nods. 'Yes indeed.'

He drops speed and prepares to pull up, considering what he should do about the Pusher. If what the woman was saying is true, they won't kill him then and there.

What should I do? Where should I intercept him? There isn't much time to figure it out.

'That's right, no time to fuck around.' The sudden voice comes from just beside his face. The Whale slams on the brake. The tires screech and the car lurches, tossing them both forward so that the seatbelts bite into their bodies.

'What are you doing?' the woman shrieks.

'This chick is too loud.' A man sitting in the back seat, thrusting his head up into the driver's area, showing his teeth. It's Cicada, who's supposed to be dead. 'She didn't like it one bit when I punched her though. Hey, does she not have shoes on?'

'You.' The Whale glares at Cicada. Then he looks at the woman. She clearly thinks he was talking to her.

248

'What?' she demands. 'Seriously, what the hell are you doing stopping here? Did you hit a cat? You're supposed to ease onto the brakes. Where'd you learn to drive, dummy? It's right up there anyway, I'll walk the rest of the way.' He's not sure if she's sensed that he's acting strange or that this is her best chance to get away from him, but she reaches for the door handle. 'See ya.' With that she gets out of the car, looking relieved. The car shakes with the impact of the door slamming shut.

'You're just gonna let her go?' Cicada sounds incredulous. Now he's in the front passenger seat.

The Whale is not at all sure what's going on. He's not questioning the fact that Cicada is a ghost. But there were none of the usual telltale signs, no vertigo or anything. And usually when he has his episodes, he loses sight of the actual humans in reality, but the woman was in the passenger seat the whole time.

'Scared you, huh? This one's different than it usually is. Know why? Because it's getting worse. You've gotten used to it. It's just gonna get worse and worse from here on out. Just like this no-good country. Anyway, glad I got a chance to see you again.'

The Whale rubs the corners of his eyes. 'You just died. Feels a little soon to be back,' he says icily.

'Shouldn't you be getting a move on?' Cicada points ahead, in the direction where the woman ran off. 'If you keep hanging around then your precious Pusher is gonna be gone.' Cicada looks genuinely delighted. 'Snatched away.'

The Whale isn't intending to follow Cicada's instructions, but he takes off his seatbelt and gets out. He stalks down the street.

'I was looking for the Pusher too, you know.' Cicada is walking along jauntily right beside him, feeling around in the back pocket of his jeans. His stride is a fair bit shorter than the Whale's, but he keeps pace perfectly. '*I* wanted to kill him. To boost my rep.'

'You're dead. Keep quiet.'

The line of parked cars is up ahead. Four of them. Sturdy-looking imported cars. They shine like black beetle shells, the antennae completing the insectoid picture.

A group of men in suits stands before a house that looks like two perfectly stacked cubes. It seems more like an office building than a house.

'Sorry to tell you this, buddy.' Cicada's lip curls. He appears to be having fun.

'What.'

'The Pusher isn't here.'

He searches Cicada's face, but the young man's ghost is just staring ahead at the house with mock importance. The Whale quickens his pace and catches up to the woman.

'Unbelievable!' She's facing down the men in suits, stamping her feet in frustration. She notices the Whale and flinches for a moment, but then regains her composure and says a bit more casually, 'This is just unbelievable.'

'What happened?'

'We came all this way, and it's the wrong place.' Hysteria is already creeping back into her voice. She tugs at her hair.

The Whale turns to one of the suits. Tough-looking, impassive. Reminds him of a well-trained military dog. 'This isn't the house?'

Cicada's ghost titters in his ear. 'The Pusher isn't here. This is too perfect.'

The suit must have mistaken the Whale for a high-up in Fräulein and answers respectfully, 'That's right, sir. No one's there. It's not even a house, it's a business.'

'A business?'

The woman smiles acidly. 'A small business. Insect stickers, apparently.'

'Insects.'

'That's right,' the suit confirms. 'We forced our way in there, but all we found inside were stickers, and some supplies for raising insects.'

'Where the hell did that kid send us?' Her voice is shrill. She's clearly flummoxed and begins chewing on her nails.

The Whale looks at the address plate on the gate in front of him. Tokyo, Bunkyo Ward, Tsujioka, Number 3–2.

'Amazing.' Cicada shakes with mirth. The Whale stares at him. After laughing for what seems like a long time, Cicada goes on: 'Relax, buddy. You still have a chance to pull this off.'

SUZUKI

'NO PHONE IN THE HOUSE,' Asagao says. 'It's not my house.'

This is unexpected. Suzuki doesn't know what to say next. He just sinks back into the chair at the dining-room table, his mouth hanging open. Asagao sits across from him, beside Sumire. Kentaro and Kojiro take a seat on either end.

Is this some kind of a joke? Suzuki's head is clouded with confusion. He tries to calm himself down, hoping that will dispel the cloud.

After listening for anything happening outside, Asagao says, 'Looks like the dangerous crowd you were so worried was on its way hasn't shown up.'

There was the noise of a car, but it didn't seem to be anywhere near the house. Certainly no indication of a line of cars pulling up to the gate and a gang of villains piling into the house.

'Looks like it,' Suzuki replies. He feels embarrassed at having made such a scene and missed the mark, but more than that he's just trying to figure out what's happening. 'But still –'

'You've been losing your mind about this *but still* for a while now,' Asagao points out.

'Big bro, you look so serious,' Kentaro says, miming a stabbing motion with his index finger.

'It's funny,' squeaks Kojiro.

'So, then, what happened? Didn't Kojiro give them the address?'

'He gave them a different address,' answers Asagao. Kojiro bobs his head in agreement.

'A . . . different address?'

'I told him to take your phone. I also told him that on the off chance anyone were to call it and ask for the address, he should just make one up.'

'When? When did you tell him to do all that?'

'Yesterday.'

'Yesterday?' Suzuki shouts back. 'That's before I even came here!' Suzuki had only visited earlier that same day.

'You were here.' Asagao looks straight at him. Once again Suzuki has the feeling of trying to see under the surface of a lake. 'You followed me to this house yesterday. Didn't you?'

'Oh, you mean then.' Suzuki nods. He can't think of any reason to conceal anything. 'That's right. I followed you here. Terahara's son got hit by a car, and so –'

'So you followed me here. I thought you might try to make a move then, but I was wrong.'

'What would have happened if I had?'

'Who knows.' Asagao plays it off like it's not a big deal. 'I figured you would come again, so I had a little discussion with Kojiro.'

'What kind of discussion?'

'How to act if you showed up. In terms of possibilities and outcomes.'

'What exactly do you mean?'

'I wanted to find out what you were after. Were you coming to kill me, or were you on a fact-finding mission? Or maybe you were just an unrelated person who somehow got wrapped up in things. After all, the target was Terahara's son. I couldn't be too careful.'

'So even when I said I was a tutor you decided to let me into the house?'

'Sure. I believed you.'

'You mean you pretended to believe me.'

'But soccer was still fun,' mutters Kentaro, seemingly coming to rescue Suzuki from feeling so deflated.

'Why did you let me in?'

'The truth is,' Sumire intervenes, 'we thought that by learning more about you we might be able to get closer to Terahara.'

Suzuki never expected to hear the name Terahara from Sumire. *I guess the wife of the Pusher knows all about the underworld.*

'The organization called Fräulein,' Asagao says, sounding almost bored. 'Also known as Maiden.'

'What . . . exactly is going on here?' Suzuki asks. 'How is your family connected to all of this? Sumire? Kentaro and Kojiro?'

Asagao's brows knit gently as he looks at Suzuki. There's something in his expression – maybe pity, maybe regret. His face looks completely open as he answers, no act or artifice. 'They're not my family.'

This is too much for Suzuki. For a short while he sits there, unable to speak. His lips move, his mouth opens and closes, but he can't find any words.

'They hired me,' Asagao says simply. 'Have you ever heard of the Performers?'

Suzuki nods. He'd heard about them from Hiyoko.

'Sumire's with them. I don't know the details. The boys are part of it too, apparently.' Asagao looks at Kentaro and Kojiro, not with the eyes of a father, but how someone might look at a team member or coworker. Or an employer.

'We used to work with Terahara, but nowadays we aren't getting along,' Sumire explains, scrunching up her eyes and looking like a university student gossiping about one of her friends. 'We wanted to make something happen, so we hired this one. Hired him for a little push. We're good actors, but when it comes to murder we're just amateurs.'

Suzuki almost yelps hearing her talk about murder.

'But Terahara's organization is huge,' Asagao says, his expression blank. 'Enormous.'

'Yes,' Suzuki agrees with a head movement that's somewhere between a nod and a twitch. 'Big, and awful.'

'And violent. Right? So after I took out Terahara's son, we expected that there would be some repercussions. There's no way they would just take it lying down. I pushed one person, but they would be ready to tear the whole city apart. Unrelated people would get pulled in. Terahara would lash out, someone would pay the price.'

'That does sound likely.' Through the fog, Suzuki recalls what Hiyoko said. About how Terahara lost his mind with rage when his son was killed.

'So I made them come after me.'

'You . . . made them?'

'When people are cornered, they become dangerous. I knew I needed to make a path for them. Leaving them a clue put them on the trail, and they followed it. As long as they were after me, it didn't seem like they would do anything too unexpected.'

Realizing the role he has played in all this, Suzuki wants to cover his face. 'So I was the bait?'

'It didn't need to be you. But I guessed that someone would follow me. And I led you here. This neighborhood, this house. It's not my house. It was empty. Rented for this job.'

'We set it all up,' Sumire says. By 'we', she must mean the Performers.

255

'And then she, and these two,' Asagao continues, looking at Sumire, Kentaro, and Kojiro, 'they played my family.'

'We weren't just after Terahara's son. We also wanted to take out Terahara himself,' Sumire offers. 'We thought this might give us an opening.'

'You're trying to kill Terahara?' Suzuki doesn't mean to say it out loud, but he must have inadvertently spoken his mind.

Sumire explains further. 'The target was the son. But we're generally unhappy with the whole Terahara operation. If we took out the boss, that would make things easier for us. So we were looking for a way in. And then you came along. So we wanted to find out what we could from you.'

'So you used me.'

'Used is a heavy way to put it,' Asagao says with a shrug. 'We put you to work.'

'What's the difference?' Suzuki sounds like he's on the edge of tears. Sumire and Kentaro find this hilarious and both burst out laughing.

'But wait,' Suzuki says, not done with his questions. 'What if when I first came here I had told Terahara's people right away, what would you have done then?' It just happened that he was afraid and overly cautious, so it didn't go down that way, but if he had told them then, Fräulein soldiers hellbent on revenge would have come here that same night. Or when he was here pretending to be a tutor.

'The first time you came, there were actually quite a few of the members of my group hidden around,' Sumire says casually. 'They spotted you, and if Fräulein had sent more people then my group would have attacked and tried to use it as an opportunity to force Terahara out into the open.'

Suzuki blinks several times, trying to think back to last night. He had followed Asagao to this house. Everything was quiet, it seemed like a completely typical residential neighborhood.

Apparently there were members of the Performers, out of sight, all around, watching him, but he hadn't noticed them in the slightest.

You never notice the most important details. He can hear his wife chiding him.

'But you came and went the same night. So I followed you.'

'You did?' Suzuki looks at Asagao. *The tail became the tailed.*

'You didn't go back to your apartment. You went to a hotel instead. I watched you report in. It seemed like you weren't happy about your task.'

Asagao is explaining patiently, but the words are barely entering Suzuki's ears. Instead he's staring at Asagao. The man's face radiates tranquility, like a snowfield that no one has set foot in, the sunlight soaking into the snow. Suzuki can almost feel it. There's nothing kind about Asagao's expression, and yet there's somehow a curious warmth. Suzuki finds himself deeply perplexed.

'He guessed that you wouldn't give up the location of this house right away, Mr Suzuki,' Sumire says. 'If he had been wrong and Fräulein ended up coming here, then we would have called on my team. Plus this house has a secret escape route.'

Suzuki shakes his head slowly from side to side, then his shoulders fall and he lets out a deep sigh. 'But,' he persists, because he still has questions, endless questions. 'Why are you telling all of this to me now? Have you given up on trying to get Terahara? Are you done with me?'

'Well, now that you know all of this, we can't exactly let you leave here alive,' Asagao murmurs.

Suzuki has a feeling like a frozen hand is stroking his neck. *They're going to kill me next.*

'Just kidding,' Asagao says lightly, raising his eyebrows. Suzuki has a flash of anger. *If that's supposed to be a joke, it's the least funny joke in the history of the world.* 'Anyway,' Asagao continues, 'it seems that Terahara's already dead.'

'What?' Suzuki is not sure he can handle any more surprises, but he can't help his voice pitching upward. 'When?'

'Just a short while ago,' answers Sumire. She peers at Asagao's profile as she goes on. 'I got a message from my team. Terahara's dead. They think he was killed.'

'By – by who?'

'Good question.' She doesn't appear to be trying to conceal anything. 'We're not quite sure.'

'It was when we were in the car, on the way back here. She called, remember?' Asagao glances at Sumire. 'That's when I found out. So we don't need to use you anymore.'

'You mean you don't need to put me to work,' Suzuki manages to reply.

'We didn't plan to tell you any of this. There was really no point. I was planning to take you home, part ways, and be done with it.'

'Then why are you telling me all of this?'

'I thought you deserved it. You seem like a good guy to me.'

'It's true, you do,' Sumire agrees.

'Yeah,' Kentaro pipes up with a grin, 'and he looks like he'd do whatever anyone tells him to.'

'Plus I enjoyed your Brian Jones reference,' Asagao says.

Suzuki heads toward the front door, feeling as though he's floating through space. There's no sense of reality. But he's made up his mind to go home. As soon as he thinks that, more questions spring up all at once – where he should go, whether his apartment is safe, whether the business hotel has any available rooms.

'It's our second time to see you off today,' Sumire says to him as he stands in the vestibule.

Kentaro and Kojiro are there as well. They both look a bit sad, but Suzuki has to wonder if that's an act too.

'Big bro, you really leaving us?' asks Kentaro.

'It's not like this is actually your house.' *We're all leaving.*

'Well, yeah, that's true.' Kentaro sounds glum.

Kojiro is holding the other boy's hand. 'You're leaving?' he asks in a whisper. Looking at them together, they do look a lot alike. Same thick eyebrows, same ears. *They're probably actually brothers*, Suzuki thinks. *And they're in a group like the Performers, at this age?* The thought upsets him. Their lives must be so far from a normal childhood. Strange and disordered, maybe unhappy, maybe grueling, but in any case something far out of the ordinary. *Where are their parents? Do they get to go to school?* He recalls Kentaro when they were kicking around the soccer ball. The joy he saw on the kid's face seemed genuine. Do you play soccer in school? Suzuki had asked, and Kentaro had looked downcast, shaking his head.

Kojiro steps toward Suzuki, standing right in front of him. He holds out his hand.

Suzuki leans down, bringing his face closer to the boy. 'What's up?'

Kojiro answers in his trademark whisper, 'I want to give you this.'

'Oh?' Suzuki looks at Kojiro's hand and sees a sticker. He takes it with great ceremony and holds it up to get a better look at it. An image of a longhorn beetle, lovely green in color. 'I can have this?' he asks, and Kojiro nods enthusiastically. Suzuki regards it reverently and realizes that it must be important to Kojiro. 'This is a rare one, right? Are you sure I can have it?'

At which Kojiro shakes his head solemnly. 'That one's a duplicate. It's the one I have the most of.'

Before Suzuki can feel any disappointment he just laughs. 'I'll bet.'

'I'll give you a ride,' says Asagao.

'Oh, no, don't worry about it,' Suzuki says, waving away the offer. He's about to add that he's sure if he gets into Asagao's car it will just lead to the next bizarre episode, when he notices the fingers on his waving hand. His head droops in frustration.

'What happened?' Sumire asks.

'Actually, I will take that ride,' Suzuki says, head still bowed. 'I want to find my ring.'

'Your ring?'

'I have to find it.'

My hero, his wife says, clapping her hands. *Did you think I'd forget?* he answers. *See, I'm doing my best, just for you.*

THE WHALE

HE TURNS TO CICADA, OR more accurately to Cicada's ghost, and asks, 'What do you mean, I still have a chance?'

'You do. A good chance, a very good chance.'

'Where?' At this point the Whale is feeling like Cicada is actually there, right in front of him, part of reality. The ghost looks more solid than the telephone pole he's standing next to.

'Where we were before.'

'Where is that?'

'Where you killed me, man. John Lennon had the Dakota House, Oda Nobunaga had Honnoji Temple, and for me it was that cedar grove.' Cicada scratches his head, seemingly a bit embarrassed about having died. 'Go back there.'

'Go back there and do what?'

'There should be a ring next to where I went down. It belongs to that guy, Suzuki. I took it off him, and then I dropped it.'

Now that he mentions it, the Whale recalls. After being shot, while lying there bleeding out from the chest, Cicada was mumbling something between choked breaths. It was just nonsense, barely coherent, but the Whale had the sense that Cicada was talking to the ghost of Iwanishi that was standing there too, and he recalls hearing something about a ring.

'Suzuki's on his way to go get the ring.'

'What makes you so sure he'd go back to the cedar grove?'

'I mean, I don't know if it'll be the cedar grove exactly, but I bet he knows that he lost the ring somewhere around there. Maybe he thinks it's in the car, or in that building, whatever. But he'll go back there.'

The Whale doesn't like taking suggestions from ghosts, but it seems worthwhile to check it out.

The presence of the Fräulein crew in the residential neighborhood is starting to draw attention. Besides the line of imported cars, there's also the woman shrieking and shouting like she's lost her mind. People are starting to poke their heads out of their houses. The men in suits are standing there dumbly, unsure of what they should be doing.

There's no more reason for the Whale to be here. Without the Pusher, he has no use for the woman, or Fräulein, or this neighborhood. He starts to turn back toward the SUV.

The woman raises her voice again. 'I'm getting a call from headquarters,' she wails, gripping her phone. 'What if it's the boss? What am I supposed to tell him?'

This is hard to watch, the Whale thinks, as he watches her take the call.

After listening for a moment, she screams again. 'What are you saying?' Then she peppers whoever she's talking to with questions, one after the next, her voice sounding more and more desperate. He can't quite hear what she's saying until the end when she shouts, 'How could this happen? Who the fuck *are* they?'

The suits crowd around her and ask what happened as she puts the phone away. The Whale also takes a few leisurely steps in her direction.

'The boss is dead.' She's not quite in a daze, but she does look exhausted. Her skin seems to have gone past white into a shade of green. Veins show blue under the surface.

Cicada's ghost whistles cheerily. 'Terahara's dead? This is too good.'

How did he die? someone asks, and her body sways as she murmurs, 'He was killed. Poisoned. They said he was poisoned.' She keeps repeating the word poison, like an incantation from a nightmare. 'Back at headquarters. His tea was poisoned. He's dead.'

'Who did it?' the Whale asks, standing in front of her once again. He sees his shadow from the streetlamp stretching out into the street. 'Who poisoned him?'

'It was those two,' she says, looking up into the night, then spinning her body so she can see all around. 'The guy and girl we'd taken. Now they're gone. Young guy and girl. The ones Suzuki was supposed to kill.'

The Whale has no idea who she's talking about. Her men seem confused as well, all the muscle in suits blinking uncomprehendingly.

She spreads her arms out and keeps spinning, like an actress in a musical.

'A guy and a girl, they called themselves Yellow and Black. They killed the boss. Maybe that was always their plan. Maybe that's what they were up to from the start.'

'Yellow and black, huh?' Cicada says airily in the Whale's ear. 'Wonder if they're the Hornet? Yellow and black, those are hornet colors. Those creepy stripes.'

'The Hornet.' The Whale says it out loud. Come to think of it, he has heard that name before. In the business, contract kills, working with poison. 'Who hired them?' he asks Cicada. Of course he knows it's ridiculous to ask a ghost that sprang from his mind for the answer to something that he himself doesn't know, but he can't stop the question.

'Who knows. But everyone wanted Terahara dead. That much is for sure.' Cicada seems to be in high spirits. 'Forget about these assholes. Let's get outta here. Get the jump on Suzuki. Settle the score with the Pusher.'

The Whale turns on his heel and walks up the road. The street-lamps cast multiples of his shadow along the concrete walls lining the gardens. By the time he opens the driver's side door of the SUV, Cicada is gone without a trace.

SUZUKI

AS ASAGAO DRIVES ALONG, THEY barely speak. There are all kinds of things Suzuki wants to say, but at the same time he feels like nothing is actually worth saying.

He sits in the passenger seat and gazes through the window into the night. It's the second time driving to Shinagawa in the same day, but now that the sun is down it all looks completely unfamiliar, like he's passing through unknown territory. Mostly he can just see the headlights from the oncoming traffic in the other direction, the white beams stretching through the darkness.

His head keeps dipping, and he realizes he's on the verge of falling asleep.

'You all right?' asks Asagao.

'I'm fine,' Suzuki answers, but there's a dull ache in his head. Must be the residual effects of the drugs Hiyoko's men gave him.

'Why were you working for Terahara's organization?'

At first Suzuki doesn't know how to respond.

'I don't know too much about them,' Asagao goes on, 'but you don't seem the type to work at a place like that.'

'Well, actually . . .' Suzuki begins, but then trails off. *Actually my wife was killed by Terahara's son, for no reason, he was just out on a joyride, so I infiltrated their organization to get revenge. Saying 'infiltrated' sounds childish, but I was dead set on it. I turned my back on my sensible, ethical life and joined up with Fräulein.* It feels like if he starts talking he won't be able to stop the words from spilling endlessly out, so instead he just sits there silently. His heart flutters like a scrap of paper on the pavement on a windy day. The feeling seems to pass, he takes a deep breath, then the wind picks up again and his feelings start churning once more. So he just sits there, waiting for the wind to stop.

Asagao must be able to sense Suzuki's state of mind, because he doesn't press.

'I wanted revenge,' Suzuki says quietly. He feels satisfied with that answer.

'On Terahara?'

'On his son. I did it for myself. I needed to get revenge. Talking about it now I realize that I was willing to do it no matter what happened to anyone else as a result. So even when it dawned on me that the products I was selling for them might be drugs, I told myself it didn't matter.'

'Seems a little selfish.'

'I kept downplaying it.' The truth is that he didn't even feel that bad about selling illegal drugs. Only when he was given a gun and told to kill those two kids who called themselves Yellow and Black, only then did he start to get scared. *Come to think of it, whatever happened to those two?* He pictures the guy's face, looking so much like one of his old students. *Are they all right?* If Terahara's actually dead, then the Fräulein offices are no doubt in disarray. *Hopefully they made it out all right.*

Suzuki follows the night scenery through the window. 'Mr Asagao. What you told me this afternoon, about locusts, do you really think that's true?' As he asks, Suzuki registers surprise that it was earlier the same day. It felt like something that happened far in the past. The conversation with his professor from ten years ago seems more recent.

'What about locusts?'

'That there are too many people, and we've become like swarming locusts, dark and violent. That's what you said.'

'Don't you think so?'

'I do get angry when I have to sit in traffic.'

'There are far too many of us.'

'Is that why you do the work you do?' Possibly on account of the drugs still in his system, Suzuki's fear of the Pusher has faded considerably. 'Is that why you push people to their deaths?'

Instead of answering the question, Asagao offers a statistic. 'Every year in this country, thousands of people die in car accidents.'

'I've heard that too.'

'Terrorists don't kill that many people. There's no such thing as a terrorist that randomly kills almost ten thousand people. And if you count all the people who are just injured in car accidents, the numbers go way up.'

'True.'

'But no one says we should stop driving or riding in cars. It's funny. In the end, human life comes second. The most important thing is convenience. Convenience is worth more than life itself.'

'You're driving a car right now.'

'Indeed I am.'

'I guess you could say that cars are like the wings that locusts grow.'

'Sounds about right.'

It's an oblique exchange. Not quite evasion, but also not a proper exchange of opinions. It doesn't foster any sense of closeness or shared understanding either, but somehow Suzuki feels satisfied.

As they pull to a stop at an intersection, a thought occurs to him. 'I don't suppose I'll ever see Sumire or the boys again.'

'Probably not. I'm sure they're already gone from that house. I imagine I'll never see them again either. We just happened to all be on the same job. Ordinarily I work alone.'

'I see . . .'

'Don't tell me you're sad about it.' There's no mockery in Asagao's voice, just a neutral statement.

But Suzuki is surprised to realize that he *is* sad. He wants to say so, but he can't bring himself to. It's too embarrassing. He had believed that they were a real family, and that they had welcomed him in. He feels deeply silly.

The light turns green, Asagao eases onto the gas, the sedan picks up speed smoothly. They pass Shinagawa Station and slip onto a dark side street. There's no traffic, probably due to the late hour. Suzuki has the sense that these two bizarre days are finally drawing to a close.

'It's probably a little late for me to be bringing this up,' Asagao says, looking straight ahead even as the building where Suzuki had been held looms into view on the left, 'but do you really think you're going to find your ring here?'

'I'm pretty sure this is where I lost it. Either in the van or in the building.'

'And you don't think it's dangerous, coming back here?'

'I haven't really thought much about it,' Suzuki answers honestly, blushing. 'I just had to do it. That's as far as I got.'

THE WHALE

THE CEDAR GROVE CONTAINS THE blackest depths of night. When he steps inside it the dark air wraps around him. With every step further in his body descends deeper into shadow. The darkness licks at him. He can feel it.

Cicada's ghost is gone. No other ghosts appear either. Lying on the ground is Cicada's body. It hasn't moved from the place where the Whale shot him dead. It doesn't seem at all gory, or even sudden. It looks completely natural there. Like it belongs there among the fallen branches and insect corpses and bird shit and cedar needles.

He looks down at the body. There's no light, but he can somehow clearly make out the details of Cicada's face, down to the fuzz on his cheeks. The eyes are open. Arms outstretched, though the right arm is bent at the elbow, with the index finger extended.

It seems to be pointing. The Whale looks in the direction it indicates: there's the ring. It's not glittering, and it's half buried in the dirt, but it's clearly a ring. He reaches down to retrieve it and wipes the dirt away.

Will Suzuki really come back? There's no reason to believe he will. The Whale leans against a knotty trunk and closes his eyes. He focuses his hearing, feels the cool air, marks his own breathing.

After some time he starts walking. He puts his hand in his jacket pocket and squeezes the worn-out paperback.

When he steps out of the grove he's standing at a road. Two lanes, one-way. No cars to be seen.

There's a light on the fifth floor of the building across the road. The rest of the building is dark. Guessing that Terahara's underlings must be doing some work up there, the Whale steps over to a streetlamp and leans against it. The lamp bends over him like a giant fern. He takes out his book. It's the best way to steady his spirit.

At length, the light on the fifth floor winks off, like the building is closing its eyes.

The Whale puts his bookmark in place, closes the book, and returns it to his pocket. He takes a step away from the lamppost and stares intently at the building's entrance. He has no sense of how long he's waiting like that, but soon enough the door to the building across the road opens and a man emerges. A voice rings out: 'It's him.' At first the Whale assumes that it's Cicada's voice, but then it sounds like it's more than one voice. Like a whole chorus of people, not shouting, but whispering to the Whale, 'It's him.' The unappreciated secretary, the woman betrayed by her lover, the newscaster who mixed up justice with self-righteousness, the politician who framed others for his own misdeeds, the young man born of an affair whose father didn't want him around, the gang member who made the mistake of assaulting a politician's daughter, the man who took contract kills and managed a talented young murderer, and more, more, they all speak at once, from inside the Whale, from outside: 'It's him.'

The man from the building becomes more visible with each step. He's slim. Hard to say his age exactly, but probably late twenties or early thirties. It's Suzuki. *Just like you said*, the Whale thinks, thanking Cicada, who isn't there. *Suzuki came after all*. He starts off to his left until he's standing directly across the road from Suzuki.

Settle the score.

He hears Tanaka's voice. *I will*, the Whale nods. *I need to settle the score with the Pusher.* And then he thinks again: *Suzuki isn't the Pusher. I don't have any business with him.* Right away another voice drowns it out: *Who says he's not the Pusher?*

It's true. This man very well could be the Pusher. Actually the chances seem quite good. *Now this ends*, he tells himself.

Even in the darkness, from across the road he can make out the expression on Suzuki's face. Suzuki looks up at him. Blankly at first. But then Suzuki's eyes open wide. Fear and doubt flash on his face.

It's over, the Whale thinks. He takes a step forward.

SUZUKI

HE GETS OUT OF THE sedan at a bit of a remove from the building. Without knowing for sure that Terahara's actually dead, he'll need to be on his guard. He decides to walk the last hundred meters.

'How are you planning to get home from here?' asks Asagao.

'I'll figure something out.'

With that, they part ways. They don't exchange any kind of proper farewell or wave goodbye.

As Suzuki makes his way slowly toward the building he gets the sense that there's no one else around. First he looks for the van that Hiyoko and the torturers brought him in, but he can't find it anywhere. He thought it might be parked somewhere nearby but a loop around the area reveals nothing.

Then he enters the building. It's not locked, but the automatic doors aren't working either, so he has to force them open. The power is off and it's dark inside. He proceeds anyway. No one is around. He feels no fear as he climbs the stairs to the fifth floor. The drive to find his ring is too strong for there to be any fear.

The lights on the fifth floor are somehow working and he carefully searches the area where he was held. He bends low as he looks, nearly crawling around the expanse of the room, eyes peeled. When he sees the corpses he has a moment of shock, but no fear. He searches the hallway, even checks the fire escape doubtfully, but all he's doing is using up energy. The ring is nowhere to be seen. He's sure that if he dropped it, it has to be somewhere around here. He retraces the path to the elevator. Nothing.

The ache in his head is still throbbing, getting worse. His eyes feel heavy. *I just want to go to sleep*, he thinks feebly, but right away shakes himself. He may not know where the ring is just yet, but if he goes to sleep he'll never find it.

If it's not in the building, it must be outside near the entrance. He heads back down to the ground floor.

It happens as he exits the building. He feels a strange emanation of force. Like supercharged air pressing in from somewhere in front of him.

At first he thinks it's from the cedars across the way, exuding their ominous darkness, but almost immediately realizes that's not the source.

There's a man standing across the road. Rooted like a great tree. A pair of hollow eye sockets, black against the blackness of the cedars.

It's the big man who took Cicada. A few hours back, he had wrenched open the door of the SUV and dragged Cicada in among the trees.

Has he been in those cedars this whole time? Cicada is nowhere to be seen. *Maybe this big man is part of the cedar grove*, Suzuki thinks. Acting as a grasping limb for the trees, finding prey and pulling it in. Catching cicadas.

The man steps into the road.

The force of it makes Suzuki go rigid. He can't move. Can't sidestep, can't turn away, can't even blink. *Where did he come from?*

The man takes another step closer. His face is obscured in shadow. Suzuki can't make out his expression. As soon as he thinks that, a voice sounds in his ear. Although not quite a voice, and not exactly the wind, and not necessarily the rustling of his clothes.

'All people want to die,' it seems to say.

When the man steps forward again, Suzuki feels a weight on his chest. A deep gloom settles on him. His breathing doesn't work – no matter how much he exhales he can't expel the air. *He's filling me up*, Suzuki thinks, watching the man, his mind growing hazy.

The darkness spreads through his body. Scenes replay from his time with Fräulein. Calling to a girl passing by. She's dressed unfashionably, clearly just arrived in Tokyo from some town in the sticks. She looks uncertain, bashful, but she follows him to a cafe. Big dreams for her life in the big city. He opens the pamphlets, takes out the samples, makes his pitch. She happily takes the contract with her. Two weeks later, he sees her in the same shopping arcade. Her hopeful smile is gone. There are dark circles under her eyes. She's being reeled in by a sex work recruiter. She looks unsteady on her feet, drained of vitality. Suzuki wonders if it's because of the products he sold her. Maybe they had some negative side effects. Maybe they're actually addictive drugs, and they're eating her up from the inside.

But he immediately pushes the thought out of his mind. If she looks sickly it's because the miasma of the city is too much for her. It has nothing to do with him, he tells himself. Then he calls out to the next passing girl.

I had to avenge my wife.

No one is accusing Suzuki, but he starts pleading his case. *I needed to work for them, gain their trust, so that I could get close to Terahara's son.*

But isn't that selfish of you? You didn't see any problem with taking a job at a shady company and doing their dirty work?

He insists that it was fine, trying desperately to convince

himself. Black smoke spreads from his chest into his throat, into his head, into his guts.

Then a piercing voice stabs at him: 'But you didn't even avenge your wife.'

The mortifying truth of it reverberates darkly. He doesn't know where the voice came from, but it's clearly directed at him.

Without realizing what he's doing, he steps into the road. At the same moment a small light appears, down the road to the right. Two lights, headlights on a car, shining in the dark. Heading his way. *A blessing*, he thinks. He takes another step into the road, then another. *I need to get in front of this car.* The feeling is deep, urgent. *I need to die.*

A sudden thought occurs to him: maybe his wife felt the same way. Maybe in the moment before Terahara's son slammed his car into her she was looking for death. She was sensitive to all the pain in this hopeless, tragic world. *Maybe she just wanted to end it, like I do now. She must have felt that way. And now I can join her.*

He starts walking toward the approaching headlights. It's a minivan.

I need to jump in front of it, he tells himself. *My wife will be so happy*, he agrees.

He's about to take another step when, just at the moment of lifting his foot from the ground, he hears another voice: 'You think this will make me happy?'

It's not an actual, physical voice. But he can feel his wife right next to him, her mouth close to his. 'Whoever said I wanted to die?' She laughs her old laugh, familiar, delightful. At least he thinks he hears it.

He jolts to a sudden halt. The minivan passes right before his eyes, missing him by a hair. He doesn't hear the engine, or the squeal of the tires on the road, or anything.

Then it happens.

The big man, who was standing on the opposite side of the

275

road, staggers forward and tumbles into the minivan's path. His long right arm flails in the air as he falls down.

The minivan smashes into him. Suzuki still can't seem to hear anything, not the screech of the brakes or the sound of the big man's body being crushed or the impact to the car or the driver's shout. Everything unfolds like a film in slow motion: the headlight shattering, the hood of the car caving inward, the man's arm bending at an odd angle, his upper body being pulverized.

The minivan skids several dozen meters to the left, coming to a stop on a diagonal.

All Suzuki can do is stand there in a daze. Once he's able to walk again, he goes over to the big man's body. There's a paperback book on the ground. It looks like it's been read many times. He bends down to pick it up, but then notices something right next to it: a ring. Fallen on the road. He brings his face close to it.

See, there you go, you found it, says his wife.

Suzuki looks left, then right. Searching for Asagao. The way the man fell, it looked like he was pushed. But all Suzuki sees is the black of the cedars, their boughs shaking as if they have something to say. He stands there in the hush of night, watching a liquid spread over the surface of the road, maybe gasoline, maybe blood. He feels like he's on the verge of collapsing. Tightly wrapped by exhaustion, and relief. His knees buckle. Before he knows it he's sitting on the asphalt. His head grows heavy and the muscles of his neck go slack. His eyes slide shut. The black of the cedars mixes with the indigo of the sky, which then blends with the cold gray of the road, and then absorbs him. *Sleep.*

SUZUKI

SITTING IN A HOTEL RESTAURANT, he faces down his plate. On the top floor of the high-rise hotel in Hiroshima, at a window table bathed in the morning sun, he skewers fried foods with his fork and stuffs his face. He chews vigorously and gulps it down.

'That right there is one loaded-up plate.'

Suzuki looks up at the voice to find a thin older man standing beside his table. Not anyone he knows. Must have been passing by but felt that he had to say something. It's hard to tell from his voice if he's impressed or just poking fun at Suzuki.

'You must have some appetite. Well, I guess you're still young.'

'It's not that,' Suzuki says, his cheeks relaxing into a smile. 'A buffet is a one-on-one contest.'

'Not quite sure what that means.'

'It's a duel. You against the food. You take your plate, consider each item, and ask, "Do I want to eat this or not?"'

'Ask who?'

'You ask yourself. And if you want it, you take it. It doesn't really matter if you end up with too much food.'

'Mm, I'd say it does matter.' The older man's smile shows a row of uneven teeth. All he has on his tray is a bowl of miso soup, some white rice, and a cut of grilled salmon. 'This is plenty for me.'

You're not taking this buffet seriously, Suzuki wants to say, but instead he just laughs and shoves more food in his mouth. The fragrance of meat in sweet sauce spreads through him.

As he works his way through his meal, he thinks about what happened last fall, more than six months ago now. *What did it all mean?*

The whole crazy episode that began with the death of Terahara's son and the hunt for the Pusher.

After it ended, he woke with a start, to find himself in Shinagawa Station, sitting on a bench on the platform. He looked around, momentarily frantic, but nothing seemed to be out of the ordinary. He had no idea what happened to the big man's body, or to the minivan that hit him. All he could do was sit there in a stupor. As to whether he had walked to the station or been taken in a car, he had no memory.

Going back to his apartment didn't feel safe, and he didn't know if people were after him or not, so instead he looked for a cheap hotel. He ended up spending a month at a business hotel in Ochanomizu. He never charged his phone, so naturally Hiyoko couldn't contact him. He looked for the longhorn beetle sticker that Kojiro had given him, but he couldn't find it.

After a month he went back to his apartment with some trepidation, but it appeared to be unmolested. He took small steps back toward living his life. Meanwhile he wandered the entertainment districts, keeping his ears open, and learned that the Fräulein organization had vanished off the face of the earth. He never learned the details, but it seemed that they were gone for good.

A few months ago he went to Netozawa Parktown, just once. Relying on his memory and his gut, he spent nearly an hour strolling by the similar-looking houses, but he never found that one house. As he walked he kept an eye out for his missing beetle sticker, thinking it might have fallen somewhere, but he never found that either.

More recently he saw a story in the paper that a woman in her twenties jumped in front of a subway train. She had apparently been behaving strangely and babbling something repeatedly. It was an odd enough story that it even got a fair amount of coverage in a sports newspaper. Suzuki thought that it must have been Hiyoko. There was a photo in the paper of high heels kicked off on the train platform, and they looked like hers. Of course, he couldn't be certain.

The only thing he knew for sure was that his wife was still gone, and he never got his revenge.

He spent several months languishing in a dark state of mind.

'What are you so depressed about?' he heard her chiding him, but he couldn't work up the energy to act on it. He stayed shut up in his apartment, wondering if the moisture he exhaled into the room would make his body grow mold.

He finally made up his mind to shake it off just a short while ago, inspired by something rather random.

He turned the TV on and it happened to be showing a program with a whole pack of dogs all crowded around their food bowls, chowing down. They were completely absorbed in chomping their dogfood, no pretense whatsoever. It shifted something inside him.

Suddenly in a rush, he went out to buy a magazine full of job listings and started looking for work. *I have to work*, he decided. The dogs were adorable, so intent on their meal, but there was also a kind of absurd vitality in it that made him feel like he needed to live too.

He found work as a teacher at an exam-prep school. It was a temporary contract gig, and there was something about the ad that seemed a little fly-by-night, but he didn't mind. The school was on a backstreet just outside of Shinjuku.

On the day before he started working, he took the Shinkansen to Hiroshima. He felt like he should kick off this new chapter of his life by having a meal at the hotel restaurant where he had first met his wife. To put himself in the right frame of mind, he would have a ceremonial breakfast, then return to Tokyo that evening as an exam-prep teacher.

In preparation for the big meal, he skipped lunch and dinner the day before. He kept his hunger at bay by revisiting memories of his wife, and going to see the peace memorial at the Atomic Bomb Dome for the first time in years.

Now, sitting in front of a plate piled high with food, he chews, working his jaw, swishing his tongue, savoring the flavors, ushering the food down his gullet.

'You do seem like you're in some kind of a battle there, my friend.' Now the older man is impressed.

'I'm digesting,' Suzuki answers through a mouthful of scrambled eggs.

'I'm pretty sure the digestion starts when you finish eating.'

'I'm digesting all sorts of things.' He's made up his mind to finally come to terms with his wife's death. 'I want to live.'

'What, uh, what do you mean by that?'

'I've thought a lot about it. About a lot of things. I suppose I feel like if I'm alive, but I live like I'm dead, then my wife won't be happy.'

'Oh, you're married?'

'If I'm going to live, I need to eat a lot. So I'm going to eat. A lot.' Stuff in, chew up, swallow down. Repeat. He has no intention of declaring himself full. That would be quitting.

If I'm going to live, I need to eat. He wants to say it again, but his mouth is full of food. He has the feeling that his wife is sitting across the table from him. She has a fully loaded plate too. She looks a bit pale and she's clutching her belly. *I can't eat it all*, she groans.

I'll finish it for you, he declares. *I'll live for you. Just you watch. I'll live like I'm really alive.*

'Well, I have to give you credit,' the man says sympathetically, a kind look on his face. 'But you know if you keep eating like that, you might not live so very long.'

Later that afternoon, after taking the Shinkansen back to Tokyo Station, he's standing on the platform to catch the train across town. It's getting close to rush hour, and there are lots of other people around him. Old people with bent backs, young people with dyed hair. They all look glum as they stand there with their bags. Bird droppings speckle the platform.

It's the middle of July, almost the peak of summer. His neck oozes sweat where the collar of his button-down shirt touches it. The westering sun bakes the station, reflecting off the glass of the nearby power company office.

Suzuki faces the tracks. On the other side is the platform for outbound trains. People are lined up there too.

He looks left and right down the tracks. The train doesn't seem to want to come. He begins to scan the people on the far platform, and then –

Right in front of him are two young boys. They're wearing the same T-shirt in different colors, and shorts that give them a lighthearted feel.

They appear to have noticed Suzuki as well. The taller one points at him. It's Kentaro. The shorter boy standing beside him grins. Kojiro.

Suzuki feels himself break into a smile, and at the same time has the sensation that a knot in his chest is unthreading. 'It's them,' he says, not even meaning to say it out loud. 'There they are.'

Sumire is nowhere to be seen. Neither is Asagao. Instead, standing behind the boys is a bespectacled man Suzuki has never seen before. *They're on some kind of a new job,* Suzuki thinks. A new role to play in their life with the Performers.

Kojiro has a large album tucked under his arm. It must be his insect sticker album. *I guess that really is his prized possession.* That much at least was true.

I lost the sticker you gave me, he wants to shout. But just at that moment an announcement reverberates through the station. The muffled voice informs the crowd that an out-of-service train will be passing through the station.

Suzuki smiles and looks at Kentaro. He suddenly doesn't know what to do with himself. The boys also just stand there smiling. He raises his hand to wave right when the train comes speeding in from the left. It rushes by in front of the opposite platform.

There's violence in it, like a river bursting its dam. The torrent roars by, completely blocking his view of the far shore.

The train seems to go on and on, which makes Suzuki feel a little uneasy. He's worried that the boys will be gone in the time it takes for the train to pass.

It finally ends, but at the same instant another train hurtles in from the right, passing in front of Suzuki.

It obliterates his view of the world, booming like thunder.

But Suzuki hears a voice. *Huh?* he thinks. From the far platform, a high-pitched voice seems to rise above the din. 'That's soooo stupid!' It's the voice of a young boy, but it's strong. Even through the clamor of the train, it reaches him.

'That's sooo stoooopid!' he hears, in a different voice. Unmistakably Kojiro's. *So you could shout this whole time,* Suzuki marvels.

A powerful urge takes hold of him, to go over to their side of the tracks, to be with them.

But Suzuki just stares at the passing train. 'This sure is one long train,' he whispers to his wife.

It's still passing in front of him.

BULLET TRAIN

KIMURA

TOKYO STATION IS PACKED. It's been a while since Yuichi Kimura was here last, so he isn't sure if it's always this crowded. He'd believe it if someone told him there was a special event going on. The throngs of people coming and going press in on him, reminding him of the TV show he and Wataru had watched together, the one about penguins, all jammed in tight together. *At least the penguins have an excuse*, thinks Kimura. *It's freezing where they live.*

He waits for an opening in the stream of people, cuts between the souvenir shops and kiosks, quickening his pace. Up a short flight of stairs to the turnstile for the Shinkansen high-speed bullet train. As he passes through the automated ticketing gate he tenses, wondering if it will somehow detect the handgun in his coat pocket, slam shut while security swarms around him, but nothing happens. He slows and looks up at the monitor, checking the platform for his train, the Hayate. There's a uniformed police officer standing guard, but the cop doesn't seem to be paying him any attention.

A kid with a backpack brushes by, looks to be eight or nine years old. Kimura thinks of Wataru, and his chest tightens. He pictures his beautiful boy, lying unconscious and unresponsive in a hospital bed. Kimura's mother had wailed out loud when she saw him. 'Look at him, he looks like he's just sleeping, like nothing even happened to him. He might even be hearing everything we're saying. It's too much.' The thought of it makes Kimura feel scraped out from the inside.

Bastard will pay. If someone can push a six-year-old boy off the roof of a department store and still be walking around, breathing easy, then something in the world is broken. Kimura's chest clenches again, not from sadness but from rage. He stalks towards the escalator, clutching a paper bag. *I quit drinking. I can walk a straight line. My hands are steady.*

The Hayate is already on the track, waiting for its turn to depart. He hustles to the train and boards the third car. According to the info he got from his former associates, his target is on the three-seater side of the fifth row in car seven. He's going to enter from the next car and sneak up from behind. Nice and easy from behind, sharp and alert, one step and then another.

He enters the gangway. A recess with a sink is on the left, and he pauses in front of the mirror. Pulls the curtain shut on the small vanity area. Then looks at his reflection. Hair unkempt, beads of gunk in the corners of his eyes. Whiskers sticking out at odd angles, even the downy fuzz on his face seems coarse. Ragged and raw. It isn't easy to see himself this way. He washes his hands, rubbing them under the water until the automatic stream cuts off. Fingers trembling. *It's not the booze, just nerves,* he tells himself.

He hasn't fired his gun since Wataru was born. He only even touched it when he was packing his things for the move. Now he's glad he didn't throw it out. A gun comes in handy when you want to put a little fear into some punk: when you need to show some asshole that they are way out of line.

The face in the mirror twists. Cracks split the glass, the surface bulges and warps, the face curls into a sneer. 'What's done is done,' it says. 'You gonna be able to pull the trigger? You're just a drunk, couldn't even protect your boy.'

'I gave up drinking.'

'Your boy's in the hospital.'

'I'm gonna get the bastard.'

'But are you gonna be able to forgive him?'

The bubble of emotion in his head is no longer making sense, and it bursts.

He reaches into the pocket of his black tracksuit jacket and draws out the gun, then pulls a narrow cylinder from the paper bag. He fits it to the muzzle, twists it into place. It won't completely eliminate noise from the shot, but on a little .22 like this one it'll muffle it down to a tiny *thunk*, lighter than a pellet from a toy gun.

He looks in the mirror once more, nods, then puts the gun in the paper bag and steps away from the sink.

A female car attendant is prepping the snack trolley and he almost barrels into her. He's about to snap 'Move it', but his eyes fall on the cans of beer in the cart and he backs off.

'Remember, one sip and it's all over.' His father's words flash through his mind. 'Alcoholism never really goes away. One sip and you're right back where you started.'

He enters car number four and starts up the aisle. A man seated just inside the car on his left bumps Kimura as he passes. The gun is safely tucked away in the bag, but it's longer than usual due to the silencer, and it catches on the man's leg. Kimura hastily hugs the bag towards himself.

His nerves spike and he feels a violent surge. He whips towards the man – nice-guy face, glasses with black frames – who bobs his head meekly and apologises. Kimura clicks his tongue and turns away, about to move on, when the nice guy pipes up. 'Hey, your bag is torn.' Kimura pauses and looks. It's true, there's a hole ripped in the bag, but nothing sticking out that could be obviously identified as a gun.

'Mind your own business,' he growls as he steps away.

He exits car four, and moves quickly through cars five and six.

One time Wataru had asked, 'How come on the Shinkansen car one is at the back?' *Poor Wataru.*

Kimura's mother had answered, 'Whichever car is closest to Tokyo is car number one.'

'Why, Daddy?'

'The closest car to Tokyo is car one, the next is car two. So when we take the train to where Daddy grew up, car one is in the back, but when we go back to Tokyo car number one is up front.'

'When the Shinkansen's heading to Tokyo they say it's going up, and trains heading away from Tokyo are going down,' Kimura's father had added. 'It's always about Tokyo.'

'Granny and Grandpa, you always come up to us!'

'Well, we want to see you, that's why. We come all the way up the hill, heave-ho!'

'But you don't do it, the Shinkansen does!'

Kimura's father had looked at him then. 'Wataru's adorable. Hard to believe he's yours.'

'I get that all the time. Who's the dad.'

His parents ignored his sulky remark, chattering away happily. 'The good stuff must have skipped a generation!'

He enters car seven. On the left side of the aisle are rows of two seats and on the right side are rows of three, all facing forward, backs of the seats to him. He puts his hand in the bag, closes it around the gun, then takes a step in, once, twice, counting the rows.

There are more empty seats than he had expected, just a

sprinkling of passengers here and there. In the fifth row, by the window, he sees the back of a teenager's head. The kid stretches out, white-collared shirt under a blazer. Clean cut, like an honours student. He turns to stare out the window, dreamily watching other Shinkansen pull into the station.

Kimura draws closer. One row away he's seized with a moment's hesitation – *Am I really gonna hurt this kid? He looks so innocent?* Narrow shoulders, delicate frame. Looking for all the world like a schoolboy quietly excited about a solo trip on the Shinkansen. The knot of aggression and determination inside Kimura loosens ever so slightly.

Then sparks burst in front of him.

At first he thinks the train's electrical system is malfunctioning. But it's his own nervous system, gone haywire for a split second, first sparks and then blackness. The teenager by the window had whirled round and pressed something into Kimura's thigh, like an oversized TV remote. By the time Kimura realises it's the same sort of home-made stun gun those schoolkids had used before, he's paralysed, every hair on his body bristling.

Next thing he knows he's opening his eyes, seated by the window. Hands bound in front of him. Ankles too, wrapped in bands of sturdy fabric and duct tape. He can bend his arms and legs, but his body isn't going anywhere.

'You really are stupid, Mr Kimura. I can't believe you'd be so predictable. You're like a robot following its programming. I knew you'd come for me here, and I know exactly what you came to do.' The kid is sitting right next to him, talking brightly. Something about the double-folded eyelids and the well-proportioned nose looks almost feminine.

This kid had pushed Kimura's son off the roof of a department store, laughing while he did it. He might only be a teenager but he speaks with the self-assurance of someone who's lived several lives. 'I'm still surprised that everything went so smoothly. Life really is too easy. Not for you though, sorry to say. And after you gave up your precious booze, and got yourself all worked up for this!'

penguin.co.uk/vintage